The Grace of Our Affecti

A writer ponders a photograph 1890s of his maternal great-grandparents and their seven children. His mother gave it to him when he was a boy and told him his ancestors' names. Since those seven had only four offspring and so much time has passed, he realizes he is likely the last person alive who can identify those in the picture.

The few extant records show the family patriarch was a Methodist minister and that his eldest son followed in his footsteps. Another son became the writer's grandfather whose troubled relationship with his daughter failed to erase her fidelity to the collective past.

Faced with a sense of obligation to his mother and scant historical evidence, the writer attempts to meet his vanished relations the only way he knows how – by writing them down. Who were his great-grandparents, Thomas and Elizabeth, and great-uncles and great-aunt – Ernest, Bertram, Horace, Arthur, Norman, and Letitia – as well as his grandfather Clement. What might have been the personal stories of consequence they did not visibly leave behind?

In order for those stories to emerge, he invents distinct ancestral voices and has his family members react to a shared set of circumstances in a single setting – the Orkney Islands – where they dramatically break free of old gender, class, and sexual restrictions. Because of his great-grandfather's profession and convictions, and the children's interrogation of religious certainties, there are unavoidable collisions in this new world between Methodist faith and secular belief, and between generations.

Accompanying the nine Orkney tales are vital sections of the novel titled 'The Frame' in which the writer questions the results of his creative efforts and the price of such invention. Haunting ancestral lives, and haunted by them, he is forced to confront what it means to try to raise the dead with words and live on through their imagined resurrection.

By the Same Author

Confronted by his own mortality and that of his paintings, artist Ben Sand reproduces several modern masterpieces on the walls of an isolated French cave so they will last for 20,000 years.

His efforts are mirrored by those of a Paleolithic girl, An, who, in her own cave, reveals through stroke and colour the physical violence and spiritual depths of her prehistoric environment.

An's visions and techniques are directly described, while the essence of Sand's endeavours is found in compelling stories that emerge from landscape and human presence within paintings by Bruegel, Goya, Monet, and others.

The result is enduring images of visual brilliance framed by lived experience that has its own place and longevity in time.

The LAST ARTIST

About the Author

J.A. Wainwright was born in Toronto, Canada. Since 1972 he has lived in Halifax, Nova Scotia where he is McCulloch Emeritus Professor in English at Dalhousie University. His areas of specialization were contemporary and Canadian literature and popular culture, including a class on Bob Dylan and literature of the 1960s.

His first novel, *A Deathful Ridge: a Novel of Everest*, was shortlisted for the Boardman-Tasker Prize in Mountain Literature in 1997, and his biography of painter Robert Markle, *Blazing Figures*, was shortlisted for the ForeWord Magazine Literary Prize in the U.S. in 2010. He has given readings from his fiction and poetry collections in Canada, the U.S.A and Europe.

Poetry Publications:
  Moving Outward, Toronto: New Press, 1970
  The Requiem Journals, Fredericton: Fiddlehead Books, 1976
  After the War, Oakville, Mosaic Press, 1981
  Flight of the Falcon: Scott's Journey to the South Pole, Mosaic Press, 1987
  Landscape and Desire: Selected Poems, Mosaic Press, 1992

Fiction Publications:
  A Deathful Ridge: a Novel of Everest, Mosaic Press, 1997
  A Far Time, Mosaic Press, 2001
  The Confluence, Mosaic Press, 2007

Biographies:
  Charles Bruce: World Enough and Time, Formac Publishing, 1988
  Blazing Figures: A Life of Robert Markle, Wilfrid Laurier University Press, 2010

Published by

CUSTOM BOOK PUBLICATIONS

Premium CLASSIC Imprint

Asia's Global Print & Digital Publisher

The Grace
of
Our Affections

by

J.A. Wainwright

ESW 1924-2011
LSW 1871-1902

Let another praise you, and not your own mouth; a stranger and not your own lips.
Proverbs 27:2

What is life? Thoughts and feelings arise, with or without our will, and we employ words to express them. We are born, and our birth is unremembered and our infancy remembered but in fragments. We live on, and in living we lose the apprehension of life. How vain it is to think that words can penetrate the mystery of our being. Rightly used they may make evident our ignorance of ourselves, and this is much.
Shelley

The Origin

The photograph rests on a small bookshelf beside my desk, all that's left of a family of seven children posed with their parents in the early 1890s by a man (presumably) from the Edison firm with offices in Leeds, Sheffield, Barnsley, and Castleford. My mother gave it to me many years ago. She had written the names of her grandfather, grandmother, father, five uncles, and one aunt on the back, but the ball-point ink faded over time, and the names remained only in my mind. Astoundingly, the seven children had only four of their own among them – my mother and her brother, and their two cousins. My uncle married late in life and left no descendants. One of the cousins was a lesbian, and the other had one son who never married. No one is left alive now except me, my mother and sister passing most recently, so unless I replace my mother's script the family faces and names will soon become anonymous.

They are standing or sitting outside their house in Yorkshire where my great-grandfather was a Methodist minister after serving in Lincolnshire parishes, long before my grandfather married and settled in my mother's birthplace, Grimsby. The photo is, of course, black and white, and they all appear to be dressed accordingly with shadings of grey perceptible in the jackets of the three younger boys. There is a tall bush behind them on the upper left side of the picture and an unattractive patch of dried grass at the lower right. The brick wall of the house is bifurcated by a four-paned window covered with a curtain or sheet to cut the glare and containing the most curious markings. On two sections of this material are hand-drawn faces that look like portraits from an earlier time, while the other two segments seem to be tattooed with dozens of faded signatures, though they could simply be the folds and creases of wear. Down the centre of the framed space, rippling out from beneath my great-grandmother's voluminous skirts is a gravel-strewn path dotted with fallen leaves and bits of weed. The overall setting is somewhat drab to tell the truth, and I wonder why this site was chosen even as I realize it's the gathering of the clan that mattered. The solid poise and definite tidiness of the sitters ultimately offsets any plainness of locale.

Seeking birth and death dates, I have explored ancestry websites where I discovered one of my great-uncles, Ernest, became a Methodist minister like his father. I can't explain why I never asked my mother for more details about him; her own father, Clement; the lives of those other uncles – Bertram, Horace, Arther and Norman; her deceased aunt Letitia

1

who died in childbirth in 1902; not to mention the old folks themselves, Thomas and Elizabeth. His funeral took place in the first year of the Great War, and she lived only until my mother was six. If the past is to escape the frame I need somehow to make up for my personal negligence and try to hear their distinct voices that I want to believe run through me like blood. From the depths of the photograph they return my gaze with a combination of strength and fragility: a profound certainty arising from their conviction of God's benevolence towards them, and an over-exposed vulnerability in their images that suggests we are but specks of cosmic dust held together by the grace of our affections for one another. Their imagined breaths must mingle with my own so belief in eternal salvation might be reconciled with faith in a very different kind of blessing.

1. In the Garden

Thomas (1841-1914)

I'd rather this picture business be done another time. I have my sermon to prepare; well, to polish really. Its subject is the growing number of work stoppages in the country as men protest their long hours for low wages, and village ways, let alone daily lives in the major towns and cities, are disrupted. Neighbour sets upon neighbour in un-Christian fashion, and those in charge, whether in Parliament or on the district council, either lack sympathy or seem oblivious to the consequences. People need to eat properly and to have a decent roof over their heads, and it is the job of the Chapel to support their cause without, of course, encouraging overly demonstrative protest or, God forbid, revolt. The bishop agrees and supports my stand that a certain dignity of existence must be granted the common labourer and his family. I believe that the part of Thomas Paine's philosophy about rights and freedoms was just and correct, though may the Lord have mercy on him for his later assertions about religion.

I have six strong sons and a headstrong daughter. Ernest has shown signs of following me into the pulpit, and I think his firm if quiet manner would serve him well. Bertie wants to study the law and has the brains to do so as well as the proper demeanour for a barrister. Arthur, despite his athleticism, is a dreamer who writes poems he never shares with me but that arise primarily out of admiration for Mr. Shelley, a lost soul whatever the validity of his verse about Peterloo. Ungainly Horace hides a sensitivity that will surely aid in his dealings with people. A small-town shopkeeper, perhaps, smiling at his customers over the counter. Clem will be a musician of some sort as he is already quite accomplished on the piano and organ and singing in the Chapel choir. Norman is still too much the young boy for any predictions, but I worry about his eyesight. Without his spectacles he cannot read the hymnbook or hardly find his place at the breakfast table. As for Lettie, she should have been a man with all her aspirations and ability to influence her brothers. She wears her hair short and squabbles on occasion with her mother and me, barring Chapel matters that are not hers to question. But God bless them all, they are decent and never flaunt their privilege as a minister's children. Elizabeth has raised them to be respectful of their elders and tolerant of weaknesses in others. Even Lettie, for all her forthrightness, never talks down to her equals and defends those who have not had her opportunities.

Will this photograph show all these qualities in those I love? I doubt such disclosure, but if any of our descendants discover it in a trunk or gathering dust on a shelf one day, I hope they will see some of the truth revealed.

Elizabeth (1843-1930)

The photographer is a fussy little man, one minute fawning and full of praise for our cooperation and the next overweening in his pride of the instrument with its bellows and heavy plates. I don't know why he's brought us out here to the garden when the parlour would do nicely, especially with its new patterned wallpaper that even Thomas has admired. 'Too busy a background,' the little man said dismissively, emphasizing that the tiny rose petals would divert attention from our faces and besides the light wasn't strong enough.

So here we are, Thomas and I, sitting rather crookedly as our chair-legs sink into the gravel. The others are standing behind. Ernest and Bertie, on the left as our grandchildren will view them, carried out my parlour chair with its plush cushion so I'd be fairly comfortable. Ernest's hand touches its back (I can feel his fingertips lightly drumming the wooden edge) while Horace, somewhat overweight, slouches against the other side. I tell him to stand up straight, but he pays no heed. To the right Arthur with his open collar, Lettie leaning sideways, her arm resting on her father's tilting edifice (she's far too casual at times, that girl, but sharp as a tack), and poor Clem in his spindly wooden chair who can hardly stay upright as the gravel threatens to swallow him whole. Norman is cross-legged on the ground.

The occasion is Thomas's twenty-fifth year as an ordained minister of God. On this summer day in 1867 before we met and married he became an Elder in the Methodist Church and began his preaching in Louth. His Chapel stood in the shadow of St. James Church whose Anglican tower is the highest in all the British Isles, but he had a goodly number of congregants who seemed pleased, along with the Bishop, by his sermons. I was born and raised just across the Notts border, and as we had relatives near Louth we would attend the Sunday service on visits to their farm. Thomas had a strong voice as he spoke of how our neighbours, rich and poor, were our kin on whom God looked down as our equals, and one day He would take us all up to be by His side without preference or any special elevation. My father and mother were pleased when the preacher singled out their daughter one bright morning at the end of service and after lunch came calling at the farm. All the children were born in Louth with the exception of Clem who arrived early when I was at my childhood home for a brief stay. So this anniversary marks the period within which we have all grown up together. I suppose I can tolerate leaning chairs in celebration.

'Smile, Madam,' the fussy little man demands, and I try.

'Thomas?' I say later.

'Hmm?'

'What shall we do about Lettie?'

'Do?'

Ernest (1873-1964)

When I was young I would sit with my siblings in Chapel and listen to my father's voice roll out over the heads of the faithful like a river raging in a storm or dance like a subtle current between their pressed bodies seeking the sea. I was the oldest boy and expected to appreciate at least the thrust of his declarations about God's welcoming mercy and the power of communal over individual devotion and belief. Seven of us in twelve years, together with our mother, means we are now a miniature congregation within the larger throng of worshippers, and, of course, expected to lead by example. Bertie, sober in nature and already in love with the rule of law, does so automatically; Arthur's immersion in his own thoughts and feelings leaves him staring at the Chapel ceiling with a slight smile on his face suggesting, for the gullible at least, that pleasing visions are at hand for all who follow his celestial gaze; Horace is deferential but often restless, and it takes our mother's reassuring hand to keep him calm; Clem quietly anticipates the music of choir and organ during the breaks in the spoken service; Norman's spectacles give him a pensive look as if the words of the sermon will turn a child into a wiser man. Only Lettie does not conform.

There is nothing obvious, no half-stifled snicker or shaking of her head in disagreement, just tightly pursed lips at certain points and a constant curling and unfurling of her fingers that seem to signal a pressure needing release. Sometimes she sighs and mother glances sideways in Chapel as I do, wondering if the audible exhalation of breath portends winds to match father's tempest or arrival at an estuary of conviction all her own. But whatever possesses her during this evident time of trial never declares itself in open rebellion, at least not in church.

I see all this but am more concerned with my own state of mind and soul. I have known for many years that I will have to carry on when father's strength fails. I made up my mind long ago to enter the ministry but will not speak openly of my decision until I am ready. I want to be completely sure on my own and not because father, followed by mother, will approve or even disapprove (perhaps thinking me not up to the task). Meanwhile, I have been reading as much as I can of Mr. Wesley and the founding of Methodism, and apply any understanding I have gained to the details of father's addresses to his flock. I will also seek a position at Kingswood, the Methodist school in Bath. No one will be able to say on the first day of my ascension to the pulpit that I am not prepared.

'Lettie,' I asked her once. 'Why do you ball up your fists so and then spread your fingers wide time after time?'

'First I want to hit the pew in front of me,' she replied. 'Then I want to fly away.'

Bertram (1875-1934)

Sometimes on school break we would all go to the seaside. Cleethorpes mostly because it was nearest Louth where father was preaching and had miles of sandy beach. While mother and father strolled the promenade above, we would race along the strand in swimsuits or on cooler days with trousers rolled, Lettie holding up her skirts between her legs, our bare feet splashing in the shallows, and our laughter ringing the salt air. One morning, winded from so much running, I began to collect pebbles washed up and left stranded by the tide. I wasn't interested in just any old stones but in those with designs etched on their faces that assured me there was history in their otherwise blank appearance and random presence on the shore. Because I couldn't possibly keep everything I had found, I had to make choices amongst them and based my selections on the smoothness of the surface and a minimum number of intersecting lines. My brothers would mock my hoarding, but the stones allowed me to organize my memories of the holiday on our return home. I would arrange them on my desk as a kind of border for the past so it would always be there.

In the developed photograph I will be taller than Ernest or Arthur though they both are older. I will hold my watch-chain lightly with one hand to remind anyone looking at us that I am a busy man and that valuable time is passing even as we remain still for the photographer. Ernest and Arthur have watch-chains as well but they are merely decorations or conveniences. The ticks of a watch for me are like those stones sounding who we are into bounded place.

In Chapel I memorize certain of father's words, ones like 'immortal,' 'everlasting,' and 'eternal' that promise God's order will never disappear. When his eye catches mine I can tell he is pleased at my attention.

Horace (1877-1942)

You wouldn't think to look at our parents sitting sturdily in their chairs that the three tall, thin boys in the back row belonged to them. Only Lettie and I have some heft. Father fills out his suit pants and jacket well enough, though it is more difficult to tell if mother has true weight or is just big-boned. But I have seen Lettie's calves at the seashore and they have muscle and curve near my own. My vest buttons are done up tightly over my bulging stomach so it's hard to sit still in church, though I know I must. Mother's touch helps me, and I try to think of other things besides my duty and how father can speak for sentences at a time without seeming to draw a breath. I like to hold things in my hands, not feel them passing by my ears. You can't grasp words for very long, and when you let them go there's no telling where they'll end up – anywhere from a piece of dirt under your nail to some flotsam out at sea that no sailors give much attention. I'd like to be a farmer and have all that hardiness of animal alive about me, or even a butcher where pieces of cow and pig stay solid as you hand them across the counter to a waiting buyer. My brothers and sister are all thinkers of one kind or another, shifting easily from thought to thought like joiners binding bits of wood without any nails or screws. They mostly ignore me because they know I can't keep up, except for Lettie who encourages me to stay the course and calls me 'little brother' with affection. Norman is really her little brother, but he's got a manner quick and slippery as the eels we catch in the creek below the bridge, so he needs no heartening.

One day I asked her why she bothers with the tallest three.

'They have their troubles, too,' she said. 'You can't always measure them on a scale, but they're there just the same.'

'Do you have troubles, Lettie?'

She smiled at me. 'I'll look to you for balance, Horace, when I do.'

Arthur (1874-1947)

Shelley was born one hundred and two years ago this month. I am sure our father would not want this fact associated with his ordination, although the date is inescapable. Of all the glorious lines in his work I am most fond of the one at the end of his last poem, still sitting unfinished on his desk when he drowned – '*Then what is life? I cried.*' My father's certainties do not assuage my doubts, and while I do not turn from the Lord completely, I am probably more of a Deist than a true Methodist, one who sees a Hand busy in heavenly spaces but no fingers pointing at the individual lives of men. I have read Mr. Darwin, of course, though like the collected poems of S. I must keep the volume hidden away. The only place where I can bring forth my questions and misgivings is in the writing of my own verse, which, for some reason, father does not forbid (little good it would do him!). I am not very accomplished yet and, if truth be told, my images and tones have a slightly Methodist ring to them, a hymnal quality that perhaps Mr. Wesley would approve while he condemned the accompanying sentiments. As for my siblings, only Lettie shares my concerns, telling me she wishes she could quote the Bard's Hamlet to our father – '*There are more things in heaven and earth, Horatio, than are dreamt of in your philosophy.*' Poor Lettie! There is so much she could do in this world were she not a woman. But I remember Mrs. Browning and George Eliot and try to encourage her.

'No, Arthur, I am not a writer like you.' Then, almost angrily, 'But I would like to be a politician and shake up Westminster's complacencies.'

'Lettie, you can't even have the vote. How could you sit in Parliament?'

'Quite well if you and all my brothers fashioned me a comfortable cushion.' She laughs to break the tension that results from most such talk between us, so seriously do we exchange our views.

'We can hardly do that,' I reply, 'but if you want a simple wooden chair, I'm sure Horace could fasten one together,'

Then she surprises me.

'*Teach me half the gladness/That thy brain must know,/Such harmonious madness/From my lips would flow,/The world should listen then – as I am listening now.*'

And I realize I will always think of her as a skylark still trying to soar despite the pruning of her feathers.

I am only a year younger than Ernest though it might as well be eons, as I'm certain he's bound and determined to follow in father's footsteps. He reads as much as I do, but the history of Methodism and the sermons of ministers past preoccupy him, and more than once he has mentioned Kingswood School where young Methodists are taught to be diligent, upright, and believe evil of no one. I think the Bible a great book but one among many.

Bertie is easily satisfied with how the world is run and wants to be part of the establishment that keeps things smoothly on track. I've no doubt he'll do very well for himself in secular ways, and given my attachment to Shelley this should be more than enough to seal my admiration and loyalty. Father seems to grant him great latitude as far as his observation of beliefs is concerned because Bertie is a fountain of knowledge about the organization of our Church and the rules and regulations that govern it.

Ernest and Bertie think Horace a rather dull fellow who will plod along without much accomplishment but without doing much damage either. What I do know is that he's very good with his hands, a skill our household relies on, what with slates on the roof needing frequent repair and the water pipes constantly groaning and thumping in our basement. Prometheus might have given fire to humanity, but it is types like Horace who keep the flame burning in the worst of weathers.

Clem could be choir-master in Ernest's Chapel one day, even if his love of music might mean the praise-song took centre stage rather than the preacher's stalwart voice. Of us all I feel he will be the best father. There is a sensitivity in his creative disposition that holds promise for his children, though they, of course, will eventually sing their own hymns.

Norman struggles to keep up with us all. Small and virtually blind without his glasses he expends a great deal of energy trying to understand conversations around the dinner-table, especially when father waxes on about the justification by Faith alone or defends the policies of Mr. Gladstone like the Reform Act that extended the suffrage and legal rights for Irish tenant farmers. I see Norman looking from face to animated face, wishing he could get a word in edgewise but not knowing yet what that word might be.

So I keep on, my small leather notebook tucked in my vest pocket wherein I pen my lyrical resistance to scriptural indoctrination that cannot trace its own inflections.

Clement (1881-1962)

The legs of my chair are sinking in the soft earth beneath the gravel. I have to lean away from mother towards father if I do not want to topple into her lap. And despite my best efforts this might happen if the photographer does not quickly finish his job. I am twelve years old, and if I stand up straight I am as tall as Lettie. She and my older brothers, with the exception of Horace, like to use words to keep dragons at bay; at least that's what I told her one day. She laughed and messed my hair.

'And how do you deal with your dragons, Clem?' she asked.

'Music hurts their ears,' I told her. 'That's why I play the Chapel organ so loudly when father lets me.'

We have a piano in the parlour that mother played when she was a girl. Now her fingers remain still, and I am the only one in the family who touches the keys. Father approves only so long as hymns are the order of the day, though he will tolerate a piece by Mozart if it is not too lively or reminds him of that 'wasteful pastime', dancing. What I told Lettie is true enough. My dragons come in all shapes and sizes, but mostly frighten me with their temptations to disobey father's rules and play really anything energetic. Mother, on the other hand, will sit by my side when he is out and keep time with her hands or the tapping of her feet as 'pagan' music fills the parlour. If walls could talk father would get an earful every night when he occupies his favourite chair to think over his weekly sermons before writing them down. Strangely, apart from mother, Horace is my greatest ally with my musical expression. He will often stand at the parlour door, his own feet in tune with the tempo and a bright smile on his lips as I trace the patterns of a fugue or, if we are alone in the house, hammer out the more basic beats of a music-hall number. Sometimes I think music is all there is in life and to subdue such enthusiasm would be a sin. But then I remember the Chapel loves the choir and organ sounding in God's name and promise myself I will keep within the bounds of its esteem. Ernest tells me I will make a fine choir-master; Bertie that my abilities will provide me with a good living; Arthur says I should have more ambition given my openness to what he calls the romantic strain; Lettie encourages me to slay the dragons with whatever means at my disposal, though sometimes I think she is mocking me for not being a true St. George of the piano.

What will be missing from this photograph is sound of one kind or another, the unceasing murmur of a family that cannot be heard above the snap of the shutter or within the moment of absolute silence frozen in time.

Norman (1883-1954)

I am the youngest, the small one who sits on the ground while everyone else has chairs or stands. Except for Clem, the older boys all wear ties and pants like father. Clem and I wear shorts and black stockings above our knees. I am the only one with glasses. If they fall off I cannot see the ground beneath my feet or mother's smile. I cannot see the wings of the butterflies I like to collect in a jar or the way the sun shines in the parlour window when we gather for prayers. But I can hear well – the buzz of other insects in the garden, father's quick breaths behind me as if he has had to run to his place in the photograph, the rustle of mother's skirts as she settles herself, and the tapping of Ernest's fingers on the back of her chair. The man with the camera keeps disappearing behind his black cloth and tells us several times to keep still. I have never heard anyone say this to father before. Usually Horace and I are the fidgeting ones in Chapel and at the supper table. Lettie calls me 'roaming Norman' even though I know enough to stay in the pew as father calls upon the Lord or in my chair as the dishes are passed around.

Because I have good ears I hear things I am not supposed to hear. Mother asks father what they will do with Lettie. Ernest asks him why if the Lord likes singing He does not like dancing. Bertie tells Arthur he lives in another world, and Arthur nods and agrees without a fight. Horace tells Clem he'd rather use his hands than his voice to get things done. Lettie talks to herself but I can't understand what she means when she says she wants to fly. No one says very much to me except to ask if I've washed my hands or is my schoolwork done or, when mother tucks me in at night, have I said my prayers. Arthur laughs and says I'm lucky because the time will soon come when grown-ups will pay me too much attention and I will grow tired of their conversation.

I am allowed to bring my butterflies to school. My sister and brothers collect things too. On the shelves in their rooms are piles of shiny stones, pretty beads, postcards of hills and beaches, and sea-shells that curve like tiny animals and hold the sound of the waves inside. I do not leave my butterflies on the school shelf but bring them home for a meal of flower bits and grass. I punch holes in the jar lid so they can breathe, but if I keep them too long they will die. My teacher says I should find a caterpillar so we can all watch it weave its chrysalis and see the butterfly be born. Father tells me if I become a naturalist when I grow up I must remember every insect and every blade of grass are part of God's purpose and mean nothing by themselves. When you study the things that breathe and grow you come to know the Lord, he says. I must not forget, he warns me, that John Wesley, who was the first Methodist minister, preached we should not heap and gather things of this world to gratify an idle curiosity. I heard Lettie tell Ernest one day that there was not enough idle curiosity in all of England to worry the Lord. He answered that she would come to no good end with thoughts like that. His voice sounded like father's in the pulpit.

Letitia (1871-1902)

O Lord though I doubt you are there at all let me rise from beneath my father and speak my mind that is so harnessed to his cause I feel like one of my brother's butterflies held in a jar waiting not for freedom but for the silencing camphor that will quiet my flight and drain my colours without mercy without end.

I lean on the back of his chair so he feels my presence my hand grazing his shoulder as if a little pressure would sweep him from his post as if a nudge might cause him to turn and ask what is my question though no answer will suffice.

I am the eldest a daughter disappointment that only Ernest relieved two years later and continues to relieve with his certain steps towards the ministry I cannot have nor want even though I wear my hair short and have a manly widow's peak to match my wide ungainly body below like a female version of Horace so we might be twins except his own head growth thrives in opposition to my stringy strands and as far as I can tell no inner voices sound alarms in his daylight or his dreams.

What have I been born to do except marry and bear children why not seven like my mother who went too far with Norman and almost died at forty while the doctor tutted at the loss of blood and told her she must take the proper measures as my father prayed in another room and allowed without saying that I might teach or nurse or serve in some capacity that held my feet to the ground and my face to the fire of obedience.

Ernest will follow Bertie will explain Arthur will write Horace will mend Clem will sing Norman will examine.

There is a wall around the garden that the photograph does not show designed to hold us in until we are so rooted here that circumstance and time will not combine to sway the faithful trees we have become but I will stand with arms outspread like branches seeking sun beyond the edge of mortared stone and dim horizons.

Branches or wings?

The Frame

Great-grandfather seems freer in mind and spirit than I expected. The Methodists, I've read, were by and large proponents of social justice and firm believers that matters of class should not dominate earthly conditions just as they would not reign supreme in Heaven. His assessment of his progeny indicates the attention he pays to them and his confidence they will not stray from safe and familiar paths. He describes all his sons as strong, so he can't be too worried about Arthur's dreaming. Only Lettie seems a possible problem because she's a young woman asserting herself in a man's world, even if, thus far, her independence of voice appears contained within the walls of home.

Until very recently I'd never given my great-grandmother any thought at all. If I glanced occasionally at the photo I saw her, with pin-backed hair parted exactly in the centre, as a stern and prim Victorian housewife and didn't catch the slight upturn of her lips I see now and, more, the hint of laughter in her eyes. It's all guesswork, of course. But my words are a kind of homage to uncertainty. Is the photographer her equal and will God allow him into her heaven?

Ernest is an observant young man who takes seriously his eldest son position, seeing himself as the responsible inheritor of his father's role in life yet clearly determined not to be a mere duplicate for the Lord. He also defines a good part of himself in terms of his perceptions of his siblings. I suppose he is already looking out for his own parishioners and determining the strengths and weaknesses of each. I hope there are not too many Letties in the crowd because she unsettles him like no other and may lead him to wonder if all in God's domain is really as certain and predictable as his father makes out. Most of all, there is concern about her apparent tendency to violence and desire to escape when he would never wish to raise his hand in anger or view any part of creation as a prison.

More than a bit compulsive and worried about any loss of personal control is great-uncle Bertie. No wonder the law attracts him. I note that after Lettie, whom he doesn't mention, he will be the first of the siblings to die. I hope it was quick because the messiness of any medical complications would have appalled him. Yet that line about the ticking watch, the beauty of capture by time, suggests the possibilities of his youth.

The kind of constancy Horace offers is hard to find. You could probably sit with him in the pub, fresh from the colonies, and he wouldn't look down his nose or stare morosely into his glass as you tried defensively to explain your shared lineage. No, he'd give what he could of himself honestly and without wavering. If there was a war – and South Africa is on the horizon – you'd want him beside you because he'd not only be able to fire a gun but strip it and clean it, and he'd tell you, without knowing Kipling, to keep your head down when all around were losing theirs. In the photograph he has a full head of thick hair, unlike his older and younger brothers with their high foreheads. I know from later pictures my grandfather Clem was bald in his forties, and I'll bet the others were thinning drastically by the time they got there. Lettie's hair isn't as luxurious as Horace's, but, unlike the rest of the family, she has a tendency to let it down.

I rebelled through my poetry but only had lay convention to oppose and never religious conviction writ large on a daily basis. There's no evidence that Arthur wrote any verse at all, though he *looks* as if he did and maybe kept it up as he grew older and the aging walls of conformity closed in. He lived through both world wars and must have found unavoidable subject matter there not to mention in the new freedoms of the 1920s that, had she lived, Lettie would have surely embraced even in her fifties. I like to think of him with his hair long and living something of the bohemian life while he offered, on occasional visits to Grimsby, an alternative vision for my mother to that of her father who, despite his music and Arthur's prediction, was rigid and domineering in his parenthood. The sensitivity Arthur saw was apparently swallowed by the need in Clem to control his children and ultimately disown his daughter, the one female descendant of Lettie who refused to bend.

It is difficult to approach Clem because he was my grandfather as interpreted by my mother all my young life. Thus he abandoned the romantic strain to disapprove virulently of my mother's marriage to a Canadian airman, banning her from his house and, when she emigrated, not speaking to her again by phone or letter for the remaining sixteen years of his life. In 1962 she woke up one morning from a dream in which he had appeared at her bedroom door. When she called out to him he did not answer. The telegram from England came that same day, announcing his death. I went to Grimsby four years later aware I was the colonial result of her damned and ultimately doomed trans-Atlantic affair. My uncle, her brother, took issue with my own social and cultural insubordinations and cut me off as Clem had her. None of this is visible in my grandfather's young face.

Not yet caught in the web of adolescence Norman remains free of cant and full of wonder. Budding naturalist that he is he observes those around him but has not yet learned to judge. Those spectacles he fears to lose are symbolic of his condition. Wearing them he sees the tiny movements of antennae and mandibles, though the lens do not reveal the rest of creation so clearly. Without them he is almost blind but hears the murmur of meaning in the undergrowth of family and a larger life.

Lettie is the key. My eyes gravitated towards her the first time I saw the photograph as if I had already, in 1966, met her daughter as an old woman in an unacknowledged Boston marriage. This distant great-cousin disliked me, ironically, because I tried with every step to douse the flames of conformity and compliance. I had thought Letitia died giving birth to this intelligent harridan whose forbidden love soured instead of sweetened her outlook, but it seems to have been a second childbirth that claimed her and the infant. She deserved better. I feel sometimes as if I am Lettie's grandson not Clem's and that the missing space between us contains all the promise her final forced surrender could not subdue. I am already rewriting that absence.

2. *Northern Dreams*

Thomas

I called them into the parlour and told them I had a surprise. The wry smile on Lettie's face suggested she could not be caught unawares – though I had shared my news only with Elizabeth – but the others waited expectantly, even Horace whose usual restlessness was not on display. About a month previously, I said, I had received a letter from a solicitor in the Orkney Islands informing me a distant cousin had passed away, one I had never heard of and who almost certainly did not know of my existence. She left no children or will, and after an extensive search for any relations the solicitor had alighted on me. Would I please confirm I was Thomas Larsen whose father was William born in 1811 in Malton, Yorkshire. I was indeed, I let him know, and learned just this past week that I have inherited her house in Kirkwall, the largest town on the islands. The older children's voices immediately rose up with questions and Clem and Norman began to dance a jig before I raised my hand to indicate I had more to say.

'Although I could deal with this matter through the post and my solicitor in Leeds, I would like to know my inheritance at first-hand. Therefore I have decided' – I nodded at Elizabeth to indicate her agreement with my decision – 'to visit the Orkneys for the next month or two and' – here I paused, rather dramatically, she said later – 'to take you all with me on the journey.'

Response was almost deafening and I had to raise my hand once again. 'But, father,' asked Ernest when everyone had calmed down, 'what about Chapel? Surely you cannot leave it for any period of time?'

'That has been taken care of,' I replied. 'I have spoken to the Bishop, and he agrees that after twenty-five years of service to the Lord, a few weeks leave is in order. I am confident I will come back refreshed and with new knowledge of the larger world for my sermons. There is a small and scattered Methodist community on the islands and I will play the role of itinerant preacher for awhile, reaching out to those who cannot attend Chapel in the main town. Meanwhile, the Bishop has arranged for my replacement here at home. Mr. Walsham will give his first sermon this coming Sunday, and we will depart next mid-week on the north-bound train.'

Clem and Norman began their dance again. Bertie asked me about intestate law in Scotland. Arthur laughed and put his arm around Lettie's shoulder. I saw her nod at something he said as she put out her hand and rumpled Horace's hair. The great boy stood there, a bit like a rock at the centre of the group, until Norman fell into him with a crash. I glanced at Elizabeth, knowing she would bear the weight of the journey and our sojourn on the islands, having left behind her house and garden and afternoon teas with the Chapel ladies as well as her almost daily ministrations to the unfortunate in our parish. But we had talked things through before my announcement, and she admitted to a certain excitement about the trip. Since a childhood journey to London, she has not ventured, with or without me, farther than Cleethorpes, which had been just a half hour by train from Louth and is another two hours from our present Yorkshire home.

What I didn't say was that I myself am not entirely confident about what will unfold. Used to having my own Chapel and the respect of an established community of faith, I am concerned about playing second fiddle to the incumbent minister in Kirkwall, particularly, as the Bishop informs me, in the shadow of the great Presbyterian cathedral of St. Magnus built as a Catholic sanctuary in the 12th century. Never mind, I assure myself, my inheritance is the Lord's will and He will provide and direct us as always. After all, Deuteronomy 10:11 – *'Go,' the Lord said to me, 'and lead the people on their way, so that they may enter and possess the land I swore to their ancestors to give them.'*

Horace

Lettie says I will have a good time on the train. She says it is because I pay attention to what goes on around me more than anyone else in the family. She doesn't mean attention to father's sermons, like Ernest gives; or to the reasons the world goes around according to Bertie's insistence; or to things that can't be seen, like Arthur dreams of. She means everyday things like the way the wind shuffles the leaves of the trees or bees coax the nectar from the flowers; the way the ponies on Mr. Whitney's fenced patch of ground nuzzle your hands as they look for bits of food; or the way Clem tilts his head when listening to a tune while the rest of us keep our chins on the level. She says there are lots of sheep and cattle in the Orkneys because the flat parts of the islands are good for grazing and that I will be able to see how proper farms are run.

'Who knows, little brother? The temptation might be too great and you'll end up staying there.' I can feel my cheeks burning with pleasure but reply that father would never allow such a thing.

She sighs. 'That's true. But let me enjoy the vision of you herding your animals, your boots all covered with dung and your eyes contemplating the prime ribs or legs of lamb you'll sell at the market.'

For a moment I see myself as she describes, only with father's approval. He'd visit often and I'd lend him another pair of boots so he could walk with me through the yard and into the fields. Mother would like to come but her skirts would drag in the muck, so father and I would walk out to the edges of my property and we'd look back at the whole place. 'You've done well, son,' he'd tell me, and I wouldn't have to think about the accomplishments of my older brothers or even Clem.

'You could live with me,' I tell her. 'I'd take good care of you.'

I see the tears glistening in her eyes. 'I know you would, Horace,' she replies, 'but each of us has to find his own bit of heaven here on earth.'

I hope I will be able to sit by the train window for a time. The others will talk their way to the islands while father and mother hide behind their books. The window will be my book and all the fields and rivers and mountains will be what I read.

Clem

I won't be able to play any music for a whole month! But, as if reading my mind, mother says there's bound to be a piano somewhere on the Orkneys and she'll make enquiries when we arrive. Father says the Chapel there is small and probably can't afford an organ, but, of course, there will be plenty of hymn-singing and perhaps I can help form a children's choir if one is not already in place. I'm not worried about the train trip because whenever I'm moving I hear music in my head. So if I get tired of antics with Norman or looking out the window I'll just close my eyes and hear some Mozart or *The Daring Young Man on the Flying Trapeze*. I have to be careful when I'm lost in the music inside me that I don't start humming along outside. Father would approve of a Mozart melody but not of Mr. Leybourne's circus ditty.

I'm not sure why there always seems to be a lot of suffering to go with art. Poor Mozart died in great pain of a fever while penniless Mr. Leybourne drank himself to death. I will keep my art within the Church and strictly govern whatever habits I have of playing and humming unholy material. That way my life will be a sober one and my health sustain me for a good long time.

Ernest has just told me there's a giant cathedral in the main island town of Kirkwall. It's called St. Magnus and was built by the Catholics in the 12th century, though now it's Presbyterian. There's bound to be an organ there, but of course I'll never be allowed inside such a place! Maybe I can sneak off one day and just walk inside as if I were of the other persuasion. I must learn their liturgy and hymnbook so I can pass muster.

Do Presbyterians have those confession boxes? Though what would I say when the priest asked me if I had sinned? Yes, Father, I have hummed a song about a man in leotards who died in the gutter. Instead of counting cattle and sheep as we race along, Norman and I should look for church spires and make a small wager on who will spot the most. I'll have to hide his spectacles.

Norman

There will be so many things to see and collect! I wonder if butterflies go that far north? Maybe not because it's colder than here. But I'm sure there will be plenty of insects and birds' eggs. Mother says the islands will be a naturalist's paradise and that the sea-birds especially will be plentiful. I won't be able to get any of their eggs because they will nest high up on the cliffs, but I will see them swoop down into the waves for fish and hear their different kinds of cries. There are plenty of gulls at Cleethorpes and lots of smaller shore-birds who leave their tracks in the sand, but mother says to expect puffins with their colourful beaks and maybe even rarer types like the albatross we read about in Mr. Coleridge's poem at school. I would not want to shoot any bird or even cage one for long. I don't let my butterflies expire in my jars so why would I keep a bird in prison until it pined so much for the skies it just gave up and died? But if I had a puffin in my grasp it would be hard not to give it a name and tame it as a pet. No, I am a proper naturalist and won't do such a thing no matter the temptation. We are all part of God's creation, as father says, birds and men alike, so no one of us should have power over another. That's what he tells me when I show him my collections. Stones or flowers are different because they don't breathe and can't feel pain, but creatures that crawl or run or fly have beating hearts like us and don't want to live in a gaol. How small a butterfly's heart must be. When I put my ear to the holes in the jar lid I hear only the soft flutter of wings.

I would like to see a seal. The ocean will be far too cold for swimming, but the seals have a special coat to keep them warm while they spin and dive for their dinners. Lettie says some of the seals are really selkies who turn partly into people when they come up on the land. They are beautiful but dangerous because they can pull humans back into the water. If I see a selkie, I tell her, I won't think about collecting it but run as fast I can away from the shore.

'Let me know where it is.'

'Would you swim away with it, Lettie?' I ask.

'Perhaps,' she replies, smiling. 'I would have to learn to swim first.'

Lettie

Oh Norman, I don't say, I would leave in an instant. And once I did I could never return to my human body or even be on the land again. I would breathe the sea in through my gills and wend my way with my lover through the deeps where even God is silent and there is nothing but freedom to enjoy.

That is of course a dream and what I will ultimately find on the Orkneys is likely a cold and miniature version of home, though I must say I welcome the movement of travel and the promise of wide open spaces in which to rove. Father will not be happy when I go off alone, and to placate him I will sometimes walk with mother or Arthur. The best company will be that of Horace who won't have much to say, but when he does will teach me to pay attention to new sights and sounds. I never really heard cattle lowing until he told me their moos and snuffles are as varied as human voices. What he said actually was that cows talk like we do to one another and just like us they can be happy, sad, angry, or merely content. I want to ask him if the Orkney cattle low with a different accent or a burr, but that would hurt his feelings. Up north there's bound to be sufficient wildlife as well for Norman's attention. He wants to put everything in a jar, except selkies perhaps. For Horace the entire world is washed up daily in a bottle he holds carefully then throws back into the sea. He would watch me swim off and nod in acceptance.

Once we're on the island I'll be fine. Mother says the house is apparently large enough for me to have my own bedroom – in the rooming house at Cleethorpes I had to share with Norman, but he's getting too old for that now. The train ride north will be difficult. For one thing everyone except for father and mother will jostle for the window. For another the chatter will be endless and I'll be expected to participate. Arthur and I can speak of Mrs. Browning or *Middlemarch* but only for so long before Ernest brings us back to earth with one of his rehearsals for a sermon or Bertie regales us with tidbits of Scottish legal history. I'm not being fair. To them, I suppose, I'm a tiresome woman who never seems to be happy about very much but whose tongue, whenever it flaps, makes sure they suspect their own contentment. Now there's a picture I've not imagined before – flapping Lettie, the predictable tormentor of her younger but wiser brothers. I must have some kind things to say occasionally, just to keep them on their toes.

Bertie

Whatever anyone might think, I am looking forward to our summer trip. Mr. Joyce has said I can work in his Bradford office while I am studying for my barrister's exams, and I will start there in mid-September. I will miss Saturday cricket with the lads and their company afterwards, but otherwise I'm free for the next few weeks and it's time I expanded my horizons. After all, if I am to represent clients in Her Majesty's courts I should be more familiar with Her territory. Thus far I have combed the Cleethorpes sands and know the narrow roadways between here and Leeds quite well.

Mr. Joyce tells me the differences between English and Scottish law are evident when it comes to criminal and family cases, but the intestate rules are much the same in both places. Nonetheless, I am interested in finding out the history of the property father has inherited and in making sure there are no caveats involved in his smooth acquisition of the house and its contents. I must ask him if his distant cousin had enough assets to pay the inheritance tax. Otherwise he will be stuck with it. The policies of the Lord come foremost in life, to be sure, but those niggling stipulations dreamed up by mere mortals can catch even the most faithful by surprise.

Meanwhile there is the train ride to anticipate. I've been down to the local station and learned the route – Leeds to Edinburgh, Edinburgh to Perth, Perth to Inverness, and Inverness to Thurso on the north coast. From there it's a ferry ride to Kirkwall on Mainland Island, which in our *Bartholomew Gazetteer of the British Isles* seems to be about thirty miles offshore. We leave Leeds first thing on Wednesday morning and arrive in Edinburgh in mid-afternoon. The train to Perth is a one-hour journey. Father has booked us in an old hotel in the city centre, and that means four rooms as Lettie must have her own. I'll be with Arthur and Horace, while Ernest will look after Clem and Norman. For the first time I wonder how much this trip will take from the family purse, but father has always managed our finances quite admirably so I assume all will be well. Apart from the question of the inheritance tax, there will certainly be property tax to pay annually; but in as remote a place as the Orkneys that shouldn't amount to much.

Out of Perth it's just over a hundred miles to Inverness on the Highland Main Line, By chance the clerk at our station has been to Inverness and tells me the journey through the Drumochter Pass is thrilling as is the crossing of various long viaducts. The trains at times reach speeds of 60 miles per hour! Inverness to Thurso by the Far North

Line is almost exactly the same distance, though evidently we stop at all sorts of isolated villages with queer names like Muir of Ord and Altnabreac. Perhaps, given what I've already learned, I don't need to take the actual trip at all!

Elizabeth

When Thomas told me of his inheritance I was pleased. My first thought was that he might sell the property and receive some funds to alleviate somewhat his concerns about the younger children's education and provide the older ones with a little start when they leave home. When Lettie marries, she will, of course, be looked after by her husband, but Ernest, Bertie, and Arthur will have to make their own way. Horace has a few years with us yet, but after that he will need to start as an apprentice in trade. Thomas soon disabused me of my idea of a windfall. He had inquired of the Orkney solicitor and discovered the house, although a large and sound one in the main town, would bring in less than one hundred pounds at sale, a useful sum to be sure but not enough to provide the largesse I had thought of. No, he had said, the idea of owning a permanent property was a pleasant one, not least because we had always lived in ministers' homes near a Chapel that were only ours until we moved on and could not be left to our family. Perhaps, he allowed, a rental arrangement could be made through the solicitor in Kirkwall, and one day we might take our grandchildren on holiday there. Then the thought came to him to see the place and have a holiday now. Any future rental income would offset the cost of our journey. I had not seen him so animated about something outside church business or the birth of Ernest as his first-born son.

'What do you think,' he asked. 'Could you manage six or eight weeks?' I knew he was thinking of my responsibilities here in the parish and whether I could arrange for someone to visit the cottage row at the edge of town where I and several others took food baskets and whatever comfort we could offer several days a week. There were the lesser matters of my afternoon teas with the Chapel women and my flower garden in bloom. Although I didn't say, it was the latter I would miss more than the dry clink of china and the conversations that never strayed from their expected course through niceties I was bound to observe. After a few questions as to when we would leave and details of the journey, I told him not to worry about me since his obligations were much more important than my own and he was the true voice of the Lord in our family and parish.

I must admit to my excitement about the proposed expedition. I have not been beyond the borders of two English counties except for my visit to London as a girl. The Orkneys, Thomas told me, are almost five hundred miles to the north and seem to be in another world altogether. I am also excited for the children. They, too, have been homebodies, and whenever the oldest boys have spoken of their future plans, they have never indicated any interest in travelling far, except for Ernest when he said he would like to teach for awhile at Kingswood in Somerset and even then promised to come back home and help start up a similar school in South Yorkshire. Bertie will find law work in Leeds, but I am surprised that Arthur with all his admiration of Shelley's travels has not yet made his case for going off to the Continent. Lettie could end up anywhere depending on her husband's desires, though it is most likely she will marry a local man and settle nearby. Yes, the trip will be good for them. There are many arrangements to be made in a short period, but we will be alright.

Arthur

Given a choice I'd rather the cousin had lived in Keswick so I could see where Shelley stayed briefly with Harriet and visited Southey, or even Wordsworth's cottage. I won't get any chance to breathe Edinburgh's air. He lived there with Harriet for a month when they eloped together. And if we were stopping overnight in Inverness rather than Perth I could visit the Culloden battlefield just a few miles outside the town. Father says perhaps on the way home.

We will undoubtedly be crowded into a single train compartment all the way north, so time for private thoughts, let alone writing them down in my notebook, will be under siege. But I do anticipate the glories of the landscape if I can steal a seat by the window occasionally. Though not the Alps, the Highlands will have their own heights and beauty, *Remote, serene, and inaccessible*, on which to gaze. Shelley's words about Mount Blanc could just as well describe the Orkneys whose distance by boat from the mainland alone is daunting. I doubt there is a decent library in Kirkwall and plan to pack enough books to last the entire trip. Everyone is quite excited by the prospect of the journey, even Lettie.

'Though it would be nice if you and I could have our own compartment,' she says. 'We could have great talks together and then keep silent for long stretches as each of us is capable of doing, unlike some whose names I shall not mention.'

'Let's be fair, sister mine. Father and mother will read most of the way and look up occasionally to see where we are. Horace, bless him, will gaze at the fields and imagine himself behind a harrow or at the smoke rising from forges and hear the hammers ring. Clem and Norman will understandably be bored after the first hour or two, and we'll have to set them playing some games to keep them occupied. Counting sheep or cattle by the tracks or something like that. The ones to contend with will be Ernest and Bertie. Ernest will muse aloud about the spiritual well-being of the islanders and his intention to influence them for the better, and Bertie will regale us with facts and figures – how far we travelled in the last ten minutes, how far we will go in the next ten, and so on.'

'You are cruel, Arthur.' Then she laughs. 'Cruel but close to home.'

For now, I am thinking of this trip as my own voyage to the Continent though not as the exile Shelley endured. I will see new places and people, and even encounter a new language in Gaelic, which will undoubtedly be spoken more and more as we move north. How I wish I had a friend, Byronic or otherwise, with whom to travel and exchange ideas and poems. Lettie is my escort, and I do appreciate her quick mind and ability to converse on all sorts of subjects. But she is still a woman with her own womanly concerns, and it is not the same thing as having a boon companion with whom to share one's certainties and doubts or discuss the world's larger affairs. I can think of nothing better when in the Orkneys than finding a public house in which to down a few glasses of ale and talk with other men about the issue of Scottish Home Rule. Of course, I've not yet downed a single glass anywhere and my presence in any public house would be frowned upon by father. As for Home Rule, I would be reminded very quickly by him that it was rejected by Irish voters just a few years ago and that one's earthly loyalty, whatever the changing state of the nation and the injustices within it, should always be to the Queen. I wonder if Her Majesty ever stares out the window of her train to Balmoral Castle and thinks kindly about Scots aspirations in her realm?

Ernest

When father announced his news I was interested in the circumstances of his inheritance. After all, it's not every day that one discovers a previously unknown family relation and is singled out for reward or benefit of a kind. I waited for him to inform us how soon he would sell the property, and when he announced his intention to travel to the Orkneys accompanied by all of us I was rather shocked. How could he simply abandon his duties here and what in heaven's name was the point in travelling to the back of beyond? I know nothing about the islands except they are off the northernmost tip of Scotland and such remoteness must mean a certain roughness to life there. When father said he would become an itinerant preacher I was even more taken aback since he had always seemed most comfortable, as was only natural, in a predictable pulpit speaking to those he knew well and who took unquestioningly what he said as the word of the Lord. Who can tell what primitive kind of Methodism the islanders practise and what dangers await him on his rounds by sea and land?

With father's recommendation included in my letter, I have written to the principal of Kingswood School applying for a position as an Assistant Teacher, which means I will not have to have a certificate to teach grammar and history, my two best subjects. Experience at Kingswood will forward my plans to eventually gain a Chapel of my own. But if a reply from the principal were to arrive when we are in the far north my failure to act promptly on his almost certain offer might prove catastrophic.

'As far as I know they have postal delivery in the Orkneys,' father says when I voice my worries. 'I would simply write to the principal and provide your new address for next two months.'

Then, surely having noticed my glumness, he throws me a lifeline. 'I will need help in preaching to the islanders. This will be a good chance for you to deliver some sermons of your own, probably in fields or by the seashore.'

Right away I begin to consider proper subjects for deprived island parishioners. *Salvation reaches to the End of the Earth. Listen to me O islands.* Isaiah 49:1.

3. Highlands

Bertie

The hotel room in Perth was rather dull. On a coin toss, I had to share the bed with Horace. Fortunately I am as a slim as he is round. Ernest read his book of sermons and didn't say much, while Arthur kept to himself except to ask me one or two questions about the speed of the trains and the highest points of our coming journey.

'That'll be the pass of Drumochter. The summit above is one thousand five hundred feet above sea level and we won't be far below that height.'

'Drumochter *gleams on high*,' he intoned, '*the power is there,/ The still and solemn power of many sights/ And many sounds, and much of life and death.*'

'Mr. Shelley,' I gather.

'The very same. Except for the name of the peak.'

He told me Mount Blanc was ten times higher than Drumochter and no train can come close. When we did go through the pass, however, he offered no derogatory comparisons but seemed as elated as the rest of us with the vista.

I am very interested in the viaducts across rivers boiling down from the heights and crossing small valleys in one swoop. They are engineering marvels as some are almost half a mile in length and have enormous spans. My guidebook tells me this, but I knew the figures before we set out from Leeds just as I knew the giant structures are mostly built of local red sandstone. Mother gasped as the curving track allowed her to see the first one in its entirety as we approached.

'How high above the river will we be?' Her voice had an uncharacteristic squeak.

'Fifty or sixty feet, at least. But there is no danger.'

'*Fear not, for I am with you*, saith the Lord.' Father patted her hand as he proclaimed these words, and she seemed much more comforted by them than by my own faith in the pillars and arches.

Clem and Norman were quite excited and wished they had something to throw out the window so they could watch it drop to the water below. Arthur held out a penny, but they scoffed and said it would disappear from sight after just a few feet.

'What we need,' Norman said knowingly, 'is a big log so we can see the splash. He looked around the compartment in vain.'

'I know, I know,' Clem yelled. 'You jump, Horace. We'll see your splash for sure.' We all laughed, except Horace and mother. 'That's enough, Alfred, Clement,' she said firmly, and we knew no further comments were in order since she only used our full names when annoyed. I should say Lettie smiled rather than laughed. If she wasn't immune to the vision of our chubby brother ballooning in the wind as he entertained his younger siblings with some airy antics, neither was she so taken that she would ignore his feelings at being made the obvious prat. It's interesting what father chooses to hear and to ignore. He didn't lower his book an inch, though I thought I saw his stomach give a little twitch of mirth when Clem spoke up.

Elizabeth

I am so pleased the children have been given this chance to encounter so much beyond the borders of home. We all must have a hearth to sit beside and hear there the comforting voices of those we love, but sometimes we must walk (or ride) out into the Lord's creation and grasp it at first-hand. I must admit I am like a child myself in my response to what I am seeing and hearing – the crowded platform in Edinburgh accented by thick Scots brogue, the wild Highland peaks and dales with the train whistle screeching each time we pass through a town or village without stopping, and now this stretch of track beside the Moray Firth stretching away to the Continent in its blue and sparkling manner beyond the steady rolling of the wheels. More often than not I put Mrs. Gaskell in my lap and peer past the heads and shoulders of Norman and Clem to the passing world outside. 'Look, look,' they cry, but the object of their attention has already disappeared and I must find my own piece of the panorama.

The hotel in Perth was quite pleasant. We were all tired on our arrival as we had taken the local train into Leeds at 8.00 o'clock in the morning, boarded the northern express without much delay, but didn't step down in the Edinburgh station until mid-afternoon. The children were disappointed there was no time to go out into the streets and see some sights, though Bertie did make a mad dash to the entrance and claimed to have glimpsed the famous crag rising above the city and named, as he could not refrain from pointing out, after his brother Arthur. I would have preferred he report back about minster steeples, like the one on the Church of Scotland cathedral which, as a girl, I read about in *Rob Roy*. Thank goodness the journey to Perth was under two hours. We took two cabs from the station with our luggage piled in and settled into our rooms. Although the dusk fell quickly we managed a stroll after our tea.

There is so much history in this city. Thomas has told me of the assassination of James 1st of Scotland in 1437 and the visit of Cromwell two centuries later. He is most interested in John Knox's denunciation of idolatry in 1559 which led to mobs damaging altars in various churches as well as James's tomb and to the Scottish break with the Papacy. Mr. Wesley took us down a more peaceful path leading to our own separation from the Church of England, but, as Thomas points out, nothing would have been possible if Rome had not been left behind in the first place.

I worry about the expense of our voyage. Three rooms in the hotel did not come cheaply, I know. To save money, I slept with Lettie. Thomas went in with the younger two, and the four older boys shared two beds. Then there were the cab fares and meals besides. Thomas assures me we will rent out the Orkney house to help offset our costs, but this income will not be provided all at once. He never speaks to me about how we manage from week to week at home, paying all the bills himself and giving me sufficient funds each market-day without any revelations as to what we might need to save for a rainy occasion. The Chapel, of course, houses us, so it is food and clothing we must look after, but I have never felt the children deprived of nourishment or proper attire. I know this trip is a once-in-a-lifetime event, and will be brief enough in the end, so perhaps I should stop worrying and enjoy its attractions.

Outside the window cloud shadows flicker across the Firth waters like startled birds.

Arthur

The atmosphere up here is exhilarating. I don't mean in this confined compartment filled with pungent smoke from father's pipe but outside in the keen air I breathe in deeply when lowering a corridor window to lean head and shoulders into the wind. It's best to be exposed on an upward grade when the train slows and the foul discharge from the stack tends to go straight up rather than parallel to the tracks. I learned this the hard way on my first alfresco venture.

I always knew what a sheltered existence we lived together at home, so the Orkney legacy to father has been a godsend. Here we are somewhere in the Highland wilds far away from our usual daily routines, drinking in countryside the likes of which we have not seen before, and on our way to a destination utterly off the map we have clung to for directions all our lives. What more could we ask? Yet I sense a slight anxiety in father behind George Eliot's protective cover and a nervousness in mother's laughter as she tends to her brood. Ernest always takes his cue from father, so anticipations of island preaching can't be easy for him despite his seemingly self-assured manner. Bertie takes his cue from the tangible world and will be comfortable as long as we're moving because he can anchor himself in speed and direction. When we arrive he'll simply measure the absence of progression and make it fit his rational viewpoint. Horace has his feet on the ground whether mainland or island, so he'll be alright. Clem and Norman will be fine as well, constantly distracted from any deeper concerns by the natural curiosity they haven't yet lost.

I do worry about Lettie. The sparkle in her eye is visible at each new turn of the track as the landscape is eternally revealed in undulations of possibility she had not suspected possible. What mythic tale of escape from custom is she conjuring beyond the simple story of a family holiday in which she has the predictable role of minor heroine? I will ask her once we are out of this damned compartment. As for yours truly, how much will poetry sustain or undermine once the quotidian has been left behind, the familiar perspective from which everything has been written or read thus far and on which so much relies? Leaning out and breathing in the atmosphere bespeaks freedom. From what I have no doubts. To do what I am not so certain.

Ernest

When the Lord surveyed the land and water he had brought forth on the third day and saw that it was good he must surely have glimpsed the Grampian range out of the corner of His eye. I know these heights are only hills compared to the Alps, but their peaks are quite imposing in the morning sun, and the clear blue sky above them is full of the light He declared into being. Yet how can such splendour be part of Eden if the grass is stunted by scouring winds, herbs and fruit trees are entirely absent, and neither creatures nor fowl are in the abundance the Good Book describes? My initial, humble response would be that even if Adam and Eve could not live everywhere at once in the new Creation, their dominion must surely have extended to outlying areas of the Garden just like this, hence the beauty of the landscape and hints of glory. But perhaps this is my pride speaking and am I witness to the world outside Eden after the fall where our first ancestors wandered without the Lord's pity. I must discuss the matter with Father when we have settled.

For generations cottage-dwellers, clustered together against the tempest in different valleys, must have been cut off from one another, speaking in tongues only family and close neighbours comprehended, and who's to say the railway has joined them at all except by lonely whistles in the night? There are probably few churches up in the hills so the Word brought by wandering preachers has been crucial to spiritual survival. I can only pray any Methodist visitors have prevailed. At least where we are going there will be a Chapel to serve as a base for father and myself. I mustn't be nervous about speaking before strangers. After all, when I go to Kingswood I will be far from home. But my congregation there will be mere boys not rough-hewn islanders whose judgments are based on turns in the weather or superstitions father warns me not to dismiss entirely. Despite their false notions, they will be good-hearted, he says, and eager to seek comfort in the Lord given the unrelenting demands of sod and sea.

When we stop at one especially desolate spot, Altnabreac, Arthur announces it is the most isolated station in the British Isles.

'How do you know that? I ask.

'It's in the guide I picked up in Perth,' he replies. '

You should know where the Lord is taking us.' He waves a slim paper volume at me and grins broadly.

'No matter where, I shall serve Him, Arthur.'

Father peers at us over the edge of his book but offers neither admonishment nor praise. He must not have heard our exchange.

Thomas

My text for the train is Miss Evans' novel *Adam Bede*, which I have read previously. She, of course, called herself George Eliot, concerned as she was with the proliferation of silly plots by women writers, though I'm sure she must have acknowledged the worth of Miss Austen and Miss Bronte (Charlotte, not Emily. I was not far into my perusal of *Wuthering Heights* when I realized its subject matter was wholly profane with no redeeming Christian values). Miss Evans has struck the right note, providing the correct mixture of the worldly and spiritual as well as of punishment and repentance. I do not think Hetty Sorrel should have been hung for her transgressions, but transportation itself was a cruel passage, and if there had been a sequel to this work we would have found a sad creature indeed on Australian shores.

Elizabeth reads Mrs. Gaskell. I agree with her that *North and South* is a wiser novel altogether than the more famous *Mary Barton*. This is because of the fairness of the author's judgment in her tale of the cotton-mills. It is never enough to deal with one side of the story, even if it is of workers' miseries and the injustices meted out by their so-called betters. In her greater work Mrs. Gaskell recognizes that some cotton employers were not so much cruel themselves as victims of a pernicious system that spared neither nor the poor nor those better off.

When I ask Ernest what he had brought with him he replies Mr. Wesley's sermons will carry him all the way to the islands, but for a little relief he had Mr. Stevenson's *Treasure Island*. I tell him he needs to broaden his horizons beyond piracy and one-legged sailors with parrots on their shoulders. Somewhat wounded, he asserts that most novels are too earthly for his taste and that he has tried to read those Mr. Wesley would not necessarily approve but that he would perhaps not condemn. Mr. Wesley was a great man, I tell him, but he passed on to his Maker over a century ago. While he might have been able to imagine Long John Silver he certainly could not have envisioned a world of the steam engine and telegraph. Did that mean we should do without such inventions?

'Father, I was thinking of morals. Surely they are timeless, and Mr. Wesley would understand the best and worst behaviour of today.'

'All the more reason to put that understanding to the test by your own awareness of the world's moral progress or lack of it.' I hold up my book. 'We have to comprehend the people and places around us Ernest, and writers like Miss Evans and (I nod at his mother's volume on her lap) Mrs. Gaskell show them to us in quite remarkable ways.'

I can see he is not convinced and resolve to leave my copy of *Adam Bede* on his bedside table in the Orkney house.

We are fortunate to have mostly bright clear days on our journey, and I am constantly made aware that when the Lord made the Highlands he did not skimp for beauty. The section of track between Perth and Inverness, a little over a hundred miles, takes us close to the Drumochter Summit which Bertie tells us is the highest point reached by the British railway system. The views are sublime. Great open slopes of purple flowers dotted by rather stunted trees and the occasional trace of a beck all seeming to be upswept toward heaven as if by an invisible wind that shakes the train windows when we slow on our ascent. We push through this fierce domain with all its attendant threats and our reward is to marvel, as we cross a half-mile-long viaduct, at man's capacity to tame the natural world in the furthering of God's plan. At one time this region would have been but desolate wilderness whose inhabitants knew little of anything beyond their immediate realm of heather and scree. Now the rail line links villages from one end of the country to the other, and a true community of Britons exists.

Lettie

I suppose we are a fairly happy lot given the circumstances. Nine people squeezed into one compartment for two days from Yorkshire to the Orkneys. In such a close space, in which there is no retreat except inside ourselves, we strive to please. At various stations mother and I buy meat pies and fresh fruit for sale on the platforms. The farther north we proceed the tougher the meat and the crisper the apples. She takes the tablecloth from her bag and spreads it over her lap, father's, Ernest's, and mine. When we have finished eating the others take the cloth carefully so the crumbs will not spill and have their repast. Then mother holding the four corners, turns into the corridor, lets two corners go, and skilfully deposits the crumbs on the dingy floor for the porter to sweep up.

I watch father reading his novel. It is, of course, *Adam Bede* he has chosen from his one-volume George Eliot collection, a stifling text with all the right penalties for transgression in all the right places. I would rather he be challenged by *Middlemarch* and Dorothea's struggle to survive under the weight of society's expectations, as well as her own. But he would not see any Methodist strain in Will Ladislaw or in a woman leaning away from the sanctity of her marriage. I watch mother's eyes flickering across Mrs. Gaskell's landscape. She has read *North and South* several times, and I wonder what comfort she finds in Margaret Hale's encounters with the misery of those trapped in the cotton mills. Of course, Margaret's father is a pastor who leaves the church to become a dissenter, another word for non-conformist, which is another word for Methodist. I think mother simply repeats her reading within the bounds of Chapel approval and father's. I have asked her to go with me to Haworth to see the Bronte parsonage there, but she always has some excuse. The Highlands through the train window are as close as I have been to the Yorkshire moors, and I can readily imagine Cathy and Heathcliff roaming over their crags and glens in a truly dissenting after-life.

Cathy pays such a price for her rebelliousness, desiring as she does a conventional marriage with all its trimmings *and* a lover for the depths of her soul. I would refuse Edgar Linton and Heathcliff alike because they would both want to own me, one like a china doll and the other like an emblem of the moors themselves. While such refusal would leave me alone, that is how I would prefer to be unless, unless…ah, what's the use? When we stop at Altnabreac and Arthur declares it is the most remote station in all of Britain, I wonder what would happen if I just walked off into the heather when no one was looking. Everything in the compartment would be just the same without Lettie. Only Horace would notice my absence. Mother, too, of course, but that is because she views me as an ally in the world of men.

'A penny for your thoughts,' Arthur says mischievously when we are boarding again, as if aware of my imaginings.

'They're worth much more than that,' I tell him, 'and, besides, they're not for sale.'

Clem

Norman has spied more spires than me. In Perth alone he counted a baker's dozen while I managed only six. It's not so easy from the train. You have to keep your eyes wide at the blur of villages behind station fences or in distant folds of the hills. Perhaps his spectacles do away with the blur, but I know he'd refuse to play if I took them from him. So I suggest another contest, one I have a much better chance of winning. 'Let's see who spies a castle first,' I suggest. What I don't say is that Arthur told me there's one in Inverness once owned by Macbeth. We're bound to see the battlements from the station, but I'm taller than Norman and have the better chance. He reluctantly agrees. We're only halfway to Inverness and he's already ten spires ahead of me.

I wonder what it would be like to play a piano on top of one of these mountains. I'd have to wear leather gloves and what would that do to my fingertips on the keys? Alright, I'll pretend it's not cold up there, so no gloves. But I can't pretend the great height and space away or there's no point to imagining the scene at all. Would the sounds of my piece rise up and be whirled away in the wind or would they float out over the peaks and valleys and settle calmly on the purple heather? If I played the accompaniment to a hymn would the whirlwind be tamed and the flowers bloom for my efforts? *There's a light upon the mountains/ and the day is at the spring,/ When our eyes shall see the beauty/ and the glory of the King.* Father says people request this selection from the Methodist hymnbook more than any other for their funerals. But I wouldn't want to perform anything sad up there even if it was to celebrate the life everlasting for the person who died. No, I'd want something more uplifting like *O Lord of hosts whose glory fills/ The bounds of the eternal hills*, and I wouldn't need a piano but an organ to make sure the music reached everywhere. I'd make Norman count all the notes then pluck them from the air and bring them back to me like the petals of those reverent flowers. Father has warned of the sin of pride and told me I won't play regularly in Chapel until I conquer it. But everyone in the family has something they're good at, and how is it sinful to love what you can do better than most?

Norman

Clem likes to win. And sometimes he cheats. The rules of the game are that both people have to see the spire after one of them sees it first, otherwise it doesn't count. Sometimes he insists I'm blind and how can he be expected to put up with that. I don't mind because he can't say all the time something's there that's not, and I find enough real spires that he can't overlook. Now he's invented a new game about castles. I know there aren't any of them out here, but there will be one in the city because that's where lots of houses grew up around the castle walls.

I like the countryside and wish I could walk in it. There are plenty of pathways beside the stone walls or across the heather even high up on the hillsides. All creatures great and small are watching the train. They have to be very careful crossing the tracks and the light on the engine makes them afraid. The birds are lucky because the sun and moon are the lights that show them their way and the tracks are never in their way. I think it is too cold for butterflies in the Highlands, but I hope they will be in the fields by the sea when we get to the islands. I like the way their wings point up in the air when they're resting. When moths rest their wings are flat.

My birthday is while we are on the islands. I am going to ask for a butterfly net. Right now I have to toss a piece of muslin mother gave me over them when they're not flying, but with a net I'll be able to pick them right out of the air. My teacher asked me why I don't pin them on a board, but I like them because they're alive and, besides, I don't want to use camphor that other boys use to make them go to sleep. When they're on a board they look like torn pieces of cloth hanging on a wire.

As we go over the big viaduct I can see birds below us. They are diving into the river to catch the fish. I know the birds have to eat and big fish eat their smaller cousins. That's why I like butterflies. They don't kill just sip the nectar from flowers and carry the pollen to other plants. Everything eats them – wasps, ants, spiders, snakes, toads, and rats. Arthur says Mr. Darwin calls it the survival of the fittest, but he doesn't let father hear him say so. I don't like Mr. Darwin.

Horace

What Clem and Norman don't know is that I wouldn't mind stepping out the window if I could float safely down and see the water rising up to meet me. I wouldn't make the big splash they wanted, but no matter. I've managed to stay near the glass the whole way from Perth to Inverness and now beyond. Finally there are some tilled fields by the sea and large herds of cattle and smaller flocks of sheep here and there. I decide to count the cattle but lose track before I reach one hundred. They are Ayrshires mostly and Aberdeen Angus. In the Highlands I glimpsed a few long-horns with their shaggy coats that protect them from the winter up there. I wanted to see a mountain-goat or two, but I think the trains scare them away. The sheep certainly scatter as the train roars by while the cattle hardly raise their heads. Bertie tells me there is only one breed of sheep on the Orkneys and that it eats seaweed. I don't know whether to believe him. When I get there I'll find out if it's true or not.

While we were going through the mountains I invented trails with my eyes that I followed to the tops and down the other side where the goats were jumping from rock to rock but sometimes would stay still so I could pat their noses and feed them some sugar. There were hawks flying and tiny creatures leaving marks in the ground as they hunted for food. I would try not to step on the searchers because, as father reminds, the Lord made them before he made us and they do not deserve to suffer because of our carelessness. I don't see how our feet can avoid the ants on our streets at home, but I would never pluck the wings from a fly the way I've seen Clem do. There's a nasty streak in him despite his love of beautiful music and the way his fingers dance over the piano keys. Sometimes I don't know why Norman is such pals with him since he collects his butterflies carefully without harming them.

Lettie sits beside me and points out the clouds that look like animals. Once we see a dinosaur with a long horn and another time a kangaroo. Arthur joins in and soon we have an entire zoo collection.

'What don't we have?' he asks. 'I know, a unicorn.'

'They don't exist.' 'They do in clouds,' he tells me.

Lettie pinches me gently. 'If you can't find one of those, I'll bet you can spot a dragon,' she says. And she's right. Suddenly one billows up complete with smoke coming from its nostrils. I begin to wonder what else we can see that isn't there.

4. Before the Flood

Thomas

There is a squall at sea when we arrive in Thurso. The ferry will not run until the wind subsides. *He caused the storm to be still so that the waves of the sea were hushed.* Psalms 107:29.

Ernest

I know what father is thinking. *For I have placed the sand as a boundary for the sea. Though the waves toss, yet they cannot prevail.* Jeremiah 5:22.

Arthur

I know what father and Ernest are thinking. *'Tis the terror of tempest. The rags of the sails / Are flickering in ribbons within the fierce gale.* 'A Vision of the Sea.'

Elizabeth

What a quaint little spot! But if it blows like this in July, I should not like to be here in the winter.

Norman

We're here. Hooray!

Bertie

A pamphlet at the station tells us the man who started up the Boys's Brigade was born here. Christian manliness and all that.

Horace

There's a flock of shaggy-haired sheep in a field by the tracks. 'Ach, they're from North Ronaldsay,' a porter says. 'Fine chops they make.' I wonder if they're the kind that eat seaweed.

Clem

Norman saw the castle first. I tell him there'll be plenty of sea-birds to count when we're on the ferry.

Lettie

There's no going back.

The Frame

Okay, here they are. But what to do with them now? The Orkneys came out of the blue, a way to get all nine out from under their restrictive environment, whatever Jane Austen might have made of it. If I had left them at home, they would have continued along their predictable paths. What else do Methodist ministers, their wives, sons, and daughters do? That's not fair, of course. There were already differences emerging, cutting edges that might have eventually drawn blood – Shelley from Wesley, Lettie from parental expectations, and so on – but there's nothing my mother ever told me to suggest permanent family damage in the real world until she left for Canada under the cloud of banishment after WWII. By that time, Letitia was forty-four years gone, and Bertram and Horace were dead; but she did have uncles Ernest, Arthur, and Norman left to advise about her father Clement. Did they say anything at all or just keep the brotherhood intact? Arthur at seventy-two had only a year left and may have been ill, but he's the one I would have liked her to have heard from. Norman was just sixty-three, but did he ever escape the role of the youngest sibling? As for Ernest, the minister who would outlive them all, was there any suspicion that my mother had had pre-marital relations with my father from the outposts of the Empire? Any hint of this would surely have met with severe disapproval.

My mother was meticulous in keeping ancestral birth and death certificates. In a tin box after her death I discovered at least a dozen of these going back to the beginning of the 19th century. She also saved her parents' marriage certificate, but not her own. An acrimonious separation from my father in 1949 meant she almost certainly destroyed the official document of her attachment to him, probably when she was finally allowed a divorce and remarried in the 1970s. British records show a registration for marriage in 'July-August-September 1945,' nothing more specific. Provided I was a full-term baby – and my weight of almost 10 pounds suggests I was – and given my birth-date, my licit conception should have occurred around mid-August of the year before. Were my mother and father married by then or not until September? Did my mother later go home to Grimsby, visibly pregnant before embarking on the former troop-transport ship *HMS Letitia*? Yes, that was the name, it's true. Was Lettie watching over me?. If so, Clement and Ernest would have done the numbers. What else but shame would have caused my grandfather to banish her entirely from his house and not speak to her for the remainder of his life? I'll never know.

These are the facts and possible truths behind the fiction I seem compelled to construct. I know so little and so little remains of the lives I am attempting to convey, but as I suggested at the beginning, the photograph alone is not enough to leave behind. I am haunted by the likelihood that I am the only one able to identify the nine people standing and sitting in the garden. Deference to what actually happened to them does not prevent their lived experience from disappearing entirely, but such obliteration is worth less than a fiction about them. If they are safe in the arms of the Lord, my efforts are either inconsequential or a desecration, but I prefer to continue as their voice within what Camus called – my great-grandfather and Ernest would have been appalled at such sacrilege – 'the benign indifference of the universe.'

5. *Keys to the Kingdom*

Elizabeth

The house is truly delightful, at least at this time of year. We will be quite comfortable here for the next six or seven weeks. After that, I do not see why Thomas may not rent out the property to a local family from year to year. I am not sure I would want to travel all this way again, but it might be good to bring just Clem and Norman back before they're too old. Out the window now I can see them cavorting on the beach below, their cheeks already ruddy with salt and sun, their tiny cares certainly forgotten. I know the others appreciate the surroundings and the change from home, but their enjoyment, except perhaps for Horace, depends in large part on a certain departure date. He attended the market cattle sale on Wednesday and Saturday past and must have impressed the farmers somehow because he was offered an unpaid position as a 'leader' or one who brings the cows into the pen for bidders' inspections. When I first saw him holding the halter of a massive bull my concern for his safety was tempered by his obvious confidence and sheer bliss at being where he wanted to be.

Ernest has begun to travel with Thomas to the villages outside Kirkwall where they are preaching to those without Chapels and bringing succour to the poorer families. It is a valuable experience for him, but I know he has ambition that will be constrained by island borders. Bertie spends much of his time at the assizes listening to the arguing of cases. Though he admits Scottish law is quite different from English jurisprudence, he feels he is preparing in the essentials for his coming career. Arthur walks a lot along the coast and returns from his treks to write endlessly, with often furrowed brow, in his leather notebook. 'It's like seeing the world anew every day,' he tells me, 'and I have to find ways to say that.' Lettie helps me shop and tend the house, but in the afternoons is content to be on her own, and often walks out along the shore. Unlike Arthur who comes home to the haven of his notebook, I sense what she is searching for lies out there in waters too deep for anchor, and I worry when she is not back well before tea. As for me, I have joined a group of ladies whose accepted task is to provide food baskets for the unfortunate of Kirkwall and the smaller, neighbouring settlements. They are a bit reserved, though their hearts are in the right place, and certainly the work they do is admirable and selfless. Thomas encourages me to slip a short biblical verse daily into my exchange with the poor.

Bertie

There was a case this morning concerning a crofter accused of stealing another man's lambs. On conviction, the penalty in the past was either death by hanging or transportation for life to Australia. Nowadays it is usually a heavy fine and, if the prisoner at the dock cannot pay, imprisonment for a number of years. In this instance, the one charged is a young islander, perhaps a little older than me, who apparently used force when the owner of the animals caught him in the act. I sat and heard him plead not guilty, a wholly expected claim given the prospective punishment, but there was something about his calm demeanour and mild manner that was compelling. Curious and drawn to his defence table, I introduced myself to his barrister and mentioned my coming service back home in the offices of Mr. Joyce. The man had a harried look as he gathered up his papers, but he stopped to shake my hand and inquire how long I had been in Kirkwall. Encouraged, I replied my residence had been but a week in length, and asked if there was anything I might do to aid in this particular case before the court. During our exchange I felt the steady gaze of the accused on us both and turned once to smile at him, wanting to show myself as an ally. His own tranquil expression didn't change, and I thought to myself he could not be guilty of a violent act even if he had taken the sheep.

'Do? Why yes, if you can pass your Barrister's examinations immediately you can take over the case on your own. Jamie MacBride here will not speak about what has passed except to admit to me he did the deed yet proclaim his innocence in court in that damnably unruffled way he has. I've no time to investigate, and I'm afraid the evidence is rather against him. Witnesses for the prosecution, you know.'

'Perhaps I could ask some questions on your behalf,' I ventured. I explained briefly that my time was my own for the next few weeks.

'You'll not find it easy, young man, being an outsider.'

'Perhaps not, but the alternative doesn't seem very satisfactory. Mr. MacBride will surely go to prison from what you say.'

He thought it over, rubbing his chin as he did so. Finally, he put out his hand and announced, 'Campbell's the name. I can't pay you for this, you realize.'

'Oh, no, sir. I'm happy to oblige.' After we shook on it, I turned to greet Jamie MacBride, stating my own name in what I thought was a confident tone. His fingers were warm to my touch and his grip was firm, but he said nothing at all. I began to wonder if my client was this taciturn what would those I wanted to question out in the countryside be like?

Mr. Campbell has given me a list of the witnesses and of others who might have something to divulge about the matter. I should say 'matters' because there is the charge of sheep-stealing and the added one of violence against the animal's owner.

Tonight at supper I told father and mother my news, stressing my belief that McBride was innocent of the assault, at least. Everyone else was there too, of course, and they all chimed in with their opinions before any parental reaction was forthcoming. Only Horace held his peace.

'Bertie's Sherlock Holmes,' Clem shouted.

'Can I help?' Norman cried.

'More Doctor Watson, I should think,' Ernest proclaimed.

'Good for you, Bertie,' Arthur said. 'I'm sure you'll see justice done.' But I couldn't tell if he was serious or not.

I looked across the table at Lettie who met my gaze evenly before standing to clear the plates. 'I envy you, Bertie,' she said quietly. I didn't like to feel sorry for her, but understood, given her housebound lot, why she might complain.

The real verdict was, of course, still to come. Mother waited for father's decision which didn't hang in the air for long. He stroked his whiskers for a few moments then brought his hand down like a gavel on the oak table-top. 'You've done well, my lad. I doubt you'll be an instrument of any real change in the course of justice, but nonetheless your efforts will be Christian ones and further the cause.'

Father, unlike my older brothers, was completely serious, and I was relieved by his praise. Confident that mother would agree with him, I was surprised by her response.

'What if you find Mr. MacBride *is* guilty of violence?' she asked.

'Then I suppose it will be a lesson not to let my emotions determine my taking a case in the future.' I meant what I said but sensed if I was so terribly wrong about reading Jamie McBride's visage there was no solid ground in a barrister's life for me.

Horace

I feel comfortable when I'm at one end of a rope. The Angus bull could pull me like a rag doll and even trample me if I fell and wasn't quick enough. But the ring through his nose is on my side, and because I never pull on it sharply I like to think he trusts me and feels the bidder's pen is as good a place to be as any. Of course, he's not going off to be slaughtered for beef steaks like the rest of the herd but to pasture amongst the cows so the eventual owner can boast of his pedigree. The farmers rely on my confidence and that I am comfortable amongst the animals. One told me I had a way with them that reminded him of a quiet collie who kept them in order without any need to bark or nip at their heels. Another asked me how long I was staying on the island and whether I might be convinced to keep on if he offered me good wages. I laughed and replied that my father and mother would never permit this, but he said if I was able to persuade them the position was mine. I asked what exactly was the position, and he answered I'd be under his foreman and no other, and that with my abilities I'd be foreman soon enough. I'm nearly fifteen and still have school to finish, but maybe I could attend a Kirkwall classroom for part of each day after my morning chores were done and before the evening tasks in the barn. It's a long way from home and I might get lonely, especially for mother's cooking. I'd have to promise father to go to Chapel regularly and never forget my prayers, but even so he'll not soon give his approval. I must think of a way to convince him especially when he's bound to declare I could do the same thing in Yorkshire and be with the family besides.

It's the island as well as the animals. There's something about the way the earth and sea meet the sky that makes me feel at home here. Father would say it's the Lord's scheme unfolding, but I just mean how my feet are firmly on the ground while a part of me rides the scudding clouds and surveys everything below. Mother understands. I can feel her watching me when I lead the bull into the enclosure. She will cry if I stay, but she will be happy for me. I wonder if my wages would let me rent the house father has inherited. That way everyone could visit whenever they wanted. I would miss Lettie most of all, but if she came once or twice a year we would have a grand time together. Maybe if she didn't marry we could live here together. But I want her to marry a good man and bring her children to see Uncle Horace.

Norman

My birthday present from father and mother was the butterfly net I wanted. It has a handle that folds up so they had it hidden in mother's suitcase all the way here on the train. I have been out in the fields and it is a much better catcher than a muslin swatch. At first I caught different coloured ones I called blues, and browns, and reds, as well as one with tiny green veins in its wings and a big one with orange-and-black-spotted wings. Mr. Garson says the big one is called the Painted Lady and teaches me the names of the others one too. He was in the field with his own net and even though he is very old he can run nearly as fast as me or maybe it's just his arms that are faster the way they swoop in a big curve through the air and pluck the butterflies from the tips of the grass and flowers. He lives here all the time and used to be the postmaster in Kirkwall. I took him home to introduce him to mother, and she says he is a good man who will teach me lots of things about my collecting.

At his cottage he has big boards with dead butterflies pinned to them under glass. I cried when I saw them, but he says it is the only way to study and compare them one to the other. I said why can't you just look at them when they're alive in jars, and he answered think of all the jars you'd have to have and how could you look at them all at once the way you can on the board and put their names underneath? He says they don't suffer if you use the camphor properly, just a little drop. When I watch him in the field I see he lets go the ones he has already and only keeps the new ones that are not on the boards. He is looking for a Small Tortoiseshell and wants me to help him because he has not seen one for a long time. They are rusty-red but have big eye spots of black and blue and yellow on each wing to frighten birds away. He says their caterpillars are even scarier because they are shiny black with six rows of sharp spikes on their backs. I ask Mr. Garson if he's a naturalist and he laughs and says we all are if we only knew it.

I like going to Mrs. Drever's cottage where Clem plays the piano. For my birthday he played a piece called 'Butterfly' by a man from Norway. When his hands went fast I could see them fluttering from stalk to stalk and when they went slow all their colours rested as they sipped the nectar. I said it was a good present but he would always hold it on the tips of his fingers, and he said he would play it for me every year until he grew up and went away. That made me happy and sad. I don't want anyone to go away. When I see Lettie walk to the end of the beach and disappear I call her name, but she doesn't hear me. Arthur disappears too, but I know he will always come back for tea. Sometimes when I am on the beach with Clem I pick up nine small stones, one for each of us. Then I look at the millions of other stones curving down the shore as the waves wash over them and wonder how God picks us out from the pile. Does he do it just like me? I hope so because when the nine stones are warm between my palms I place them carefully back on the ground and tell myself I will never forget where they are.

Arthur

I have a plan; well, not a plan, actually, but an idea. I will try to write a poem every day that we are here. It's ambitious, I know, but I'll have a lot of time on my hands and there's the fact everything is so new. How can I avoid this dramatic landscape, not to mention the endlessly restless sea? Then there are the people living out their daily lives in front of me, much like at home, but with an intensity I haven't seen before. Of course there are doctors and lawyers, shopkeepers, and such, but even they dwell within the circle of those exposed to hardship and danger – the fishermen the chief exemplars with their scored palms and faces, but the crofters too; not the wealthy farmers with their large, fenced-in properties but the simple workers of the fields whose bodies and souls are battered by fierce winds and always open to injury of bone or spirit.

I walk every day along the beach or on paths that rise and fall with the rock formations to end on cliff-tops high above the waves and provide spectacular views of the firth. Sometimes Lettie accompanies me, but she mostly respects my need to be alone and follows branching tracks through gorse or harrowed ground to her own solitude. When we are together we talk of many things, but our conversation always seems anchored by household concerns and who we are and can be in relation to our parents and siblings. I suppose we can't escape this and never will until we break off to start families of our own.

'You're much more likely to marry before me,' I tell her. 'If I ever do.'

'Why's that so, do you think?'

'Because it's the way of the world, Lettie, for women at least.'

'Perhaps I'll stay a spinster forever or become a nun. Are their Methodist nuns? I've never thought of that before.' She pokes me in the side and laughs loudly. A red-legged partridge rises from the grass nearby.

'I don't think there are, and father is certain not to let you convert to papist ways.' I am always happily surprised at the play of Lettie's mind and by her ironic exercise of opinion, but this time she shocked me with her no-nonsense assertion.

'I doubt he could stop me if my mind was made up.'

'You're not serious,' I gasped, then wondered at my aversion to such rebelliousness and daring. Was my own quest for independence a sham if I was not prepared to test it in like fashion? But what could I do? I have no interest in joining a holy order of any kind, and I can't afford travel to Italy or Greece.

She patted my arm. 'No, I'm not serious, dear Arthur, at least about passing the rest of my days in a nunnery. But one thing I am certain of. I will not marry because father and mother want me to or in the absence of true feeling on my part for a man. That's not the way of the world for me.'

Later, I write down the gist of our exchange in my notebook then strive to fix her exact words on my page. Of all of us, Lettie I feel has the most potential to rise above the ordinary, but because she is a woman that potential has the least chance of being realized. I hope she does meet someone she can love and whom father and mother approve of. That combination is likely her only way to happiness. Whatever she may say, I cannot believe she would be satisfied to grow older without companionship to comfort her heart and mind, especially after I leave home and her favourite Horace does as well.

As tides make haste at appointed hours
All are powerless to ignore
The rushing currents of our lives
That bear us lost from shore to shore

From summit high I watch the waves
In patterns endless dance and crash
Against the rocks that suffer them
In ages now and of the past

What place has love in this vast scene
Or hope to leave a trace behind
Of glance or touch or even child
All human ways that are a sign?

I have bought another notebook in which I will put the poems exclusively. As with the first volume my name and home address are on the inside of the front cover in case of loss. If I am going to be a writer – and that is what my determination to record my island sojourn surely indicates – then my words must not disappear. They are a long way from Shelley's but remain my own small contribution to intellectual beauty as much as I can make them so.

Lettie

If I did become a nun these islands would be a good place for my convent. Not here in Kirkwall but on a height of land above the sea with a small field behind where I and my few companions could grow our vegetables and perhaps some pear or apple trees. I like to imagine myself tending these crops peacefully and later sitting in a courtyard's pool of sunlight and meditating on God's grace in the world. Ha! It's too cold for such lush growth and, besides, I wouldn't last a week in such a place. I only conjured up the possibility of my retreat to tease Arthur and because he seems to believe that no matter my good intentions I don't have a chance to escape the marriage role assigned to me. As for the other choice of spinster, that's preferable because in my loneliness I wouldn't be confined to a single spot and would be free to travel and meet a variety of people.

Arthur speaks of going to Italy or Greece when he can afford to. What would he say if I got there before him? I may not know Shelley's work like he does, but in books at home I have seen the frescoes of Giotto and the paintings of della Francesca, and these are enough to pull me towards Tuscan towns and villages. There is that third choice, of course, the path of inevitability father and mother have in mind. Somewhere out there, apparently, the right man is waiting for me, the one with the truly Christian outlook, the secure employment, and the ability to tame wild Lettie. I don't mind attending Chapel each Sunday as there are many things to be learned from the ways God is present in the world, even if it is one's father mostly defining those ways. Well, he and He give me food for thought at the very least. As for a steady income, who would not want that, though I would shun ostentation of any kind in my home or elsewhere. But the taming of wild Lettie will never occur because it would undoubtedly mean not just physical but spiritual submission far beyond what is demanded of me by the Lord.

When I walk out beyond the beach leaving everyone behind and make for the headlands with their stunning views of other islands and the ocean I know stretches away to the Pole, it is not to lose but find myself. Any man who would accompany me on such journeys would do well to consider me his equal, however my skirts might drag in the dirt or be torn on pricks of gorse. He would do well to talk to me with a gentle though agile tongue that would ignore no subject for my sake or his own for that matter. If I am not to leave him behind, he will not prison me in any way and help me find she whom I seek as best he can, as I will help him discover the self he searches for. That is what will make us different from Cathy and Heathcliff because all she can do is refuse while all he can do is possess. I cannot explain this to father and mother. They want me to have an uncomplicated ordinary life, but how plausible is that if they open their eyes to each of us they have borne and raised. Ernest is no mere replica of father as I think will eventually be shown. Bertie has a compassion that has already revealed itself in the case of Mr. MacBride. Arthur will write himself away from our closed circle, I am convinced. Horace will simply remain Horace and that will be enough to assure his independence. Clem's love of music is stronger than his love of the Lord, and it will carry him into a new realm where father cannot follow. As for Norman, his position at the end of the line has meant he has gained from us all. This and his pursuit of natural beauty will provide his escape.

This morning I came upon a cottage tucked away in the folds of a vale leading down to the sea. There was no smoke rising from the chimney and no dogs barked so I knew the owner was away. From the stone path that led to the door I could see a small wharf jutting out from shore and farther out on the water the trace of a sail. I sat on a bench by the garden gate and watched the sail until it vanished in a trick of sunlight.

Clem

I was very disappointed to discover no piano in the house, but mother has found one for me in the home nearby. Now that she has realized my abilities, Mrs. Drever, the elderly widow of a music teacher, is content to hear me play without instruction, though occasionally, to give her credit, she does suggest a fingering technique or pace to a glissando that I cannot help but take into account. She has given me the key to her cottage so I might practice whenever I like regardless whether she is at market or visiting friends. Sometimes Norman comes with me, but he never really listens and is more content to explore the few small rooms though only the main one is really at our disposal. The first day he was quite excited to discover a collection of sea-shells, large and small, with whorls and pale colours that, he says, are unlike anything he has found at Cleethorpes.

The furniture is dark and heavy with tartan cushions to soften the chair-seats and table-tops covered with finely-knit doilies that look like spiders' webs. Mrs. Drever has given me permission to make tea in her absence, though I must be careful with her china pot and cups. With Norman around I don't bother because something is liable to get broken. When I mention this to him he is quite affronted, reminding me that a pianist isn't the only one with a delicate touch. A naturalist, he says, must handle all sorts of things like birds' eggs or butterflies' wings with care, and the last time he looked all the sea-shells were intact. I suppose he's right, though there's nothing as fragile as a note coaxed from an ivory key. My real quest is for an organ, but it seems the only one in the town is inside the great cathedral. I'm afraid to ask father for permission to enter this Church of Scotland that was once a bastion of the Roman faith because I know he'll refuse. So strong is my desire to glimpse the pipes and maybe even touch the stops, however, that I imagine defying him and sneaking through a side door.

We spend a lot of our time on the beach, which isn't the sandy stretch of Cleethorpes but a rocky shelf higher up and a pebbled ledge below where the waves grind down anything in their way. Bertie has come along with us and collected a few stones, the ones, he says, that shine whether they're wet or not. But he's busy in the courts most days, so Norman and I wander together sometimes more than a mile from our house. Although it is near mid-July the water is still very cold, and although we are barefoot and walk in up to our knees I would not want to go in any farther. Bertie says if you fell off a fishing boat, you would die from the cold in minutes.

The Chapel minister, Mr. Taggart, has introduced father to the congregation and invited him to speak from the pulpit. I could see how pleased he was to have been asked. Mostly, though, he and Ernest do their preaching where there are no pews or even church buildings. Fishermen's sheds or farmers' barns are what we use, Ernest says, and often as not the open air.

'Do you sing hymns?' I ask.

'Of course, though many do not know the words right through.'

I would like to accompany them and perhaps direct the musical throng, but he says they are a simple crowd who would not take kindly to being led by a boy, whatever his supposed accomplishments as a choir-master. I know he is mocking me and is perhaps nervous about his own performance before the multitudes. I will approach father sooner or later. The cathedral is one thing, but a request to attend a Methodist service is quite another.

Once, as a joke, I ask Norman how many stones he thinks there are on the beach.

'Oh millions and millions,' he replies without hesitation.

Annoyed by his certainty, I suggest he count them to be sure, but he just laughs and says it would be like counting the stars at night.

'We'd lose track and have to start all over again.'

When I play the piano there are countless variations on a theme or in the subtle bending of the notes in any one piece. Like smooth pebbles beneath my fingers or the eternal winking of stars.

Thomas

We have been here for three days, and the wind has not stopped blowing. Our ferry ride was a difficult one. Elizabeth remained below on a bench outside the ladies' commode. The boys played cards and occasionally came on deck where I stood by the rail to ask how much longer we would take. Lettie, granted her sea-legs by some naval ancestor, stood near the prow throughout the voyage to take the wind and foam in her face without flinching. She was the first to spy land ahead, and I could see the crew were impressed with her pluck if her brothers were not.

We sailed past the Old Man of Hoy in slightly calmer waters and the rocky tower was an impressive sight indeed.

'Has anyone ever climbed it?' Norman whispered.

'It's impossible,' Bertie told him. 'Too steep and treacherous.'

'I don't know,' Arthur replied. 'If they can conquer Mount Blanc and put an observatory on its peak, why not scale a piece of rock under five hundred feet high?'

'It's a steeple,' Ernest said, 'fashioned by the Lord, and is not meant for climbing.'

Then Arthur surprised me by quoting lines from Shelley that actually seemed to support Ernest's view: *Thou hast a voice, great Mountain, to repeal/ Large codes of fraud and woe; not understood/ by all, but which the wise, and great, and good/ Interpret, or make felt, or deeply feel.*

When I commended this choice of his poet's words, he smiled. 'I must read you the entire work, father.'

The Reverend John Taggart knew of our coming and made sure my cousin's house was in order for our occupation. It is a pleasing stone building on the edge of Kirkwall with a view of the bay and wider sea to the north. There is a large hearth in the sitting room where we will burn peat on cooler evenings. Elizabeth is pleased with the kitchen which has a wooden counter top set in its middle, for cutting fish as Mr. Taggart told us. The children wandered the rooms quite happy with what they found – plain but solid furniture; knotted plank floors apart from the stone-paved kitchen; painted pictures of cliffs and waves, fishing smacks and harbours; and, above all, an atmosphere of peace and contentment. I never knew my cousin, of course, but have a strong feeling of kinship already.

'Look how the light glows and dances through the panes,' Lettie exclaimed as she paused in front of the sitting-room windows.

'I daresay a rainy day won't provide the same effect,' Ernest said.

She patted his arm affectionately. 'Just a different one, brother drear.'

How old is the house, father?' Bertie asked.

'I'm not exactly sure, but from the style, I'd say well over a hundred years.'

Arthur picked up a photograph of two elderly women side by side on the front step. 'One of these must be our cousin,' he said. 'In their eighties at least, whichever one she is. I'll wager she lived here her entire life, and her parents before that, so you're probably right, father.'

This morning we attended Mr. Taggart's sermon in the Chapel. A short man, he stands tall in the pulpit with his rasping voice and piercing gaze. His subject was the growing unrest among the local fishermen who feel the Glasgow and Edinburgh buyers are cheating them of any profit when the seasons for herring and crab are already quite short. In the harbour of Stromness on the south coast there are, he says, over a hundred boats sitting idle in protest. I was curious as to how he would introduce the good Book and very pleased when he recited 1 John 3:17 – *But if anyone has the world's goods and sees his brother in need, yet closes his heart against him, how does God's love abide in him?* He went on to declare that because the Lord had given us dominion over the fish of the sea, it was our responsibility as Christians to share the wealth we take from the waters and never seek gain at the expense of others. I have arranged to go with him to Stromness this coming week to speak with the men on the docks and provide what advice we can to aid in their efforts. He also tells me there are many men on the outer islands, more isolated from one another, who are also struggling with the southern buyers and who need to hear the message of Chapel support. We must try to find a way to reach them. Meanwhile, at his request, I will visit as many people as possible between Kirkwall and Stromness, taking Ernest with me to spread the Word.

Ernest

The first days I went out with father I was quite nervous and glad to have his great wisdom and skill in dealing with a congregation. Although, applying that term to a rag-tag collection of villagers and outliers does a disservice to our Yorkshire faithful. Those we meet with listen respectfully but without much fervour, and the occasional murmured 'Aye!' is a welcome response in the midst of a sermon. Father says Mr. Taggart preaches as often as he can in these hinterlands, but that for many weeks on end the people who do not journey into Kirkwall or Stromness on business are left to their own devices as far as praising the Lord is concerned. When I look into the faces of the men and their families, I see simple strength and goodwill but also a kind of bewilderment that life need be so harsh and demanding. They farm or fish, depending on the time of year, neither herd-owners nor large boat captains but lonely tillers of the field and skippers of dories that never venture too far from land.

The first time I spoke father stood to the side, nodding his head as if to punctuate my expression of purpose and belief. He left it to me to choose my text, and I settled on 1 Corinthians 13: 4-7 – *Love is patient and kind; love does not envy or boast; it is not arrogant or rude. It does not insist on its own way; it is not irritable or resentful; it does not rejoice at wrongdoing, but rejoices with the truth. Love bears all things, believes all things, hopes all things, endures all things.* I told them that through a community of Love they would find joy amidst their sorrows and reward for their pains, and that such Christian solidarity would bring peace and contentment to their lives. Then I led them in the hymn, 'Love Divine, all Loves Excelling,' written by Mr. Wesley's brother Charles:

> *Love Divine, all Loves excelling,*
> *Joy of Heaven to Earth come down,*
> *Fix us in the humble Dwelling,*
> *All thy faithful Mercies crown.*

Few of them, if any, knew the words, but it is the job of the preacher to sing loudly and with great conviction so the unlearned choir will follow at least the tune with hummed conviction. Later, father told me I had done very well and said that particular hymn had been Christianized by Mr. Wesley from an opera about King Arthur. It was very appropriate to my sermon, he said, but perhaps we should both look to the Scottish hymnbook for the inspiration of song.

I am not fond of Mr. Taggart's preaching. For one thing, I can sometimes barely understand him through his thick accent. For another, he seems fixed on attacking anyone not from the Orkneys who threatens the well-being of the islanders. That is all very well, but surely there has to be compromise on both sides of a dispute. Prices for fish should be fair, but the fishermen should not shut down their own livelihood and take food from the mouths of others. I will leave the Stromness affair to Mr. Taggart and father and practice the Word with those who not only work hard but do so with little expectation. *Come to me, all who labour and are heavy laden, and I will give you rest.* Matthew 11:28.

Several times I have passed the remarkable edifice that is St. Magnus Cathedral, but have yet to summon up the courage to go inside.

6. Sanctuaries

Horace

I've made up my mind and have spoken to mother about my staying here. At first she tried to discourage me, but then she saw my disappointment and a tear came to her eye as she told me she would think things over and I was not yet to say anything to father. I know what I am asking. If he were to let me stay, father would not only insist on my weekly Chapel presence but also on my finishing this coming year at school. But he would be most concerned about my well-being amongst strangers and that no one take advantage of me. The man who offered me wages and the promise of a foreman's position one day is Mr. Spence. When I met him at the market the next week he said he would board me in his own home and that his wife and three young sons would welcome me. I told him I had yet to speak to my father but said it would help if he allowed me to attend school for part of the week until the spring. I was pleased when he had no objection, saying my chores and responsibilities on his farm could be carried out in the mornings and evenings for the time being. Then I raised the most important question with some trepidation.

'Perhaps you know my father is a Methodist minister and devoted to the Word of the Lord. I do not mind, but he will want to know what religion you follow.'

Mr. Spence cleared his throat. 'I am a Presbyterian, Horace, and attend St. Magnus twice on Sundays. But I am no proselytizer of my own faith and believe every man is free to worship as he secs fit. I will be happy to discuss these matters with your father. I might add, I attended school with Mr. Taggart, and he and I remain well acquainted to this day.'

This last remark gave me more hope than I had expected. If Mr. Taggart would recommend Mr. Spence to father I would be halfway to my new home. I mentioned the possibility to mother, and she seemed pleased, saying she would speak to father on his return from Stromness where he is busy with the fishermen's protest for a few days. However satisfied she might be with Mr. Spence's godliness, though, I can tell she is still reluctant to let me remain. I need another ally.

Just as Mr. Taggart will work on father, so Lettie might help me with mother.

'Are you sure you want to do this, Horace?'

We are walking along the beach where an offshore wind flattens the water and swirls it into unexpected patterns that ripple into one another then disappear.

'Yes, I want to live here even though I know I will be lonely at first when you all have gone.'

I am excited to say this to her because such loneliness will mark the start of my new life, but also because saying it somehow suggests it is possible even if the test that is father has not yet been passed. Then I try to explain to her how the island makes me feel as if my own life is a life worth living as the wind blows over it and the sea pushes and pulls it into new shapes. I stumble with the words, but she understands.

'I do know what you mean. There's a freedom here that's not at home. I'd like to stay with you...'

'Would you, Lettie?'

'...but I can't. My own freedom must find another form, and I can't predict what that will be, not here but perhaps in a place like here.'

I feel crushed for a moment by her refusal, but then am buoyed by her support for the rest of my dream. 'You will speak to mother, won't you? If you are on her side, she will help sway father.'

'You have great faith in a pair of women, don't you? Well, with you we'll be three against one. And maybe we can even rope the others into our cabal. Probably not Ernest and Bertie, at least until father agrees, but Arthur certainly. As for Clem and Norman, they'll just wish they were you and whatever noises they make will serve as a choir behind the main voices.' I hugged her and told her I loved her.

She pushed me back gently but held my shoulders and spoke as if everything had been worked out. 'I shall miss you, little brother, and I want you to promise you'll host me once you become foreman and have a place of your own.'

'When you've found your freedom?'

She laughed. 'Yes, once I've done that.'

Thomas

Two days ago I accompanied Mr. Taggart to the harbour at Stromness. The port was filled with fishing boats, sails furled, and I hadn't realized there were so many belonging to the island. When I remarked on this, Mr. Taggart told me quite a number of them had come across the firth from Hoy and South Ronaldsay. We met with the organizers of the protest and learned the men are determined to stay idle until the southern buyers admit their efforts are worth more and pay them a fair price for their fish. One leader in particular, Rory Parker, appears to be quite militant and says he will burn his boat before he allows it to sail again for a pittance. When I asked how their families were surviving, he shrugged and admitted it was hard. But it seems the other islanders are in sympathy with the fishermen's plight and are supplying basic necessities for the time being.

'Of course, we must go light on the grog, so a dram of whisky must last that wee bit longer,' he declared amidst some hearty laughter from his colleagues. I refrained from replying that such temperance might be a blessing of sorts.

Apparently, they have an arrangement to sell their herring and crab only to certain buyers, a binding agreement – although no actual document appears to exist – that means the price is not flexible through the demands of a larger market. Mr. Parker tells me that after selling his catch, paying his crew, and putting aside a little money for the upkeep of his craft, he has almost nothing left to feed himself, his wife, and five children.

'All we're asking for is decent earnings,' he says. 'None of us go out there' – he gestures towards the firth – 'expecting to become lairds, but we do expect enough to keep body and soul together.' He nods at me. 'The soul is your department, sir, but in my opinion it's in real trouble if it hasn't a full stomach behind it.'

Once again, I bite my tongue. His image is somewhat vulgar, but a man who exposes himself to danger on a regular basis and has to worry about where his next meal is coming from is bound to drift from the Lord. For all that, he is goodhearted, and the other men certainly respect him. Right now their mood is determined but still optimistic. Mr. Taggart emphasizes to me that if the protest continues for any length of time things will become very difficult indeed. The other islanders have only so much they can provide, and the men may have to leave the harbour to catch just enough to sustain their families. According to the agreement, they must sell a certain percentage of what they haul in to the buyers, no matter how small, so there will be a monetary cost, as well as one of principle, to their attempts at mere survival.

I ask Mr. Taggart if I have his permission to speak about the protest when I am in the countryside with Ernest, much as he is doing in Kirkwall on Sunday mornings and in Stromness later in the day. I am an outsider, after all, and there are some who might take umbrage with the insertion of yet another southern voice into their business. He replies that

I must preach on what I see fit and that it is precisely a southern understanding of their plight that will show them not all from the nether regions are scoundrels. Ernst baulks a little when I inform him later that day that we are entering the fray on the side of the fishermen, but I respond that these islands in their beauty and simplicity are a kind of holy place, a temple of land and water, if you like, reflecting the Lord's beneficence, and remind him of Christ's exhortation to the money-changers in the Gospel of Matthew— *My house shall be called the house of prayer, but ye have made it a den of thieves.*

'I hadn't realized you feel that strongly about it, father.'

I hadn't realized it myself, but fairness is as fairness does, and those men on the Stromness docks are only seeking just compensation for their labours. I indicate I will think on a sermon about this matter. Some hours after our exchange Ernest finds me, still rather weary from my journey, turning the pages of the Good Book at the parlour table and offers me a starting point from Psalms 140: *I know that the Lord secures justice for the poor and upholds the cause of the needy.* I thank him for this contribution and encourage him to preach on these words at the next opportunity. My energy renewed by such faith and filial devotion, I turn back to my own search for inspiration.

Arthur

What extraordinary things a little travelling has done to our family! Father is knee-deep in Orkney politics since the Scottish government is now threatening to step into the fishermen's protest and the locals are up-in-arms about this. It seems that mainland welfare is being affected by the work stoppage and the interests of the buyers will take precedence. Ernest has apparently blossomed as a preacher. Though I have yet to hear him speak, father says the outlying villagers have nothing but good things to say of him, and he is always eager to perform. Bertie is involved in his case of sheep-stealing and assault, and though he can't speak of any details he assures us there is much more to the matter than meets the eye. Clem, Norman, and Lettie remain much the same on the surface, though I have the impression the boys have grown up considerably in just the short time we've been here. Meanwhile, Lettie seems reasonably content with her lot as a preacher's only daughter since the preacher is away many days at a time, and his wife is usually busy with her Chapel crowd bringing assistance to the poorer families along the coast and inland.

The big news is, of course, Horace and his quest to be an Orkney farmer. Mother, Lettie, and I are on his side, and we, together with

Horace's enthusiasm, have a good chance, I think, of winning father over. It appears Mr. Taggart could be something of an ally as well because he will apparently attest to Mr. Spence's character and standing in the community, and that can't help but influence father's decision-making. His main concern will be, rightly, Horace's tender years. Fifteen, which is what he will be in another month, is a very young age to leave home – and not just that but live hundreds of miles away in a remote spot. Mother, Lettie, and I will speak of Horace's maturity as often as we can, how he has always had both feet on the ground, and so deserves the chance at least to try this independent life. Whatever his position, Father will have to make up his mind very soon.

As for me, I continue my homage to this wondrous place, though my words struggle to match my daily discoveries – sinuous sentences of kelp, letters of flight formed by ducks and geese, and the rocks' rough alphabet in the soil. I haven't shown my poems to anyone, not even Lettie. I'll seek her opinion once I have collected enough for a volume and can only hope she won't be too stern a critic.

Fiery drops of heaven
Flaming into the sea
To draw us in their wake

Each sunset evening
From our new home's safe lee
Promise our souls to take

To burnished headlands where
They'll ever set us free
If simple prayer we make

To God where He is found
In proof of what must be
For love of our soul's sake

I must be my father's son although I do not think of the Lord when the sun sets or rises, or dwell on the lot of any souls that might exist beyond this earth's horizons, but because here I am writing something

Clem could set to music and have his Chapel choir sing. Ah well, perhaps the true priest is a poet, though in father's eyes it is sacrilege to say so.

Elizabeth

This morning with our baskets in hand we visited the house of a crofter family in need to discover it was the home of the very man Bertie is helping to defend against the grievous charge of stealing young lambs from his neighbour. Robbery with violence, I must add. Jamie MacBride's young wife is caring for their two small children, twin girls, and trying to look after their rough patch of land while he remains in the Kirkwall jail awaiting his trial. Her sweet disposition belies her grief and her strength in the face of his apparent wrongdoing. She refuses to accept her husband's guilt and is determined to give evidence in his defence even if he will not, but what words can she possibly offer that will save him?

'It is his honour at stake,' she tells us. 'But I have said to him the well-being of our children comes before that, and I cannot afford to lose him to a mainland jailhouse.'

'Would you not go to be near him?' I inquire politely, for Bertie has told me if he is convicted his sentence could last a number of years.

'Perhaps,' she sighs, 'but I think of the hardship on our babies and on my aged parents who live but a mile off. Besides, I am determined to tell the truth, and the court will surely listen.'

The interior of the cottage is sparsely furnished with just a table, four chairs, and a bench before the fireplace. A standing cupboard against a wall holds but a few dishes. On a tartan rug covering part of the floor the children play quietly. There is a spinning wheel in one corner, and when she sees my glance at this instrument, her eyes light up. 'Yes,' she says, 'I spin enough wool to provide us with socks and sweaters and to barter a bit with the neighbours so we might occasionally have some meat for the table. We have eggs from our hens and milk from the cow.'

When I ask her, thinking to be of help to Bertie, what prompted the stealing of the lambs, she lowers her gaze and does not reply. The following moments of silence are quite uncomfortable, and I can feel the two ladies beside me grow restless. Finally, she looks up and gives an answer of sorts that I am still dwelling on.

'The truth is there is more than one truth,' she tells us mysteriously. 'I will say no more until the day I take my oath before God and defend my Jamie.'

That night I inform Thomas of her rather remarkable statement. 'Well,' he replies, 'Mr. Wesley said He designed plain truth for plain people, so let us see how that pertains to her testimony. I think Bertie knows that different versions of what happened in a case always emerge whatever oaths are sworn.'

'Should we tell him what she is thinking?'

'No, what comes out must do so naturally. Perhaps Mr. MacBride himself will save her the ordeal of a court appearance by speaking up.'

I remain troubled by my visit. It is difficult enough to see the suffering of the poor despite their admirable retention of dignity. Now I must contend with this young woman's struggle to defend her husband as well as put food in the mouths of her babes. Even if Mr. MacBride is guilty as charged, should he not be able to work off his punishment here where he was born rather than elsewhere in the country? I pray for him and his family nightly when I have finished asking the Lord's mercy for my own brood.

There is another matter that greatly concerns me. Horace has confided that he wants to remain here and work for his living on a local farm. He would be directly under the foreman in charge of the animals and has been promised advancement should he prove worthy. At first I told him it was a pleasant dream but he wasn't from here and should settle close to his roots, then I saw how his face fell and knew that he had counted on my support.

'Let me think on it, Horace. But we will not say anything to your father while I do so.' He is not quite fifteen, and my heart is already breaking over such desire, though whether from its uselessness or possible realization I cannot decide.

Ernest

When I was very young, about seven or eight, father took me to York Minster Cathedral, which looked like a giant castle to me, and announced before we entered that I was about to see a great testimony to man's pride and false worshipping of the Lord. I remember the high stone arches and stained glass windows with their pictures of the saints and the curved staircase the minister had to climb to the pulpit. We didn't stay long, just enough time to walk down the main aisle where I stared up at the altar and heard father say there was no need for priests to separate themselves from their congregations by wearing fancy robes or surrounding themselves with ceremony. When we left the bells were ringing in the towers. I looked back over my shoulder at this beautiful bastion of the enemy and thought how small our Chapel was in comparison.

Now, drawn by its imposing outer edifice, I am sitting inside another foe's stronghold, though I doubt there is much difference between the established English and Scottish churches when it comes to forms of worship. The vestments and rituals are all descended from Rome's style and authority and the capacity of popes to demand fealty like kings. But despite my preference for simplicity in the preaching of the Word and the joys of speaking in sunshine on village streets or in the shelter of a barn with the rain beating on the boards, the feeling of true refuge here cannot be denied.

The stained glass is as wondrous to the eye and easing to the soul as at York. Pillars and arches rise in splendid arrangement above statues of Viking warriors alongside the accustomed array of saints, but this strength and adornment are not alone what provide the sense of refuge. It is something I cannot quite put my finger on but surely bound up in the history I have read about in a printed pamphlet available by the entrance. The original Catholic cathedral, begun to honour a canonized Viking, was expanded over two centuries then saved from destruction during the Reformation and taken over by the Church of Scotland. What brought me here were the exterior trappings of the more recent past, but what holds me now are traces of that less striking, original building within this larger edifice. My lasting impression is not of size or spire but of a smaller 12th-century asylum against a world of threat and dissolution in which people could rest behind the strength of measured sandstone buttressed by God's infinite mercy. Where they could close a thick wooden door against the elements and open a portal on a safer, kinder world.

Father would say I have lost myself in the kind of false worship to which he alluded so many years ago, confusing outward appearances with inner revelations of glory. He took me to York Minster to teach me a lesson and would assume from my lingering presence here that the moral has been lost. Perhaps so. But I wonder if a plain Methodist Chapel built not long before one's own birth can summon up the same feelings of sanctity and security as this ancient site. As if in retribution for such thoughts, I hear his voice back then as we descended the cathedral steps. 'Acts 17:24, Ernest – *The God who made the world and all things in it, since He is Lord of heaven and earth, does not dwell in temples made with hands.*'

The Bible I always carry with me is open in my hand, and when I find the passage I am looking for I say the words aloud even if he cannot hear me – '*Let them construct a sanctuary for me that I may dwell among them. Exodus 25: 8.*' There must be a way to reconcile these verses.

Clem

This morning I summoned up the courage to enter St. Magnus by the front door. It is so much larger than our Chapel or any place of worship I have ever seen. The stained glass is very beautiful, especially one huge round pane filled with figures lit up by the sun, and the stone pillars are like giant trees supporting the roof so high I had to crane my neck painfully to see it. But I was interested in one thing most of all, and in the overwhelming space filled with distractions of Viking saints wielding their swords it took me more than a few moments to find the organ hidden behind a decorative screen. It was all I could do to keep my fingers from its keys, especially when I looked up to see the vast rows of golden pipes hanging from the wall as if suspended by the invisible chords I could hear playing in my head. How I longed to sit down and let the music roll out into the nave, all of it hymnal, though accompaniment to a Mozart mass is what I would have most liked to provide. My ears filled with such sounds and my eyes loath to leave the keys behind, I turned to step outside the screen only to spy Ernest sitting in a pew about thirty feet away.

Shocked and fearful of this discovery I hastily retreated and tried to think. I had come for the music, but what was he doing here? Father would be with him, of course, so it must have to do with church business, some sort of discussion between Methodists and Presbyterians. But the longer I stood there, and the longer Ernest remained, the more obvious it became that he was alone. Sitting with his legs crossed and one arm resting on the back of the pew, he looked very peaceful, and I had to struggle to hold myself in place and not reveal my presence. He could defend himself with father in ways that are beyond me, and if he were to inform on me his own price to pay would surely not be as great as mine. But that is not why I remained concealed. I felt it would be rude to interrupt him so calm was the look on his face that it matched the expression of a haloed saint in a window above his head.

Perhaps he is at prayer, I thought, but cannot kneel down in this 'refuge of pomp and ceremony', as father described it when we passed by one day and I marvelled at the grandeur. Perhaps he is preparing a sermon on the differences between such grandeur and the plain beauty of our Chapel. After all, to know the enemy you have to enter his camp. I wondered how long I would have to stay hidden, but after a few more minutes he stood up, stepped into the aisle, and walked towards the altar. I took this opportunity to escape, not looking back until I was in the streets again and saw the closed door of the cathedral behind me. As I made my way home I couldn't help but wonder, had I played that Mozart piece, if Ernest would have heard it in his reverie and my music and his sublime thoughts would have been as one.

That night at supper father asked him what he had done with his time while the fishermen's protest had occupied him and Mr. Taggart in Stromness.

Ernest replied confidently. 'I gave great thought to what I will say this Sunday when I preach in Settiscarth.'

'And what is that?'

'With your indulgence, father, I would prefer to speak of it in a day or two when all is clear to me.'

Father nodded in agreement, but I already knew my brother was buying time since his visit to St. Magnus was a secret.

Lettie

I have visited the cottage above the sea several more times, but there has never been anyone at home. I don't know what I would say if there were or how I would explain my wanting to meet the owner of this place. I only know it is a comforting spot and I can sit on an old wooden bench by a rose bush and look down the vale to the wharf where I imagine a boat was once tied up and perhaps will be so again. I have cupped my hand against more than one window pane to see what is inside, but the views of the interior are limited because of the angles and reflected light. What I have been able to see are bits of wooden furniture seemingly as old as the bench, a narrow set of stairs leading to a loft, and a bookcase filled with volumes whose titles I cannot discern. It pleases me to think the occupant of such a special place for me, perhaps a fisherman, is a lover of books, and I am very curious what his tastes are. Of course, I am assuming a great deal here. Why should I assume it is a single man who reads and lives here alone or that he is out there somewhere on the sea gathering in his nets or sailing into the wind. He could well be married. No woman would be on a boat, of course, so there is the matter of his wife. Is she in town every time I come to visit? In fact, I tell myself, the occupant could be a widow or spinster who inherited the property from her husband or father and is simply away for a period. Naturally, I could make some inquiries, but I prefer to wait out the mystery that I hope will solve itself before we leave the island.

This morning I walked down the beach and followed the by now familiar path towards the headland that marks the vale's edge. As I approached the cottage I heard a dog bark and saw a young woman step out the front door, open the garden gate, and walk toward the town and me. I waved immediately, not wanting her to think me suspicious in any way and because I felt a tinge of guilt at having physically intruded on what must be her place and for holding it, even for such a brief period, in my esteem.

She returned my sign of goodwill as the dog, a brindled collie, rushed up to prance around my feet, barking fiercely until it heard her admonishment and let me pat its head.

She was slim and a little taller than me with a fairer complexion. I smiled as we shook hands and introduced ourselves. 'Lettie,' I said, 'short for Letitia, which only my mother calls me when she is angry.' 'Margaret,' she replied, 'Margaret Muir.' She laughed. 'You must have a last name too.'

When I told her she announced immediately that it was a Viking name and that made me a descendant of the original Orkney raiders and therefore of St. Magnus himself. I was a bit taken aback by this information. As far as I knew, no one had said anything to father or mother about such a connection. Surely Mr. Taggart would have mentioned it or Bertie's Mr. Campbell. But I had no reason to disbelieve her so infectious was her peal of laughter as I stood there somewhat bemused by this certainty about my distant past. Her voice with its light burr appealed to me as well as her friendly manner, and I thought with some hope we might be friends.

'Where are you headed,' she asked after a moment.

How could I tell her of my destination or explain my attraction to her cottage? But, at the same time, I wanted to learn what I could about the place that had drawn me to it more than once. So I tried quickly to tell the truth without giving it all away.

'I have walked along this path in the last two weeks just to be outside and discover what I can about the island.' I pointed to the cottage. 'There has never been anyone at home, or at least that I noticed, but it seems such a pleasant spot.'

She looked over her shoulder and nodded. 'It surely is, though I don't spend nearly as much time at home as I should.' She nodded toward the tangled roots and vines in her small garden.

'Why is that?' I asked.

We were standing in a slight dip in the path that allowed me to see the cottage but not the full extent of the vale leading to the water. Margaret took my arm and drew me to higher ground where I could look down to the wharf. There was a sailboat of some kind bobbing beside the planks.

'Is that yours?' I gasped, rather shocked at the connection of her previous words to this craft.

'Yes,' she declared, 'every inch of her. I call her the *Tom Paine*.

I knew, of course, who Mr. Paine was and of his fame as the author of one of father's favourite texts, the hallowed *Rights of Man*, and of the infamous one he derided as unnatural and unchristian, *The Age of Reason*. But for the moment I was more interested in this woman's prowess as a sailor than in the boat's pedigree. Though I said nothing, the surprise in my eyes must have been obvious. She brushed some bramble twigs from her skirts and, giving a little curtsy, held them wide.

'This is the Margaret Muir who goes to town,' she said, standing up straight and smoothing the fabric. 'Proper if not prim. I find it easier to soothe people's feathers than to ruffle them, though if they ever came aboard they would find a captain who wears pants.'

'Pants,' I responded stupidly.

'Yes, and rubber boots and an oilskin jacket as well.'

I tried to regain my composure. 'But what do you do out there?'

She opened her arms and smiled. 'Why, Lettie, I see the world.'

Bertie

I cannot understand Jamie McBride. He will only repeat what Mr. Campbell told me, that while he may be guilty of the charges against him he is an innocent man, and then has nothing more to say. I have asked him to explain the contradiction of his words that I might be of help to him, but he simply smiles and does not reply.

'And your wife and children, sir?' I said to him in his cell in a somewhat exasperated tone. 'What of their fate if you remain silent?' I know she wants to speak up in court, and I have only just learned from Mr. Campbell that coverture does not apply in Scotland so a woman can testify for or against her husband. Were she to have something crucial to say, it might make a difference, but I cannot imagine what that could be. She wasn't present for the beating or the theft.

His face darkened and for a few moments he appeared to consider the obvious merit of my question. He replied in that maddeningly calm voice Mr. Campbell says is his finest asset, insisting he'd win over any judge and jury in the land if he used it to defend himself.

'Their fate has already been determined by my actions, and my silence is such as to keep them from further disturbance.'

Despite my pleas he turned away to stare out the window at the firth gleaming in the distance.

So I have begun my 'investigation,' searching out the witnesses to the alleged crime. I say alleged because, despite his admission, no one actually saw him take the lambs or attack their owner, Roger Nicholas, even though the cuts and bruises were visible on the man and the animals were discovered slaughtered and cut up at Jamie MacBride's house, the wool neatly piled and various parts ready to be cooked and eaten. When accused, he did not deny or affirm anything. I mean first to speak with his wife about what she will say in court.

'Yes, she has said she will speak up,' mother affirmed, describing her visit to the McBride cottage. 'But she also insists she will say nothing to anyone until she takes her oath.'

In order to gain whatever advantage I can when I meet her, I decided to approach the several persons whom the prosecution has ready to testify.

The first was Mr. Leslie, a neighbour of both men, who told me he heard the victim shouting on his property at someone the night of the attack, and a few minutes later saw Jamie McBride walking away from the farm in question with a bleating lamb under each arm.

'Walking, not running?' I asked.

'O aye. You'll never see young Jamie in a hurry. He rarely breaks his regular stride for anything except maybe a barn or house fire when we all have to pitch in right away.'

'Is that all you saw?'

'That and the dead creatures the next day when we went with Roger to Jamie's cottage.'

'Did Jamie explain himself to you then?'

'No. Just smiled and said Roger knew why he had been bowed and bloodied and that the lambs were part of the payment.'

'Payment for what?'

'He wouldn't say when pressed. Roger went to the Constable, and he arrested Jamie later that same day.'

The 'we' who had accompanied Mr. Leslie were named Brown and Allan, and they provided the same story, only Brown offering a new bit of information. He said he asked Roger what the 'payment' could have meant, but Roger only scowled and accused Jamie of being mad and deserving to be hung. Given such evidence I can't think how McBride's wife could put anything in the way of a conviction, but must, as a matter of course, speak with her anyway. Mr. Campbell should have all the facts at his disposal.

Mrs. MacBride is quite pretty with high cheekbones and a dimpled chin. We sit in the main room of the tiny cottage with the two young children at our feet before a peat fire. She insists on serving tea and it comes in an old brown pot alongside two chipped mugs for which she makes no apologies. I want to say it is no different than our kitchen at home when we don't have guests, but I *am* her guest and so keep mum about her service. I feel, though, since I am a stranger it would be rude to move directly to business, so I ask after her health and how she is coping given the circumstances.

'Oh, I'm fairly well, thank you, sir. The neighbours make sure we want for little, and we have our hens and milk cow.'

'So you have no sheep of your own?'

'No none at all. We must trade for what wool we need for my spinning wheel.'

Playing the lawyer I respond immediately, 'Is that why your husband would steal sheep from another farmer?'

She remains silent for a long time, and I listen to the chatter of the children as they roll a small rubber ball back and forth between them. Finally she sighs and delicately sweeps a strand of hair away from her forehead. 'He didn't steal the lambs. He just took what was rightfully ours.'

It doesn't make sense, but I leap to the only possible conclusion. 'You mean they belonged to you?'

'I feel so, yes. But I will say no more until I have sworn my oath.'

'Please Mrs. MacBride. Your husband's fate will surely rest upon this matter of ownership. Anything you can tell me will be of great help to Mr. Campbell.'

But she shakes her head firmly, and I know I will get nothing more from her that day. When I return to the office and make my report, Mr. Campbell shakes his own head but with a great deal less resolve. 'I don't know,' he says. 'The man won't say anything at all, and the wife promises to speak only when she is sworn. Meanwhile she leaves us hanging. I will make some queries as to the ownership question.'

I remember that pretty face and wish I had good reason for a return visit.

Norman

Today I found a Small Tortoiseshell butterfly! Mr. Garson had told me they feed on stinging nettles, and I discovered a patch beyond where we had hunted before. There wasn't any wind, and I sat in the grass keeping very still because then all sorts of insects and birds will come near thinking you are a tall stick or something and are not afraid. Ants crawled over my shoes and little buntings flitted by looking for grubs. In the distance I could see flocks of seabirds whirling above the cliffs. I was thinking it might be nice to lie down and have a nap when out of the corner of my eye I caught a flash of colour and there were the rusty-red wings edged in blue and dotted with black and yellow markings. I held my breath and brought my net to rest on the top of my leg as the butterfly hovered above a tall stalk of nettle then settled for its meal. Mr. Garson had showed me how to move my arm so slowly it would seem just like another piece of grass swaying gently in the wind. Only there wasn't any wind, so I moved slower than ever. Just as I got the net above the stalk the meal was over and the wings parted and fluttered. I snapped my wrist sideways and down and with a loud shout caught my prize. Taking it carefully between my fingers I lowered it into my jar with the holes in the lid.

When I showed Mr. Garson what I had brought him, he was very pleased. He held the jar, turning it round and round so he could see every bit of what he called 'my beauty' over and over again. I was so excited I didn't think about what would happen next. He put the jar down on the table and picked up the camphor bottle with its tiny dropper.

'No,' I cried. 'Not yet!'

He smiled and put the bottle down.

'Norman,' he said in a kind voice, 'we have spoken about this. What is the point of finally finding such an extraordinary creature and letting it go?'

'Can't we let it live for a while and just watch it?'

'Yes, but eventually you'll just have to stop imprisoning it in a jar and either let it go free or...' He nodded at the boards on the wall. 'It belongs in the collection.'

'But it is so rare,' I pleaded. 'What if we're killing the last one?'

'Then we're saving the last one for others to see its beauty and that it has been part of this world. Unless we do it will disappear entirely.' He was silent for a few moments and I didn't know what else to say.

'I tell you what,' he said, 'I'll let you decide. The butterfly can stay in the jar overnight. You go home and think things over. In the morning if you want to set it free you'll just have to twist off the lid.'

I said thank you and walked back to our house slowly, trying to decide if I was really a naturalist. I wasn't a collector, I knew that now, only a boy who liked to hold onto what was very special for a bit of time without pinning it to a board. But how could I hold in my mind all the butterflies I had ever caught? How could I describe them to people who had never seen their shapes and colours? A naturalist had to do more than try to remember the shades of a butterfly's wings, didn't he? I decided to ask mother and father what I should do.

They both listened to my story. Father stroked his whiskers and said, 'We use God's creatures in all sorts of ways, Norman. Think of the cattle and sheep we eat as well as fish and fowl. Think of the fur-bearing animals we kill to keep us warm in winter. The Lord gave us dominion over them. If Mr. Garson went out and slaughtered butterflies willy-nilly, he would be a cruel and wanton man. But he is trying to preserve what attracts us to the butterflies in the first place and to record details about them. That is an important thing to do.'

I wanted to tell him that what attracted me to butterflies was how their colours danced in the breeze, but mother spoke up and said this for me.

'I think, dear, you love their motion and moving with them as you try to capture them with your net.'

I nodded, thankful that she understood. But she wasn't finished.

'Yet don't we really see their beauty when they are still, hovering on a stem of grass or petal of a flower so we can study the designs on their wings and the patterns of their colours? Mr. Garson's board lets us do that for more than a few seconds.'

'Mother,' I cried, 'why can't we have both? But I knew I had to choose between motion and stillness.

The next day I told Mr. Garson I wanted to keep the butterfly until I had found another just like it. Then I would let it go and he could mount the second one.

'What if there isn't another one out there?' he asked.

But I pretended not to hear him.

The Frame

So I've got them all started in one way or another. Thomas whose interest in justice for the fishermen is tempered somewhat by their rough manners and earthy Christianity; Elizabeth whose concern for Mrs. MacBride is compounded by her husband's refusal to speak up; Ernest who is straying from familiar paths while expanding his religious horizons; Bertie who stands firmly on the law in every issue but is clearly attracted to a married woman; Horace who, as yet, has gone far beyond his brothers and sister in self-discovery; Arthur whose poems represent both an effort to articulate longings and disguise their implications; Clem who puts music above everything else including the sonorous rhythms of his father; Norman who is asking questions about life and death that might eventually give pause to his Methodist parents; and Lettie whose vision has just been expanded beyond anything she has been prepared for by her family or her incipient rebellion against it. Of course, Thomas and Elizabeth have the added responsibility of needing to make a decision about Horace – he in a rational manner and she more emotionally. Not that I would place the measured response over the more demonstrative one because I think she is more intelligent than he is receptive to feelings.

The story or stories belong to them now; whereas when I started out I seemed to be the one in charge. But that original custody of character and event was based only on a photograph, a take-off point not enough to support a narrative unless it illuminated stories more intricate and revealing than the bare facts of nine faces and names.

7. Singing Among the Branches

Thomas

At first on our preaching rounds Ernest and I walked to nearby settlements, but for those farther away we soon had a horse and cart at our disposal courtesy of Mr. Taggart. We were able to travel once around separate southern and northern circuits on the Mainland Island, bringing the Lord's Word to two or three villages a day, which kept us from Kirkwall for more than a week. Ernest has gained a great deal of confidence in his public speaking and is now more than capable of going out on his own. Given my concerns for the fishermen in Stromness, I have suggested he do just that and search out new locations, even travelling to nearby islands such as Shapinsay or Hoy. He is quite eager to do so, and I have helped him choose fitting subjects for his sermons, leaving it up to him to select the biblical verses that will best emphasize his message. He doesn't need more than one or two topics for discussion since repetition will strengthen his effectiveness and the villagers rarely see members of other settlements, if at all.

We determined first on 'The Lord helps those who help themselves,' which most think is taken from the Bible but in fact cannot be found there. Ernest is pleased with this subject because it means he is free to rove through the Good Book and introduce those verses he thinks best in support. The other basis for discussion, and which seems so appropriate for our surroundings, is from a man of God whose Meditation I recalled from my schooldays. Mr. Donne wrote, 'No man is an island entire of itself. Each man is a part of the maine.' Perhaps I don't have the words quite right, and the inadequate library here has been unable to help me, but the gist is correct. I have encouraged Ernest to underline the importance of community under the Lord and how, as Mr. Donne said, the bell tolls not for individuals alone but for us all.

So it is decided. Tomorrow he will head south to the port of St. Mary's where he will take the ferry to South Ronaldsay and on to Hoy. Mr. Taggart has provided him with a letter of introduction to the faithful on the islands and is confident they will offer him suitable accommodation. I am off to Stromness with Mr. Taggart to attend a gathering of the fishermen and various officials to try and settle the dispute.

The air in the meeting-hall was thick with pipe-smoke whose sweet-sickly odour hovered over the smell of woollen trousers and sweaters dampened by the steady drizzle outside. Things did not go well. Firstly, the three officials were all sitting behind a table on a dais at the front of the hall while the men were packed into standing rows beneath them. There would be from the outset an evident 'speaking down' to the crowd. The men were restless, feeling that they were there to be lectured to rather than to have an honest exchange about the reasons for the protest. I saw Rory Parker in the front row and thought to myself he'll be the one to lead the charge.

First to speak was a leader of the island council who, most probably because he was local, tried to strike a note of appeasement, saying he and most of his fellow councillors felt the men should be treated fairly and that no one wanted their families to suffer. He was listened to politely until he stated that in order for such fairness to be achieved they should return to work and leave matters to the council who would bargain on their behalf.

'Bargain!' shouted Rory Parker. 'They've had enough of a bargain from us already!'

There was a great cheer and stomping of feet at that, and I could see the councillor was disturbed by the response to what seemed to him a reasonable position. The second man to opine was the buyers' representative from Glasgow who unabashedly instructed the assembly on the finances of the fish trade, telling them of the costs of shipping their catch to the south and of selling it at market. It was impossible, he stated, to charge city customers more per pound. They simply wouldn't pay a higher price.

Someone behind Parker yelled that maybe they'd be better off without fish in their diet, and the red-faced speaker huffed that they were only cutting their own throats, a most unfortunate image to have employed as the first remark in response indicated the level of hostility in the room.

'I doan' know about the cutting of throats, but I'd as soon gut you than any more herring,' a voice cried from the middle of the pack, and the crowd surged forward to the dais. Just when a riot seemed about to break out, the third man at the table stood and raised his hand. The men quieted a little, knowing he was the government member for the northern district and therefore their voice in the Parliament. I don't know what they were expecting, perhaps a message not just from Edinburgh but from London beyond, some universal declaration on their behalf. But I knew any fishermen's rights were not to be found at Westminster, and his subsequent words proved me right.

'I have been authorized to tell you the protest must end immediately, otherwise...'

'Otherwise, y'll lose your job, won't ye?' Rory Parker said loudly but evenly.

But the politician was undaunted. 'Otherwise,' he continued, 'there will be arrests. He pointed a finger at Rory Parker. 'And you and your like, sir, will be among the first to be jailed.'

For a few moments the men took in this threat. Most of them, I suspected, knew there must eventually be a return to work and that any offered rise in the price they received for their catch wouldn't meet their needs. But it was important that their complaints be acknowledged and they be given *some* recompense, no matter how little. Instead they were being menaced by the rule of might without any hint of justice. After the brief silence a murmuring began that rose to a hum and then a growling from a hundred throats, and I recognized the charge was being sounded. Rory Parker and his immediate cohorts were at the edge of the dais and Parker's hand was around the ankle of the government member when the doors at the back of the hall burst open and at least a dozen constables burst into the room brandishing billy clubs and shouting for the men to disperse. They cut a swath through the centre of the crowd and headed straight for Rory Parker. I suspect he had wanted to be on the stage from the beginning, but at this point it was his only route of escape. He leapt up and past the three startled speakers and disappeared behind the curtain at the rear of the dais. The men on either side of the constables backed against the walls, and Mr. Taggart and I were briefly rendered immobile. I greatly regretted being unable to speak to anyone at all, let alone the principals of the event, but I must admit I was concerned for my own safety and that of Mr. Taggart when the constables, clearly frustrated by the loss of Rory Parker, began swinging their truncheons.

Men fell with bloodied faces while others, amidst the uproar, shoved their way towards the doors or to the exit taken by their fleeing leader. Taggart and I slid along the wall protected from the clubs by the mass in front of us and managed to find our way to the street but not before the shoulder of his jacket was torn and an elbow slammed painfully into my cheek. We were staying that night at the home of a Chapel elder and made our way there withdrawn into our own thoughts until I asked him, 'Where will Parker go?'

'There are many who will give him shelter this night and for as long as necessary,' he replied. 'I think the more important question is what he will *do* now that he has been targeted as a leader and singled out for arrest. He is very important to this struggle, and without him I fear the men will be hard-pressed to continue.'

'Will you be able to discover his whereabouts? I believe we should try to talk with him.'

'Yes, I think I can, but he may not agree to see us. He is, as he told you, more concerned with the stomachs of his family than with their souls.'

'Then we must convince him they are one and the same. *For my flesh is true food and my blood is pure drink.*'

'Yes, but he'll ask if such verse will put real food and drink on his table,' Taggart replied. 'I think he might surprise you with his knowledge of the Bible and declare that his enemy has planted tares amongst his sheaves of grain that taint both the bread for his children and the whisky for his own lips.'

I wished to save discussion about the twisting of this parable from *Matthew* for another time. At present we needed to see if any kind of harvest could be found for the fishermen.

Elizabeth

Mrs. MacBride is a curious creature indeed! I have been to visit her on two more occasions, bringing a basket of food each time. She is certainly grateful in that regard as it is clear, despite her talk of neighbourly assistance, she and the children are having a difficult time of it while her husband awaits trial. I have not pressed her on the case, but she continues with her allegiance to the idea of there being more than one truth, which I have taken to mean that Mr. MacBride is somehow innocent despite admitting to his guilt. She has been officially summoned by the court, she told me, and will appear in ten days time to defend his 'honour.' But it seems that is not as straightforward a characteristic as we might assume.

On the first occasion she volunteered information to indicate she was involved in the decision to take the sheep from the flock of Mr. Nicholas and that he deserved to be beaten.

I could hardly believe my ears. 'You mean you encouraged your husband to steal an animal, the charge for which is a heavy fine and perhaps years in prison?'

'I mean that I was the reason he did it,' she replied. 'As I was for the beating.'

'How is that possible?' I asked, further shocked by such admission. But she would say no more.

I went straight to Mr. Campbell's office after leaving the cottage. When I told Bertie what she had said, he shook his head as if to clear away the puzzled look on his face. 'I cannot believe this is true, mother. She has concocted a story to share the blame for the theft and to shift the responsibility of the beating to Mr. Nicholas. I had hoped her evidence would vindicate her husband, but the court will simply hear this kind of testimony as special pleading and dismiss it. No, he has admitted to both crimes, and if he is innocent there has to be a better explanation. Hard facts will determine his fate not the loyalty of a good wife.' He paused and rubbed his chin for a moment. 'Unless,' he whispered almost as if to himself, 'unless some kind of self-defence can be proven. Is it possible, I wonder? I'll tell Mr. Campbell everything you've said. He'll know best how to proceed.'

The next time I visited her, I was determined to get at some of those facts and be of service to my son. After she had poured me a cup of tea from a brown pot that had seen much service, I spoke to the issue directly.

'Mrs. MacBride, you must realize that your blaming yourself before the court will make no difference to your husband's position. I'm afraid there can be nothing done about the lambs, as he took them with or without your involvement, but my son says if it can be shown he acted in self-defence in the beating of Mr. Nicholas, perhaps his sentence can be reduced.'

'He acted to protect me,' she said.

'To protect you?' I was a little angry at her providing dribs and drabs of information and leaving me always to ask more questions. Then she said something that I thought might open a door for Bertie and Mr. Campbell.

'His honour was my honour, and that's what I will tell the court.'

'Thomas,' I said that night in the privacy of our bedroom, 'do you think Mr. Nicholas is guilty of some unseemly behaviour towards Mrs. MacBride and that is why he was beaten?' I had provided him with the exact details of our exchange over tea. 'Bertie says even if this is so, it will be hard to prove because it will be her word against his and, rightly or wrongly, the court will be inclined to believe the man.'

'Why would Nicholas do such a thing? The community here is so small, and everyone knows everyone else. He could not expect to get away with such an offence. And there is still the matter of the lambs. MacBride clearly stole them and slaughtered them for the fire. There are witnesses to that.'

'I don't know what to say about it all. I only know she's a woman well in control of her thoughts and that almost everything she says on the subject comes as a surprise. Even a learned judge will be hard pressed to deal with that.'

He touched my arm gently. 'There is another matter that should concern us more.'

I knew he was speaking of Horace and sensed, in his own position as family judge, he had come to a decision. Lettie had urged me to influence him as best I could in Horace's favour, and I had tried, saying that if a mother's heart could let go a child perhaps a father's could as well. Though Thomas, good man that he is, has never much been swayed by his heart's demands since I have known him.

'You know I have thought about this a great deal, Elizabeth. Mr. Spence is a decent man, and Mr. Taggart has spoken on his behalf. But while I am confident Horace would be happy working with the farm animals, I feel he is too young for the time being to leave home. There is the matter of his spiritual safety, and at fifteen the surroundings of a Presbyterian household would perhaps be too influential.'

I started to speak, but he held up his hand. If I was expecting a biblical verse, I was disappointed.

'I am prepared to consider the matter in another year or two if he is still set on the suggested course, but for now he will return to Yorkshire with us.'

Though happy not to lose Horace to the islands, I was disappointed that Thomas had not understood the depths of our son's desire to stay here. Ultimately, the decision was not in my hands, and it would be better for all if I held my peace. But in my own depths a small fear lingered that the matter had not yet been settled as Thomas willed.

The next morning at the breakfast table with everyone in place, he told Horace of his decision.

Ernest

I took the ferry this morning from Mainland Island to South Ronaldsay. It was bright and clear when I left the port at St. Mary's, but within a few minutes of embarkation a wind came up from the southeast followed by heavy clouds and fierce rain. The boat swayed and dipped in the troughs of waves, and the few passengers in the single interior space – a large cabin with wooden benches along the walls – huddled in small, grim groups that partook in little if any conversation. I felt queasy until the storm passed even though my early breakfast before leaving Kirkwall had consisted only of an egg and piece of toast. Mother insisted on packing me a lunch of cold sausage and fresh bread along with two Orkney apples, Orange Pippins she called them. I wondered aloud if there were any oranges called Apple Pippins, and she laughed and said she'd try to find some for me.

Yesterday when we were all gathered round the table, father gave his decision about Horace. Lettie and Arthur protested a little, but we all knew once father's mind was made up there was no going back. I am disappointed for Horace who will inevitably find work akin to that he was offered by Mr. Spence, but not at all surprised that at his young age he is not being allowed to venture out on his own hundreds of miles from home. Later I saw him in the garden weeping on Lettie's shoulder from the heavy blow, but there was nothing I could do or say that would take away his pain. The only thing he could cling to was father's promise to revisit the issue when he turns sixteen.

Father told me of his adventure in the fishermen's hall in Stromness. It sounds dangerous to me, and I was glad the constables hadn't caught Mr. Parker in the building because there likely would have been more violence. Father is built like a barrel, but even the stoutest of staves can snap from too much pressure. He and Mr. Taggart are still trying to find Parker, though what will happen if they do I'm not quite sure. It's best he handle this alone, or with Mr. Taggart only, rather than take me along. I still have mixed thoughts about the situation and a feeling that father steered me towards the two sermon topics for my trip so I would see the light. I can hear him say that the fishermen are trying to help themselves, and surely their united effort runs along the lines of John Donne's admonition. Nevertheless, I am more comfortable with battles for men's souls than with skirmishes for their earthly preservation.

Once landed on South Ronaldsay I seated myself in the back of a horse-drawn wagon, there as a kind of public transport to and from the ferry, and clopped along to the largest settlement, St. Margaret's Hope, where I was to board for two nights before heading south to Burwick where another lodging awaited me.

An elderly couple, Mr. and Mrs. Gibbs, were my hosts. She fed me well at tea, and he told me once the letter had come from Mr. Taggart he'd organized three meetings where I would preach my sermons – one in the square down the street from his house, one in Widewall halfway to Burwick, and the final one in Burwick itself. I knew from studying the map I had brought with me that it was no more than a few miles to each of these two villages so I declined his offer of a cart and told him I'd be happy to walk to my destinations.

'As you can see,' I said, pointing to my feet, 'I've a pair of stout hiking boots for that very purpose.' Then it occurred to me I hadn't thought to take them off on entering his house and, apologizing, I stooped to the laces.

'Not all young sir, not at all. There's no muck on them. The only reason mine aren't in their usual place is because at my age my feet complain more than yours.'

He told me his son, John, was a fisherman whose boat was tied up at the Stromness docks and asked me had I preached there. I told him no but my father had and his face brightened at the possibility John had heard him.

'He's always given his attention to the Good Book, he has. He carries his with him wrapped in oilskin and says it is a comfort to have it with him during the lonely hours at sea.'

I asked him how the Methodist population on the island compared to that of the Presbyterians, and he replied that our side held their own though the St. Magnus people were always out and about in their visits and making inroads by taking young children and their parents on trips to the great cathedral.

'You've seen it, at least from the outside, I'm sure. It's enough to turn a man's head let alone that of a youngster.'

I was sure my face turned red at this remark and forced a cough as if my tea had gone down the wrong way.

'Are there any Chapels on the island?' I asked.

'None but the open fields and barns when it rains,' he said. 'But I think hymns ring more clearly in the high rafters and fresh air. When people are closed in by stone and slate during their worship, they can't properly hear the music of the Lord.'

'*Beside them the birds of the heavens dwell; they sing among the branches.* Psalms 104:22.'

He seemed pleased, as I had intended, by the scriptural support of his position. 'Amen, young sir, amen.'

The next day at noon I spoke to a crowd of two dozen, mostly old couples and young women with children because, as Mr. Gibb told me, the majority of the men were off in Stromness with John. They listened to my lesson about each of us being 'a part of the maine,' nodding as one at that line and when I quoted Mr. Donne about the tolling of the bell for all of us together. The local Presbyterian church was a modest affair without a tower, and I doubted many of them had heard a single bell of worship more than once or twice except in the far distance. At first I was pleased to think my words (or Mr. Donne's) had conjured up the sound, then I recalled the sponsored trips to Kirkwall and knew it was more likely any imagined tones were echoes of the St. Magnus carillon.

We sat on the grass at the edge of the square and shared a lunch made by Mrs. Gibb for the three of us. Mr. Gibb introduced me to several villagers including one old man who claimed his father as a boy had heard Mr. Wesley preach in Thurso.

'That was a grand day for him,' I said.

'Yes, Mr. Wesley spoke on the failings of human knowledge, as I recall father saying.'

I knew this was the 69th Sermon as recorded in Mr. Jackson's edition. *But although our desire for knowledge has no bounds, yet our knowledge itself has.* I didn't mention this, however, because the sharing of the old man's memory seemed more important for the moment. He went on to speak of how his father had considered voyaging to the American colonies, given Mr. Wesley's descriptions of the rich soil for crops and abundant wildlife for meat supply.

'But it's a good thing he didn't, or my chance to hear your own preaching would have been lost now, wouldn't it?'

I smiled at his compliment and such association with the great man.

Bertie

'He did it to protect me,' she declared finally.

'Then you must tell me what took place and why.' When mother revealed what Mrs. MacBride had said, I left the office immediately and made straight to her cottage. If something untoward happened between her and Nicholas and Jamie MacBride took his revenge, as any man would, he would not pay as severe a penalty for the deed, perhaps none at all. Of course, as I indicated to mother, it was one thing to allege this and quite another to put her word against that of Nicholas. It meant an uphill battle to prove her husband's innocence. There was still the matter of the lambs, but first things first.

Alright,' she said in a determined voice, 'I will tell you what I intended to save for the court. But promise me my words are for you and Mr. Campbell alone so that my husband may be helped.'

'I do promise,' I replied, aware that the judge would have wanted all indications of evidence to be offered in testimony in his hands before the trial.

'I have known Roger Nicholas,' she began, 'since my girlhood. He was sweet on me then, and I didn't mind his pleasant attentions, handsome man that he is although some years older than me. I stepped out to dances and the like with him and other lads, but when my Jamie arrived from Westray my roving days were done. The other lads dropped away, but Roger would not give up. During my engagement time he would meet me on the paths to Kirkwall and plead his case, and sometimes there would be a bouquet of flowers on my doorstep when I returned from the fields. All I could repeat to him was that my heart had decided.

'Jamie is not a meek fellow, but he is not one to put himself forward. I think he was uncertain of my love right up to our wedding day and so did not admonish Roger or tell him to be gone. We invited him to the wedding, of course, but he did not come. I knew he was disappointed and perhaps even angry within me but felt such feelings would pass.

'His house, as you know, is not far off and on the way to town, so it was impossible to avoid meeting him almost daily unless I stayed indoors. He would pass with a nod but say nothing, and gradually I became used to his silence and almost preferred it to any sham inquiries after my health or empty words about the weather. Things went along like this for several years. It was when I had the girls that Roger's behaviour to me changed completely. He would never speak if we met in a crowd, at the market for instance, or if Jamie was with me on the paths, but when he passed me alone he would mutter words under his breath and make his misery clear. It was unpleasant, but bearable. I spoke to Jamie about it, but all he said was to tell him if Roger ever said anything untoward.'

She sighed and rose to her feet. 'I'm sorry,' she said. 'I should have offered you some tea.'

I motioned her to be seated. 'Not at all, Mrs. MacBride. Your story is much more important.'

'Please call me Alice.' There was a spot of red in the centre of each cheek and a thin line of perspiration on her upper lip. Surely my voice shook when I replied, 'And I am called Bertie by my family and friends.' I smiled to put myself at ease as much as her. 'Please continue.'

'Very well, then. About a month ago I met Roger not far from his gate, and he astonished me by stopping and telling me he was sorry for his behaviour. He should have been more of a gentleman, he said, and wished myself and Jamie all the best when we were married. He inquired after the children and asked their names which he would have already learned in our small community. I was greatly relieved at this turn of events and even went so far as to imagine him and Jamie as friends, perhaps sharing a pint in the pub, though Jamie rarely went there, preferring a bottle of stout now and then at our kitchen table.

When Roger said he had a tardy wedding gift for us, I was delighted, and when he added that the gift would like to meet me, I was naturally curious, and asked whatever did he mean? He turned to his gate and extended his hand toward his house.

'Come and see,' he said genially.

Perhaps I was foolish to go along, but our relations had been under such a cloud for a long time and I wanted to embrace the proffered peace. We walked up his path, but as it crested the little rise before his door he steered me to the small barn with a bright red rooster weather vane on its thatched roof. Once inside, after the bright sunlight outdoors, it took me a moment to make things out in the gloom. Eventually I identified a harrow, a pile of wood cut for the fire, and the outline of two or three small stalls.

'Over here,' he called from a stall entrance, and I went quickly to where he stood. Inside were two small lambs each perhaps a month old, their wool thick and tightly curled in white whorls lighting up the enclosure like lamps that would never burn low. I clapped my hands and exclaimed at their loveliness.

'Not so much a wedding gift, but a present for each of your girls,' Roger said.

I was so happy at his generosity that tears came to my eyes and my hand went out to touch his arm. 'You're a good man, Roger.'

Instead of a simple return of friendship, he grasped my wrist and pulled me toward him. Suddenly his mouth was on my lips and then to my ear, and I heard him murmur that he loved me still and could do better for me than Jamie. Somehow I pulled myself free and ran to the door, crying aloud sounds that made no sense except to suggest my fear and feeling of betrayal. Fortunately, he did not follow. When I reached home, Jamie was there, and when I told him what had happened his lips narrowed into a hard line and he set off after Roger, despite my protestations. By his lights the beating he meted out was deserved, though the cost has been too great.'

I was angry on her behalf and at Jamie MacBride that he hadn't simply defended himself by telling the truth.

As if reading my mind, she said, 'Jamie didn't want any gossip about me. That's why he didn't speak up and doesn't now. He was sure Roger would have nothing to say about the matter for fear of being charged himself.'

'And the lambs?' I asked. 'Why did he give Mr. Nicholas an excuse to have him charged?'

'He said they were just the gift promised, but we would eat rather than raise them and so nourish ourselves with his deceit.'

'You must say all this in court just as you have told me now. Surely if you do that your husband will break his silence. If you each confirm the other's version of events, it will be two against one. I am sure, under the circumstances, the beating will be understood, and he will be set free on the charge of stealing.'

'I am afraid you must rely on me only,' she replied.

I could not accept this and swore I would go to Jamie MacBride's cell that very afternoon and convince him to speak up.

'Now, shall we have some tea?' she said, as if there were no hurry.

Horace

Everyone is upset at father's decision. Well, Clem and Norman are too young to say anything or to care, really, but Lettie and Arthur complained aloud that it wasn't fair to keep me from doing something I love, until father declared he would hear no more on the matter. Bertie took me aside and remarked he wouldn't know what to do if he were forbidden to practice law, and Ernest told me I was a good lad who deserved my chance at happiness, even if I was a bit young to start out on my own. Mother walked down to the shore with me after father had made his position clear and held my arm as we made our way over the rocks to a patch of sand.

'You know he wants only the best for you.'

'Yes, I know, mother.'

'And there is the great possibility you can come back here when you turn sixteen. I will keep after him about that.'

'Do you think Mr. Spence will remember me?'

'I am sure he will. I will speak with him before we leave, and you must write to him during the next year. Meanwhile, you can gain some experience by working Saturdays and after school on a farm near home. That will stand you in good stead with any future employer.'

I am sure if Mr. Spence attended our Chapel father would feel quite differently. He never says anything about the Presbyterians, but I know he is worried I might go over to St. Magnus. I don't have the courage to tell him that I find the Lord's presence more in the eyes of dumb animals than in any holy text or prayer. A barn is no different than a church or chapel, after all, as Jesus was born in one and visited there by the shepherds and wise men. When he looked up from his cradle he must have been comforted by the sheep and cows whose home it was. Perhaps what I should do is try to find a Methodist family to live with not far from Mr. Spence's farm. I am determined to stay one way or another.

When I mention this to Lettie, she promises her support.

'We must make inquiries about a suitable family that will meet father's approval and about your schooling here, but let's keep things on the sly for now. Don't say anything to anyone, including mother, until we have prepared an argument he cannot refute.'

She hugged me and tousled my hair when she let me go. 'It will all work out, little brother, you'll see.'

In the meantime I continue to help Mr. Spence every day. He says he is disappointed but assures me the job will be waiting for me whenever I return. Most people think of mucking out the stables as dirty work, but I don't mind it. I use a pitchfork to shake the heavy manure from the straw and throw the waste in an old hay-cart in the yard. The pile never gets too large as Mr. Spence's men spread it on field where he has his small patch of grain and he sells the rest to other farmers for their crops of oats and barley. My main task is to see to the cattle and horses, herding them out of the barn each morning and back into their stalls in the evening when I fill their troughs with hay and water.

Best of all is when I lead the animals into the buyers' pen in Kirkwall, holding them steady so they look their best until a fair price is gained. Mr. Spence has a prize Angus bull he is that proud of he tells me I must wear a jacket and tie the day he lets him go, though he adds it is not likely he will do so. It does not matter what I wear, stained or clean, the creatures know I am their friend and never try to shake their traces. He says I must have some secret to keep them so in line, even the bull when I move it to clean its stall, but there's no mystery to my talking to them whenever we are together. Although they can't answer me with their tongues, their eyes provide reply enough, and that's when the Lord's presence is most real to me. Even if I had the courage to tell him, father wouldn't understand how this is so.

Arthur

The patriarch rules his tribe
Mother, daughter, sons
He cannot read their dreams
Where all is lost or won

In desert or in green
They follow him in line
No pace the pattern breaks
No step is out of time

He is no more than king
His word no less than writ
One day they will rise up
Throw off the holy bit

What an uproar would ensue if I suddenly said at the breakfast table or at tea, 'I've written a poem about father,' and then read it to the gathered congregation. Or perhaps there would only be silence as the face of rebellion, even revolution, erupted from behind the usual mask of civility. I would be banished in either event, of course, having put the god of poetry before Him that chose my father as his instrument in Chapel and home alike. I would hurt mother terribly, but as for the daughter and sons, except for Ernest perhaps, they would not suffer much from such insurrection whether they spoke up or held their peace. Lettie would join me, I am sure, as I joined her to try to influence father's decision about Horace.

It is unjust. Anyone can see the boy is made for this place. No one else wants to stay when the holiday is done because we all have those dreams to follow that are larger than what the Orkneys have to offer. Larger, but not at all superior. Horace might aspire to nothing more than mucking out stalls and rubbing down horses after they have run the fields all day, but that is honest ambition on display and should be praised not passed over. In one of his pamphlets Shelley said, *Labour and skill and the immediate wages of labour and skill is a property of the most sacred and indisputable right.* In other words, what Horace desires is the equal of anything considered holy, be it Methodist, Presbyterian, or some strange faith we cannot contemplate. But I know better than to argue this with father or to expose my own ambitions too soon. When I did read the poem to Lettie she warned me of its disruptive power.

'You could only say such a thing aloud if you were prepared to assume your own independence and never cross father's threshold again. Think on it, Arthur. Are you prepared to take that step and break mother's heart as well?'

We are too alike for me not to be aware she spoke of her own position within the family as well as mine, but when I asserted this she said only that we would all have to make choices, like Horace, one day. And because we were older it was likely father would have no power to restrain us. Not even her, a woman.

'Would that make our departures any easier?' she asked. 'Or mother's pain any less?'

'When will you choose, Lettie?'

But she would not answer directly. 'You're fortunate to be able to put your longings into your poetry. Your words and images are a shield between you and outright discontent. I don't have that ability and have to build a different kind of defence.'

'What is that?'

'The experience I seek father cannot imagine.'

Clem

I have decided to write a piano piece for Horace. When father told him he couldn't stay here I could see the sadness in his eyes though he didn't offer any reply. Lettie and Arthur certainly had something to say, but father cut them short after only a few moments of protest. I wanted to speak up on his behalf though it wouldn't make any difference at all. He's not three years older than me, and even if I would never want to remain on the Orkneys, I know it won't be much time before I strike out on my own. Maybe not at fifteen, but not so long beyond that. Besides, he's such a good chap and deserves to live and work where he is happy. The only bit of comfort he can take back to Yorkshire is that father says next year or the year after is a possibility. None of us are surprised by the edict from on high. What we can't understand is how mother accepts it without a murmur.

Father would dismiss my words, but he won't be able to dismiss my music. When I've finished, I shall announce that my new composition is for Horace and play it without further comment. There will be seven movements and no orchestra, of course. Horace will be the centre part with Ernest, Bertie, and Arthur on one side, and Lettie, Norman, and me on the other. I have already begun to compose on Mrs. Drever's piano. Norman has asked me why I am starting and stopping all the time and what I am writing in my notebook propped above the keys. I tell him I'm learning a new work and, not to worry, he'll hear it when I'm ready.

'I've never seen you write anything down before. Why do you have to do that this time?'

'It's different from anything I've played, and longer. I have to keep track of all the notes.'

He doesn't mind really, as long as he gets to explore amongst Mrs. Drever's knickknacks and I play him a familiar tune before we leave. I get on best when he's not with me even if Mrs. Drever is puttering about in her kitchen. She's a bit deaf, I think, and more than a bit tone-deaf if truth be told. The piano belonged to her husband, of course, and even though she can read music, having learned as a girl, she plays it only occasionally herself. Because I need to work steadily without interruption I've taken to spending more and more time at her cottage. Father takes no notice, especially as he's away so much, but mother is pleased I'm practising every day, though she worries too that I'm not getting enough fresh air. I wonder if Mozart's mother worried about him as well. He was composing little piano pieces when he was five and playing in public before crowned heads soon after that! I don't want to travel as much as he did, but I wouldn't mind being famous for my music. Well, every composer has to begin somewhere, and this is what I am doing now.

The opening movement is about Ernest. I am trying to find a way to show how he rarely strays from the path set out for him and how his life revolves around God's and our father's words. The tone must be unswerving and serious like the verses of the Bible, but if it is too heavy and repetitive it will drag itself down. Then I remember my oldest brother in the cathedral, the last place on earth I would have expected him to be. Notes of escape spring to the tips of my fingers and interrupt the predictable flow. I must draw them out to reflect not only freedom but that unusual calmness in his manner as I observed him in the pew. It is only fair that this hidden side of him be displayed even if my family listeners will never guess its origins. But perhaps I'll announce the title of each of the sections before I play them. It will be my way of telling Ernest I saw him there.

I haven't been back to St. Magnus, but the Viking statues and organ's lure are always in my mind. The other night I dreamed of playing my finished work with those mighty keys and stops. The church was full of strangers who were not concerned with any Methodist intrusion but only with the themes and variations emerging from the pipes. I was soaring on the wings of sound until Father suddenly appeared in the nave and marched towards my veiled spot behind the curtain, his footsteps pounding the instrument into silence, echoing in the great stone space like repeated notes to mark my doom. Just as his hand reached out to pull aside the protective screen and expose my heresy, the choir in the loft above burst startlingly into song and froze him like a statue. I fled into wakefulness with the words of a strange hymn on my lips – *The Lord has kept me for another day* was the first and only line that I repeated in my relief over and over again.

Norman

The Tortoiseshell died yesterday. I found it in the bottle looking like it was asleep, but I knew it wasn't. I took it to Mr. Garson who held the jar for a long time before he unscrewed the lid and turned it upside down so the butterfly fell out onto the soft tablecloth. 'I guess God wanted it to be pinned to the board,' I said. 'I hope it's not the last one. I hope there's one out there with its wings spread in the wind.'

'That's a beautiful thought, Norman. I don't think it is the last one, but maybe you should get right out in the fields to make sure. If you spot one, we'll let it be, don't worry.'

I wondered why the colours of the wings didn't fade even though all his butterflies were dead.

'That's why I cover the board with a piece of glass,' he said, 'to keep the air from changing things.'

'But we breathe the air all the time and it doesn't change us.'

'Yes it does, son. It just takes a long time to do so. You're only ten so your face is smooth and soft.' He pinched his cheek. 'But look at my wrinkled and rough skin. That's from being in the air for so long.'

I thought about what he'd said. 'Is that why people are buried in coffins?' I asked. When I was little I saw my grandmother lying in her coffin before they put her in the ground.

'Yes. The coffins are to preserve the body like the glass does for the butterflies. But even a coffin can't protect things for more than a few years.'

'But there's no air down there.'

'There is, Norman, in the earth. Not enough for us to breathe but enough to change our bodies.'

'I'd rather be a butterfly, then,' I said. 'That way I could keep my colours forever.'

He smiled, and I thought there was something else he wasn't telling me.

I'd heard father say many times that we die to rise up into everlasting life. Colours never change there, but I still didn't understand why God wouldn't just come down to earth so we didn't have to die and our colours stayed the same. When I told father this he smiled.

'But He did do that, Norman. He sent His son to dwell among us and then sacrifice himself so we would not die.'

'Are the angels in heaven like butterflies, father?'

He didn't smile this time but looked at me as if I had asked the most important question of all. 'I think the Lord would be pleased by your comparison, Norman. Perhaps indeed he put butterflies on this earth so we would glimpse the archangels Michael and Gabriel now and then.'

When I told Mr. Garson what father had said, he replied it might be so, but he believed in the butterflies' beauty by itself and that it was because things didn't last forever that such beauty was so special.

'But how can it be by itself?' I wondered. 'Doesn't God make it?'

'You mean it's the Lord who giveth and taketh away?'

Father had said this many times too, so I nodded in agreement.

'If that's the case, Norman, we should be grateful for the giving that lights up our earth. As for the taking, which includes transporting us up above, I think it was the angel Gabriel who said, *For with God nothing shall be impossible.*' He laughed. 'I suppose you and I will just have to wait and see.'

I think Gabriel is a Tortoiseshell with his wings spread in the wind.

Lettie

I have been out on Margaret's boat! After our first conversation, I returned to her cottage on several occasions to sit on the bench beside her or inside before the peat fire if there was a cool mist. She was born and raised there, her mother dying from a fever when she was a girl and her father only two years ago from an injury he suffered in a fall. She inherited the property along with two vessels, a large fishing smack that had provided their livelihood and a smaller sloop only sixteen feet in length, the one she had christened the *Tom Paine*. She sold the smack to a would-be herring fisherman in Stromness who promptly lost it in a storm though he and his crew miraculously survived. I could see the sloop moored at her wharf below the cottage.

We sipped our tea and spoke about her losses as well as of my own family.

'As you can see, I'm an only child and cannot imagine growing up like you among such numbers.'

'It would have been easier if I were not the only girl. Being the eldest helps, I suppose. But sometimes I have felt overwhelmed by the chatter of boys.'

'You were never lonely, I'm sure. When mother died father hired a housekeeper for the times he was away, which were often. She was a well-intentioned woman but tight-lipped. I was mostly left to my own devices and spent a lot of time outdoors. Thank God he taught me how to sail. The sloop was always there for my escape from the ordinary. He made me promise, though, not to go out more than a mile offshore and only on clear days. I'm sure he feared for me but knew it was the only real pleasure I had.'

'Did you have any fear for yourself?'

'Not really. He taught me well, and the boat always felt like part of my own body as she cut through the swells. I did listen to his warnings about the weather, but once or twice I was caught by a strong off-shore wind or a sudden mist cut me off from sight of land.'

I listened amazed at her calm description of circumstances that for me would have meant instant death. Of course, I would not have been out there in the first place and felt inadequate in the face of her ability and envious of it at the same time.

Not long after this exchange she took me down to the wharf and showed me the sloop at close-hand. It is a very sleek vessel, painted bright blue, with a single mast that holds what I have come to learn are the mainsail and headsail, both red ochre in colour. When not in use the mainsail is wrapped around the boom, and the smaller sail is reefed around what is called the forestay. Each of us was in skirts that blew like sails themselves in the on-shore breeze, and as we patted them down she announced she never stepped aboard except, as she had indicated earlier, in proper gear of pants and oilskin jacket.

I looked at the rocking craft and saw the white-caps farther out with gulls swooping down upon them from on high. Well, you'll never get me out there, I thought, though something inside me quivered at the prospect. As if she could read my mind, she said, 'I have an old pair of trousers that will fit you if we roll up the pant legs and an extra jacket that belonged to mother. I daresay we can find you a pair of gumboots as well.'

'Margaret,' I cried, 'I can't swim!'

'That makes two of us, Lettie my dear. It doesn't matter. If we went over all the weight would drag us down.'

We returned to the cottage where I shook off my attire so familiar it seemed a second skin and donned, for the first time in my life, a thick pair of trousers with rolled-up cuffs. Above I pulled on a woollen pullover and a stained outer coat whose sleeves were too short. Too short for what, I wondered, having no idea what was in store for me once we left the shore behind. A pair of her woollen socks fit me perfectly, but the boots were at least two sizes too big.

'Not to worry,' she said. 'You won't be walking far.'

As we left I caught a glimpse of myself in a glass by the bookcase. What a muffled, over-sized creature I had become. Somewhere inside the waterproof disguise was an old Lettie I could barely recall, one who had always thought she cut a figure of resistance to the commonplace in life and scorned the safe and narrow. Now this new uniform could not hide my nervous anticipation and unavoidable awareness that I was venturing into the unknown. How I longed to own Margaret's composure as she made her way confidently down the path, one moment pointing out the puffins on the headland rocks and the next laughingly deriding men's dark superstitions about having women on boats.

As she hoisted the mainsail I stood on the wharf and watched the canvas sheet smoothly unfurl from the boom to rise up the mast. When it was flat against the sky, her nimble fingers tied a knot to secure it in place and she beckoned me on board. I stepped gingerly down, acutely aware my two feet had always been firmly on the ground before this, except when splashing in Cleethorpes shallows. It seemed as if I was abandoning the earth entirely for the water that covered so much of it, but my faith in Margaret remained firm so I took her welcoming hand to find my balance and become a sailor.

She placed me on one of the built-in benches along each side and, her right hand on the tiller and her left holding a rope linked through a hole to the tip of the mainsail, told me I would have to duck my head and shift over when she 'came about,' which meant the sail and boom were swinging across as she turned into the wind. At first we moved slowly over a fairly even surface, heading towards another island I knew was Shapinsay. I kept my eye on the white-caps not far ahead and wondered for the first time if I would be seasick. Years ago, father had described to us his own voyage to the Isle of Man on a vessel smaller than the Thurso ferry and how his queasy stomach left him 'green about the gills' with no choice but to lean over the rail for most of the voyage.

'We'll sail with the wind,' Margaret said. 'That way it won't be so rough.'

In a few more minutes she turned the boat and yelled at me to duck. I did so just in time as the boom sliced through the air towards me, and then, staying low, awkwardly scrambled over to what was now the high side. We were moving quite fast and I looked back at the shoreline racing by, the headland cliffs bright with sunlight that glinted off the windows of isolated cottages behind them. The clarity of the air was startling, and far to the east I could make out the grey mass of Kirkwall houses where my parents and brothers dwelled in blissful ignorance of such adventure. At the tiller Margaret was smiling happily, beads of salt water running down her cheeks, and I thought how beautiful she was and how strong.

'How are you, Lettie?' she shouted.

'It's wonderful!' I cried, tightening my fingers around the wooden rail as the *Tom Paine* bounced through a swell and smacked into a wall of spray. My hair had come undone and was hanging in wet strings about my shoulders, but I didn't care. The speed and wind in my face were what mattered, and the rugged grace of my captain.

We stayed out an hour or more and sailed far enough north to see the surf breaking on the Shapinsay coast before she motioned to a pile of gathering clouds to the west and steered us home. It was only when I hauled myself onto the wharf, knees scraping the rough planks as I made to stand, that I realized I had not inherited father's gills.

8. All the Animals

Ernest

Yesterday in Lyness on Hoy I met a man who claims direct descent from St. Magnus himself. I had delivered a sermon to my largest crowd, perhaps forty people, which is no small feat on an island of less than three hundred souls, and was pleased with the response. They became a full-throated choir when I led them through 'Rock of Ages,' a hymn written by Reverend Toplady who, although converted to Methodism and a follower of Mr. Wesley for some years, eventually became a Calvinist. Therefore, father says, the intended meaning of two lines of the hymn is unclear. In Chapel we sing the end of the first verse as *Be of sin the double cure/Safe from wrath and make me pure*, while Calvinists prefer *Save me from its guilt and power*. I heard these conflicting tongues in my choir, some of whom at least must have been Presbyterians and perhaps even Episcopalians.

I was standing with a small group discussing the tenets of my sermon when an elderly but sturdy parishioner with a shock of white hair and strong jaw-line appeared at my side and waited patiently for the end of our exchange. One senior member of the Methodist community had just expressed his concern that Mr. Donne had written far too many poems about physical lust and his European travels rather than verses that served the Lord, and I replied that I thought these reprobates were from his early days.

'You mean when he was still with the Church of Rome,' the objector asserted. Father had never mentioned to me that Mr. Donne was a Catholic before he was ordained in the Church of England. Taken aback, I was thinking rather desperately of a way to cover my ignorance and reaffirm the common Christian value of his later *Meditation*, when the white-haired man beside me spoke up.

'Now, Geordie, ye'll be looking through the wrong end of the telescope. The young man is not suggesting Mr. Donne was without sin himself, just that he had a few thoughts worthy of our notice.'

Regaining my composure, I offered what I thought were appropriate lines from the Book of Romans. '*For all have sinned and fall short of the glory of God*,' I said, prepared to provide further commentary.

But the by now red-faced Geordie expostulated loudly. '*Be not wise in thine own eyes: fear the Lord, and depart from evil*. Proverbs 3:7.' He then turned on his heel and drew away his companions with him.

My ally chuckled and put out his hand. 'Roddy Erlendsson,' he said good-naturedly. 'Pay no attention to Geordie. He argues with every preacher that comes through, which isn't too often, after all, so we should allow him his day in the pulpit.'

'Ernest Larsen,' I replied clasping his palm and wincing at the strength of his grip despite his advanced years.

'Ah,' he said, 'a Viking just like me.'

We retired to the village inn where I had taken a room, and during a meal of overcooked lamb's leg and potatoes, plus a glass of stout for him, he admitted to having been raised Presbyterian and told me the story of St. Magnus.

It seems the Orkneys became Christianized in the 10th century when the king of Norway ordered the islanders to be baptized at pain of death and the ravaging of every village with 'fire and steel.'

'Not much of a welcome into the fold, was it?' Mr. Erlendsson suggested when he had provided this information.

'No,' I answered, thinking of Christian soldiers marching roughshod in their vestments of war.

'It was his fellow Vikings who were the settlers the king threatened, and, after their conversion, they kept up their own bickering amongst themselves for the next hundred years. Magnus, whose last name was my own, was an earl of Orkney who preferred the singing of psalms to the raiding of enemy shores. His cousin Haakon got fed up with his holiness and made him a martyr in 1115. Haakon didn't want to get his hands dirty so he ordered his cook to lay on with the axe.'

'But how did Magnus become a saint?' I asked.

'Oh, there were miracles having to do with a green field springing up over his grave, the restoration of sight and such things when he was prayed to. Such fervent talk and belief had their influence. The great church in Kirkwall was begun not long after his death, and there are, in fact, more than a dozen St. Magnus cathedrals scattered across the continent. But to make a long story short, my blood was his blood that was spilled all those centuries ago.'

I was enthralled by his tale and asked, quite naturally, if he attended service at the cathedral when he could.

'Aye, I go there on occasion, not to listen to the lessons from on High, but to sit for a while in a pew and think on Magnus's statue and those other likenesses of warriors past. It's a magnificent spot, is it not, regardless of one's faith?'

For the second time in my sojourn my face was burning as I saw my own occupation of a pew near the Viking saint and felt again my overpowering yet strangely peaceful attraction to the majesty of a church that was not my own.

'We're a strange lot, aren't we?' he continued. 'Given your name, one of your ancestors might have been present when Haakon ordered the execution, but almost certainly present on those raids the saint protested.'

'Perhaps so,' I said. 'But how are we strange?'

'Because most of the time we pay the past no attention. Our distant relations are strangers to us though we do not exist without them. You and I are perhaps cousins joined by our heritage, but we are asked to dwell more on our sinful present and future lives.'

I enthusiastically took up the cause I deemed right. 'Even if we cannot change the past, we can affect where we are going. Our grace is attained, Mr. Wesley said, 'by works of piety and works of mercy.''

If I thought I could win him over with my own devotion and learnedness, I was wrong.

'Tell me something, have you been inside the cathedral?'

After a slight hesitation, I replied that I had, providing no further information.

'Then you must know what I'm speaking of. There you are, a Methodist, sitting in a Presbyterian bulwark unable to disregard its stained glass and statuary but, even more, the sense of shelter and consolation that have been handed down through the ages. You can understand the solace and protection such a structure provided even to those who did not actively seek God.'

He wiped the gravy from his plate with his last piece of bread and chuckled again. 'My sermon is finished,' he said. 'But I hope when you speak to others you will not let them forget where they come from and ask them to mull over how it shapes their road to come.'

As I lay in my bed that night in a room above where we had eaten and conversed, I considered how on my first visit to the cathedral I simply sat still not thinking about why I was present or what I could possibly be looking for, and how I had felt an acceptance by the church that involved no interrogation on its part nor encouraged any of my own. I remembered looking at the statue of St. Magnus and feeling grateful he had existed, even if I could not have explained the reasons for my gratitude. Had father discovered me in my pew, he would have found an Ernest who, as Mr. Erlendsson suggested, was more involved with the sustaining power of earthly inheritance than the supremacy of eternal life.

93

Clem

I will have to change some of my musical intentions for Ernest. He's told father that he wants to visit the cathedral, and there's something different about him since he came back from Hoy and that other island. He seems, I don't know, more inclined to stray from the path I always saw him on, though if he does I don't think he will do so foolishly. It's hard for me to understand why, but I like him more this way.

Yesterday he asked me if I'd like to come to the cathedral with him on one of his visits. Before I could reply, he said, 'The organ pipes are a sight to see, Clem. They keep the organ itself behind a decorated screen so you can't tell if anyone is sitting there unless the pipes are booming.'

I realize he's just admitted that, like me, he's been inside. But why isn't he worried I might bring that up when father's around? Did he see me that day when I saw him in the pew? Is there room for me now to say aloud that I've already thought of asking the minister or, better still, the organist, some questions about the instrument I'd like to play?

'Ernest...' I begin, but just then mother enters the room and begins to ply him with questions about our canonized Viking descendant. Perhaps it's best we keep our secrets to ourselves, another matter that is making his section of my composition more complicated.

I will leave some things sketched in roughly and move on to Bertie soon. He's not marching down a path as much as a wide, paved road that he built and owns. There are people he meets whose expectations of him are never disappointed and conversations he has that always win the day. And yet, and yet...his confidence about the MacBride case contains some jarring notes I cannot explain but will have to address somehow. So if he and Ernest are no longer entirely predictable, what about the rest of my family? I have already heard father agree to Ernest's proposed visit to the cathedral, which I would never have foreseen. Who is the rock, then, the constant refrain of my piece? It must be mother, and I will have to find a way to include her. That means father too, of course, so my work is getting bigger all the time.

Mother is right about one thing. I do have to get outdoors more often. Not just for my health but because I see and hear things there that become part of my music. The other day I left Norman on the beach playing with some boys from the town and wandered along the coast alone. The gulls were wheeling and crying above me, and I saw more than one of them plummet to the waves and rise from the surf with breakfast in their beaks. They glide so beautifully in the wind I can almost hear it rippling under their wings in a rush of sound that is powerful enough to hold them in place yet so soft not a single feather is ruffled by its passing. I also hear the irregular clicking of stones as the small rollers surge across them and withdraw. It is as if they are talking to one another secretly in a way I can appreciate but not decipher, much like the members of an audience who don't write music themselves but know what they are hearing just the same. Then there are the swaying grasses whose apparent language is silence but whose form is a crescendo of green song heeded only by my inner ear. I listen to single stems joining into notes and measures as I walk on.

'Listen, Norman,' I say, and play him Ernest's section, glossing over the rough patches so he will not notice their unevenness. When I've finished, I ask him, 'If the music was a person you know, who would that be?'

'Is it me?' he says, very pleased with his guess.

I have much work to do.

Lettie

Margaret let me take the tiller this morning, and we skipped over the sea merrily and without incident as if I had been a captain all my days. It is invigorating out there with the wind and sun on our faces and the feeling of so much power immediately beneath. The manner in which sudden gusts and the grip of unseen currents can pull the boat every which way is shocking. One moment everything is secure – we are a half mile from land, but I can make out the smallest details of houses and fences in the bright air and all around are glistening ripples of water that provide buoyancy and passage – and the next we are sailors 'Flotsam' and 'Jetsam' tossed about like scraps as the sloop tilts alarmingly on its side and we are threatened with a complete capsizing. We have no life vests, and I know if we went over and were unable to scramble back aboard immediately we would either sink like stones or die quickly from the cold. Such a fact does demand attention to distant lines of cloud and a readiness to 'come about' without a moment's delay, despite our exhilarating sense of freedom.

We have been to some small uninhabited islands, really nothing more than mounds of rock and sand a few feet high that must be submerged in any storm. It is romantic to christen them with names that will never mark any map – *Margaret's Pastime, Lettie's Lair*. We haul the boat up on their transient shores and have picnics of apples and cheese from our canvas bag. I could do this every day, but because of mists and rough weather it isn't possible, so at such times we tend the garden or sit on the bench or inside by the fire, cups of tea at hand. Early on, I presumed to ask her how she survives – there are only so many vegetables she can grow in a season and she keeps no animals. She replied that her sale of the fishing smack had brought her some funds, but her regular income is from a property on the edge of Kirkwall she inherited from her mother's side of the family. It is a fenced-in tract of land with a large barn and pen she rents to the farmers who sell their livestock there.

'Just enough for food and clothing, as well as the upkeep of the cottage and *Tom Paine*.'

'Why, I know the place,' I said. 'My brother Horace works for Mr. Spence. He has a way with animals and walks them – cattle, bulls, and the like – into the enclosure where others shout out their bids.'

'That's the spot. I don't go down there often, but when I do I'm pleased it's my space. I've met Mr. Spence. He's a good man, and fair as well. Does your brother like his job?'

I told her about Horace's wish to remain here and father's decision on the subject.

'I'm sorry to hear it,' she said. 'It's usually the young ones who are leaving the islands, not wanting to stay.'

One rainy afternoon as we sat before the fire listening to the wind whistle in the chimney, we spoke of the books on her shelves, nearly all of which she seems to have read. There are novels by Jane Austen, George Eliot – 'Now there's a woman who certainly wore pants!' Margaret declared – Stevenson, and an American writer, Hawthorne, I have heard of only vaguely. She handed me *The Scarlet Letter* and said I must read it.'From what you've told me of your family, you'd better keep it from everyone except your brother Arthur.'

Alongside the novels are a few collections of poetry including a little volume of Shelley's verse that mirrors Arthur's well-thumbed copy.

I noticed essays by Coleridge and Arnold as well as travel books by Mrs. Graham and Mary Seacole, a mulatto woman, Margaret told me, who lived an amazing life. She learned about the benefits of herbs for illnesses and wounds in her native Jamaica and eventually journeyed to the Crimea where she cared for British and Russian soldiers alike. I have borrowed this one as well, promising to read it after I have done with Mr. Hawthorne.

The bookcase stretches from floor to ceiling and takes up most of one wall. I think I could spend an entire winter here and not finish a single shelf. When I tell her this, she laughs happily.

'I'm rarely lonely with them to keep me company,' she says. Some I've read two or three times – like Mrs. Seacole`s *Wonderful Adventures* and Mrs. Browning`s *Aurora Leigh* – but I'm sure there are still a few hidden higher up I have yet to discover.'

'You have a wonderful life, Margaret,' I told her. 'My own in bustling Yorkshire seems so dull and predictable in comparison.'

'You don't find my routine of books, garden, and sloop at all boring?' She tried to keep a solemn face, but I could hear the mischief in her voice.

'You know I don't.' I was immediately discomfited as if I had trespassed not on her feelings but my own.

'I shall miss you when you've gone, Lettie.'

'Tell me more about Mrs. Seacole,' I said quickly.

Tonight, inspired by her summary of an amazing life dedicated to others but not without its personal suffering and wider controversies, I put Mr. Hawthorne aside and began Mrs. Seacole's description of her experiences in the Caribbean and Europe. To my surprise, she dealt with her first thirty-nine years in the opening chapter, which I read as my lamp burned low. It seems she was the daughter of a Scottish soldier and a liberated Creole woman, the combination providing her with a light complexion, and took advantage of her freedom of movement by visiting London twice before she was twenty. She did eventually marry, but the entire period from their engagement to her husband's death six years later is condensed into only nine lines at the end of the chapter. Margaret has told me much of the book details her experiences in the Crimea where she met Florence Nightingale. I am looking forward to that but hope to learn more about Jamaica and other Caribbean places as well.

Mother has become curious and even concerned about my almost day-long absences. I am not ready to share my new-found experience with anyone, not even Arthur, and told him, when he noticed the Hawthorne, and asked if he might read it, that I had borrowed it from an old woman in town. To placate mother I will make sure to spend most mornings at home, helping around the house and walking out with her to the shops. Margaret has suggested we sail across the firth to Shapinsay and stay the night. There are standing stones from ancient times there and the grand structure that is Balfour Castle built by the family that owns most of the island and rents out its property to tenant farmers. I want very much to go but would be hard-pressed to explain such a vanishing.

Norman

I have decided if I am going to be a naturalist I have to learn about other creatures as well. Mr. Garson told me I should watch the seals that swim in the bay and rest on the rocks in the middle of the inlet at the end of the beach. He said I should take a notebook and write down what they do and what sounds they make and anything else about them that I think is interesting. When I say I don't have a notebook he pokes around through a drawer in his desk and pulls one out and gives it to me. I like the red leather cover with the little gold design of letters that spell *RG*.

"Robert Garson," he says, and gives a little bow. 'My parents gave it to me for my tenth birthday.' He asks for it back and rips out some pages. 'You need to start clean,' he says, and not bother with what I was like when I was your age.'

I sneak up on the seals' territory after circling around to the far side of the inlet where the rocks are closest to the shore. They must be swimming underwater because I can't see any at all until suddenly the smooth head of one appears on the surface followed by another then a third. Their fur is slicked back as they emerge and clamber up on the same rock, barking at one another as if to say, 'Watch it, this is my spot!' One of them with a big nose has a fish in his mouth – or maybe it's a her, I can't tell – and tosses it up in the air before catching and swallowing it whole. The two others look a little sad that they didn't get a share. They lie with their chins resting on the rock, their wet fur glistening in the sun and their tails curving upwards. I write all this down in my notebook and make a drawing of them on the opposite page. I'm too far away to see their whiskers but put them in anyway. I wish I had some crayons so the different shades of grey and white in their fur would show up. They're not the same as the colours in a butterfly's wings, but they're pretty, even so.

'Those are grey seals, you saw,' Mr. Garson tells me. 'And the one with the big nose was probably a bull. You should see if you can spot some harbour seals. They're brown and black and have noses in the shape of a V.'

'What kind of fish do they eat?'

'Mostly herring, I should think. That's what's available around here, though I'm sure there are some other species they consider delicacies.'

'They don't live on the rocks all the time, do they? Where's their homes?

'In caves you can't see at the bottom of the steepest cliffs on the north side of the island. That's where they raise their young before they take them out into deep water.'

'Have you ever seen a cave?'

'Once or twice. It's risky to try to go there because of the cliffs and the slipperiness of the rocks at the bottom.' He stuffs some tobacco in his pipe and holds a match to the bowl. 'There's also the selkies,' he says.'

'My sister told me about them.'

'Did she tell you they're very dangerous?'

'Yes. They can pull you into the sea, and you might never come back.'

'Most naturalists don't believe in them.'

'Do you, Mr. Garson?'

'When I was your age I didn't think much about selkies at all, though I'd heard the fishermen's tales about them. I just wanted to see how seals acted and try to get closer to them.'

I was about your age, Norman, and just as curious. My father always warned me away from the caves beyond the other side of the bay because he knew I was after the seals. 'You'll get down there and there'll be no way back up,' he told me.' There's no route for a boat to get ashore with the waves pounding the rocks every minute. So even if we suspect you're there, fallen and broken, we won't be able to get you out.' I knew he was right, but I was determined to have a go. One Saturday morning when he and my mother were at market and I was supposed to be on the football pitch, I packed my knapsack with some fruit and bread and a bottle of water, along with a length of rope, maybe fifty or sixty feet of it. I'd scouted along the top of the cliff before and knew there was a break in the rock that led downward through the precipice, cutting off about a quarter of the descent. This I followed until it ended far still above the crashing surf where I saw something bobbing that could have been kelp-ends on the surface.

I tied one end of the rope to a jutting piece of stone and the other around my waist then lowered myself down. I was very pleased at my progress and excited about finding the forbidden caverns when the rope ran out with me hanging perhaps twenty feet in the air, the salt mist washing my face and stinging my eyes and my outlook grim. Of course, I could have hauled myself back up, but I needed to rest for awhile before my hands and arms would hold my weight, and the rope was already cutting into my waist like a vise. I managed to swing myself across to a thin ledge and stand shivering on the narrow refuge it offered, knowing full well I couldn't stay there long. Indeed, the wind picked up and was threatening to pluck me from my perch at any instant. After bearing the onslaught for a minute or so, I decided to swing back into the centre of the cliff and begin my climb. As I did so I felt a slight give in the rope that dropped me a foot or so and then, before I could react, it all came looping towards me, and I fell.

I should have died on those rocks but somehow managed to land between two spear-like formations on a pile of sea-weed that seemed placed there for the purpose of catching small boys who had gone too far. My breath was knocked out of me and perhaps I even passed out. When I opened my eyes I was on my back and the cliff was staring down at me cold and unblinking. I knew how lucky I was to see it. I turned over on my stomach to survey the rest of my trap, the desolate meeting of rock and water that permitted no escape on foot and the furious array of crest and troughs that meant no rescue by sea was possible. Then I saw a seal slipping along the stones towards the water. But it wasn't a seal because just before it disappeared beneath the surface I saw it had long hair and arms like a girl's above its grey coat and tail fin. It was then a feeling pierced my heart and bones that I had been spared one kind of death only to meet a dark fate reserved for those who trespassed on a selkie's territory.

I became terribly afraid that if I did not leave her alone she would return to spirit me away like the stories said and looked around desperately for an exit route. Then, as tears of despair and fear welled up in my eyes, I saw the end of the rope hanging by my side. Surely its presence by my fingertips was a miracle, though later I would provide a rational explanation to myself that it had become caught at the top of the cliff before its length had been fully paid out. It hadn't broken but merely unravelled its tangled twenty feet or so. Without a backward glance to the water, I grabbed hold of my beanstalk and slowly hoisted my aching body to the top. It took a long time to reach safety, and it was only when I was within the haven of the slanting rock-break that I turned around and gazed down at the site of my ordeal. Perhaps it was because I had heard many fanciful tales of selkies around the winter fire when I was a little boy that I discounted what I had seen on the beach-stones. My imagination had been overwrought, and what I had glimpsed was undoubtedly a seal frightened by my arrival from above. It was just a matter of luck with the rope, wasn't it?

No one else has heard this story, Norman. I want to spare you the over-reaching that nearly cost me my life. You should remember my folly and watch the seals from a distance.

'But you do believe now it was a selkie?' I asked him.

For a long time he didn't say anything, and I wondered if he was angry at such a question. Then he smiled at me and put out his hand to gently touch my shoulder.

'Perhaps it was,' he said. 'But if so, I don't know whether she didn't see me or just swam away to leave me to my own devices. It's something I never wanted to put to another test.'

Horace

I am feeling very sad, and Lettie says it is only to be expected. This morning Mr. Spence had to put down his favourite horse, a Clydesdale mare named Bess. She had been pulling a plough on the edge of a field when she slipped sideways off the border and snapped her foreleg against a buried rock. The ploughman had seen her hooves trying to keep purchase in the wet soil but reacted too late. He could only watch helplessly as her weight wrenched the handles from his hands and the blade spun about to cut the air like a scythe. When Mr. Spence and I arrived, she was standing on three legs, the useless fourth held free of the ground but twisted at an angle from her knee. I could tell she was frightened because of how fast her rib cage went up and down and how the steam from her nostrils formed a thick cloud about her face that the sea-breeze could not shift.

Mr. Spence patted her muzzle and tried to soothe her with some quiet words. Then he bent to look more closely at her injury. After a few moments of inspection with a light touch of his fingers, he sighed and said, 'There's no use in sending for Mr. Peverel. It will never mend properly.'

He sent me back to the farmhouse for his firearm, which Mrs. Spence took out from a locked cupboard near the back door. 'It'll not be easy for him,' she said, and I could tell she was upset as well. 'He's had that horse for many years.' Then she handed me two bullets. 'Just in case,' she told me.

I had never carried a rifle before and was surprised at how heavy it was, the well-worn stock soft against my palm and the long barrel pointing to the ground. I could feel the weight of the bullets in my sweater pocket. My thoughts were in a bit of a daze because Mr. Spence and I had been mending a pasture fence only half an hour before, and he had been telling me which of his livestock had been with him the longest. There was Percival, the prize bull born in his barn over fifteen years before and descended from Grey-Breasted Jock, the first Angus himself from Mr. Watson's farm in Aberdeenshire. And there was Bess that he had purchased as a foal and was now almost twenty years old. She was a gentle soul, despite her great size and strength, he said, and I knew that was true. I had seen her pull a sled piled high with stones for a quarter mile without a misstep and do the same with wagon-loads of seaweed hour after hour. And I had watched Mr. Spence's young nieces and nephews sit on her back as if she were a docile pony beating a safe track in a fairground circle.

'I'm attached to them both,' he had said. 'My children are near grown and will soon be gone from the house, but these two are still with me and will be even when they can work no more.' He laughed. 'Of course, that's a different kind of thing for Percy than it is for Bess, and he's bound to slow down sooner, though you never can tell.'

Now here he was holding the weapon I had brought him, faced with Bess's death and having to bring it about himself. We had undone her traces and pulled the plough away, and she stood suffering patiently on the verge with the sunlight dappling her red-brown coat and her tail flicking away the flies. I could see lines in his face where I had not noticed them before and a grim determination in his eyes as he stroked her neck and spoke to her in a whisper I could not make out. Whatever her pain and discomfort, she nuzzled his cheek and made a small snuffling sound as if to signal her contentment he was at her side. Then I heard him say, 'I'm sorry, Bess.' Without hesitating, he stepped around in front of her, pressed the barrel to her forehead, and pulled the trigger. I was but a few feet away and the roar deafened me, which is why I watched her fall as silently and softly as a feather would settle on the earth. Her hind legs twitched once or twice then she was still. Death had frozen Mr. Spence as well. He gazed down at her without moving, the smoke seeping from the barrel's end, his lips pressed together in a tight line of grief. I remembered how he had as much as called her one of his children and did not know what to say.

'We'll put her in a pit at the edge at the edge of the main pasture,' he told the ploughman. 'On the high point where she can glimpse the sea.' Then he turned to me. 'You mind what you've signed up for, Horace, in the life you've chosen.'

I wanted to remind him of all the years of happiness he'd had with her but could only think of what father might say – that in the end we are all, men and creatures alike, feathers in the hands of the Lord. I know our happiness pales beside our coming glory above, but I mean to ask father if there are any horses galloping through heavenly fields. I've heard him preach often enough that only men and not animals have immortal souls.

When I told Lettie about what had happened and Mr. Spence's sorrow, she took my hands in hers and said Bess and Percival were special animals indeed to have lived as long as they had. 'Most of the time,' she reminded me, 'we raise them only to send them off to slaughter.'

'Never horses,' I replied, though I knew we did sometimes.

'But they cannot live as long as we do, and finally we have to put them down.'

'Even if they're like our children?'

She blinked and looked at me curiously. 'Yes, even then.'

When I asked father if Bess might be in heaven, he thought long and hard. Finally he opened his Bible and ran his finger down a page right at the end. 'I don't employ the Book of Revelations often, Horace, but here is the one called Faithful and True who sits upon a white horse when heaven opens. *And the armies which were in heaven followed him upon white horses, clothed in fine linen, white and clean.* Chapter 19, verses 11-14. These are the armies of judgment at the Apocalypse, so the horses have an important role to play in the new heaven and earth.'

'Does the Bible say anything about feathers?'

'You are testing me today, are you not? Look to your Psalms. There may be something there.'

I read forty-five pages, more than I have ever done before, and then I found the words that let me sleep. *He will cover thee with his feathers, and under his wings shalt thou trust his truth shall be thy shield and buckler.* 91:4.

Arthur

Horace told Lettie what happened in Mr. Spence's field, and father too. His melancholy couldn't be ignored at the supper table, especially when Clem and Norman pestered him for details, word of his experience having gotten around the household. I have seen dead pets, cats and the like, and even a deer lying by the side of the road after a coach-and-four passed over its hindquarters, but to witness a deliberate killing must take its toll, and Horace's attachment to animals would make such an event particularly shocking. Lettie says Mr. Spence told him the mare was like one of his own progeny. Horace has heard often enough about the kingdom of heaven belonging to little children so naturally he asked father if that meant there were horses up above. I didn't hear his eventual theological reply, but whatever it was, I am a poet and cannot disregard the boy's struggle to understand the collision between love and violence.

The horse does not turn her head
The master is he who blinks
Waits patiently for what will come
Into close death she'll sink

The shots ring clear and clean
Eyes wide the horse dies down
The master's after-life
Is like an open wound

Those who hold the power
Twixt life and death decide
Must pull the soul's trigger
Whether in heaven they ride

I have decided to write to the publisher John Murray in London and provide a sample of my efforts. Years ago, of course, the company printed *Childe Harold's Pilgrimage*, and as Byron describes it, he woke one morning to find himself famous. I do not have any pretensions on that score, but it would be nice to have one's work read and appreciated. I believe Mr. Murray also published Miss Austen's writings, which might somewhat mollify father's hostility to profligate poets and to the appearance of Mr. Darwin's *The Origin of Species* under the Murray insignia. I doubt it but will persevere. Perhaps there is a Scots publisher who would respond favourably to my rendition of the Orkneys – whatever its partialities, I know! There is the *Blackwood's Magazine* out of Edinburgh. That way I would not have to wait until I have sufficient verse for a collection but can see one or more individual poems more quickly onto the page.

It is strange, but each time I write a poem I wonder if it will be the last time I do so. I have the strongest conviction that while the words lie waiting to be discovered in my mind, there is not an endless supply of them, and there will be no warning when they run out. Did Shelley have such doubts, and is that why he managed to write so much in the short span he had? I know *The Triumph of Life* was on his desk when he drowned in the Gulf of Spezzia, cut off in mid-sentence as it were. Perhaps he pushed himself into the storm because he sensed he would be unable to complete his thought or answer the final question he posed – 'What is life?' I am hardly in the same position since I lack his genius and my brief exile from England is not eternal, but I still worry about the source of my creative well and its depth.

Lettie seems distracted much of the time. Happy, but not as open with me as usual. When I tease her about her sun-lightened hair and wind-burned face, she only smiles and does not have much to say other than that the outdoors is good for her. She's always off for several hours at a time now. Perhaps she's found an Orkney beau and that's why I'm not invited along. I've half a mind to follow her on one of her walks.

Ernest returned from his southern preaching tour a new man. He appears much more confident in himself than before and speaks with father about Chapel matters almost as an equal. He told us he met a man who claims descent from the Viking they named the cathedral after, and he's interested in discovering all he can about the history of the relationship between the Vikings and Christianity. That means, he said to father in our presence, he would like to visit the cathedral and speak with the minister there as well as with any others who might provide him with information on the subject. To my surprise, father agreed, and to my further astonishment – and everyone else's – announced he had met the Bishop of northern Scotland and the Orkneys when he was in Kirkwall the week before.

'He and Mr. Taggart have known one another since they were boys in school, and though we spoke not of the holy scripture but of the fishermen's cause and our differences there, it is clear he is a man of strong character and faith who believes in his church as much as we do ours. I hope he gained an equally favourable opinion of me and the Chapel's pursuit of justice.'

Bertie continues with the MacBride case, which comes to court in a day or two. He is convinced Jamie MacBride will walk free and his accuser will face some charges himself. He is clearly enamoured with the wife but will not own up to it when I press him.

'She's a lovely woman,' he says, 'and I respect her courage deeply. I am sure, when all this is over, they and their children will be more than content together.'

'And if he happened to be convicted?' I ask in pretended concern. But he knows my intention and parries it like the lawyer he will become.

'Then, as any loyal wife would do, she will wait for him.'

The evidence against me is apparently damning, as he adds, 'You're too much the poet, Arthur, always looking for things beyond the facts.'

Clem is up to something. He spends all his days at Mrs. Drever's cottage where, Norman says, he plays the piano constantly and writes things down in his leather notebook. I think mother knows about it because he always has a word or two with her when he comes home in the evening. I ask Norman for further information, but he just answers with a question for me.

'Have you ever seen a Tortoiseshell butterfly, Arthur?'

'Not that I'm aware of. Why?'

'They look like angels,' he says, and the innocence on his face takes my breath away.

Thomas

Taggart and I found Rory Parker in a house by the docks. It took some time because people were reluctant to step forward for fear of informers in their midst. Finally, one man approached us outside the Chapel and gave us directions in as broad a Scots accent as I'd ever heard. We waited for darkness before setting out.

'I dinna naow that Rory would approve,' the man had said. 'But he might ha' need 'o the Lord to snatch him from a right fix.'

The stone house was dingy in appearance and a bit run-down, but the woman who answered our knock was tidy enough, her white hair held back in a bun and her apron spotless. When we identified ourselves, she beckoned us inside, saying that, though Presbyterian herself, she knew well who Mr. Taggart was and that I was no stranger to the fishermen. There wasn't much furniture in the ground floor room, but a low fire gave off a friendly heat and a kettle was singing on the hob. She invited us to sit down, poured us mugs of tea from a Brown Betty, and set a plate of biscuits on a stand between us. Her name, she offered, was Morag Connery, and she was Rory's aunt.

'He thought you might turn up, Mr. Taggart. Angus, who told you where to come, sent word he'd spoken to you. Rory may be less of a believer than that old scoundrel, but he won't turn down help from ones the Lord inspires. I'm one of seven sisters, so those in search of him have more than a few places to stop before they find him out.' She sighed. 'But they'll be here soon enough.'

Just then we heard footsteps on the floor above and a few moments later Rory Parker's boots appeared on the stairs, which were so steeply inclined toward the low ceiling that his feet were almost at the bottom before his head was visible. He nodded at both of us and sat on the edge of the hearth as we occupied the only two chairs in the room. Mrs. Connery busied herself in a large alcove that was kitchen and mud room both.

'I thank you for coming,' he said. 'No one else has been along.'

'What about Angus?' I asked.

'He sent word by the boy who brings the bread, a wee chappie they wouldna suspect.'

Taggart spoke up. 'Have you any plans to get away, Rory?'

'As ye can see, we're not far from the harbour. There's constables lined up down there, I'm sure. Someone will let me know when I can slip through their lines and get aboard a smack.'

'Where will you go?'

'They be thinking I'll head for the mainland, but it's to one of the outer islands I'll go – Papa Westray or North Ronaldsay. They're wild and it's easy enough to hide in the bracken if you see a sail on its way.'

'We'd like to help,' I said. 'It might be some time before you can safely take a boat, and meanwhile the authorities will close in on Mrs. Connery's home.'

'Aye, that they will. D' ye have anything in mind?'

Taggart and I had talked this over and agreed the loft of our Stromness Chapel was best, reached by a ladder and trap door at the back of the hall. Our regular presence would be taken for granted so a little food could be brought in without suspicion as could anyone wishing to help him escape. When we conveyed this to Mr. Parker he stroked his whiskers thoughtfully and asked Mrs. Connery if he might have a mug of tea as well, which she brought shortly.

After taking a large gulp, he chuckled and looked up to the rafters. 'I'm not a believer, y' know. My father tried me with the Presbers when I was a boy, and Aunt Morag still does the same, but they haven't won me over yet, maybe because the minister at St. Magnus has spoken against our struggle. When I first went to sea, the crew were all of your faith so I followed along on Sundays, but somehow the Lord and all his ways didn't settle with me. It will be an odd path of flight for me to pass through a Chapel. No doubt y'll simply tell me the Lord moves in mysterious ways.'

'He does that, Rory,' Taggart replied. 'But we're not here to win you over, just to give you the chance to fight another day. What the buyers and politicians are doing to you and your lot is not just.'

'It's good of ye to say so. When shall we move this old sinner, then?'

'As soon as possible, I should think,' Taggart said. 'You can't have much with you. Why don't you wear my coat and hat and go now with my friend. I'll stay with Mrs. Connery and another cup of her fine tea for awhile, then make my way alone. If you take Wallace Street and on past the cemetery you'll get there quickest.'

'I'll just get my kit, then. Nothing more than an oilskin and boots, but I'll need them after the Chapel.'

We thanked Mrs. Connery for her hospitality while he went upstairs, and when he returned shortly with a canvas bag over his shoulder she hugged him fiercely.

'Ye'll be coming back to me, Rory Parker,' she told him with as much confidence as she could muster.

'When the time is right, be sure of that,' he said, then turned and bent to the hearth. With a brush of his fingers he spread a bit of ash and soot on each cheek, darkening down his fair complexion. 'Just one of many disguises,' he declared with a smile.

I went first and saw there was no one about. He followed, and we set off to the corner of Wallace Street, not speaking a word as we then made our way east up a hill and alongside the cemetery fence beyond which a few gravestones flickered dimly in the starlight. The Chapel with its white clapboards was a more evident marker, and it seemed as we approached like giant beacon not only for those on the run but for their pursuers as well. I took him to the side door soon opened with Taggart's key. Once inside we found the ladder in a storeroom behind the pulpit and leaned it against the side wall that gave access to the trap-door and loft. 'I'm afraid a chamber-pot and blanket are the best we can do for your needs.'

'More of a luxury than is on a boat, that's certain.'

'In the morning, Mr. Taggart or I will bring you some food. You can tell us who best to speak to at the harbour. By the way,' I asked, 'what will you be able to accomplish from the outer island?'

'The struggle has only just begun,' he replied. 'There'll be a place for me in it again. Thank you for your help despite being a mainlander and an Englishman to boot.'

'The Lord knows no borders, Mr. Parker,' I said, perhaps a little too sanctimoniously for my own liking. 'Besides,' I added, in an attempt match his wry sense of humour, 'I know who'll give me the best price on herring in the future.'

'That you do, sir, that you do.' He shook my hand, climbed the rungs, and pulled up the ladder. The trap-door clicked shut behind him. A few moments later, I heard the soft thud of his boots as he took them off.

Elizabeth

Thomas has confided in me his efforts to help Mr. Parker. I know he is uneasy about breaking the law because Mr. Parker has been charged with 'public mischief,' a polite way of saying 'leading a riot,' and his punishment, if he is caught, will be severe. They will want to make an example of him, Thomas says, and all because wealthy buyers, who are no different from landlords with their tenant farmers, won't allow the fishermen to make a decent living. When he stands in the Stromness pulpit this Sunday and preaches from Proverbs that *the Lord secures justice for the poor but the wicked have no such concern*, he will certainly be aware Mr. Parker is part of the congregation and that there are probably spies for the buyers listening as well.

It has been two nights and days since he brought the fugitive to the Chapel, and we have supplied him with food and drink from our own kitchen. I do not begrudge him this sustenance but worry he will be discovered and Thomas charged with a crime. The authorities know we Methodists are sympathetic to the fishermen's plight and they are bound to watch us closely for any sign that we are sheltering Mr. Parker somewhere. Thomas concealed bits of food on his person and carried water in a flask that fits easily in a pocket, but such secret methods cannot go on forever. I know the constables are still guarding the harbour, and Thomas has said he and Mr. Taggart will likely have to smuggle Mr. Parker out of town so he can be picked up somewhere along the coast. I know his cause is just, but I will be glad when I no longer have to imagine him lying still and silent on the loft floor just a few feet above my husband's head.

Meanwhile, life in our house goes on as usual. We have now been here more than three weeks, and though I have become somewhat attached to the island scenery and the friendliness of the townspeople towards us, I shall be glad to see Yorkshire again. Ernest is away to the south preaching on his own. We have had a letter from him telling us of his success and how he feels he has found his feet as a preacher. He still talks of working at Kingswood School but emphasizes that the sooner he is able to have a Chapel of his own the happier he will be. Bertie remains involved with the MacBride case which will be coming to court any day now. I continue to visit Alice MacBride who, Bertie says, has told him a story the court will not be able to ignore. He cannot divulge the details but hints that it is Mr. Nicholas who is the guilty party. When we are together I do not speak of the matter to her but ask instead what plans she and her husband have for the future. Her affection for her two children is clear, and I suggest again it might be better for the family on the mainland, not just because her husband could be in gaol there but to get away from Mr. Nicholas and any gossip about the case.

'Oh, we could never leave home,' she says with a surprising conviction she had failed to express previously. 'We were both born and raised here, and the girls as well. It is Roger Nicholas who will have to leave. As for idle gossip, I have no time for it. Jamie and I are strong enough to withstand malicious tongues, and we have enough good neighbours to support us. You have been very generous with your baskets of food, but there are others who help out more than I can say.'

I cannot but admire her strength in the face of her ordeal. When I ask if she will write to me when we have left the island, she smiles and nods. It pleases me to think of keeping some contact with this place.

Of course, my contact would have been Horace had Thomas decided differently, but I would have been very nervous leaving him behind. I must say he has taken things quite well and continues to work cheerily for Mr. Spence. I believe he is counting on a more favourable verdict this time next year. If he still wants to come back when he is sixteen, I will do all I can to persuade Thomas to grant his wish.

Arthur is writing every day and seems quite content. He has told me he would like to travel to the continent after working for awhile and saving some money for such a trip. Perhaps he'll teach for a period, he says. Not at a place like Kingswood but as a private tutor who can provide young boys with a good grounding in the literature of our country – Shakespeare, Tennyson, Browning, and of course the ever-present Shelley.

'I'm not sure your father would approve of Shelley's verses ringing the halls of home,' I tell him.

'Oh, I agree,' he says. 'I would go to the homes of my students *Like a poet hidden/ in the light of thought,/ Singing hymns unbidden/ Till the world is wrought/ To sympathy with hopes and fears it heeded not.*'

When I ask him if we will see his own poems one day, he replies that he will be proud to read some of them to us when we are home.

'Why not all?'

There are a few, he says, that father would find too secular in their nature. They are for earthly posterity, he says mischievously. Though I am determined to press the matter, I banish from my mind the shameful thought of poking around in his room in his absence.

There are two creative minds in our house! Clem has just told me a great secret. He is composing a piece in Mrs. Drever's front room, which he says is for Horace but is really music about all his brothers and Lettie as well. He has sworn me to tell no one, and I have promised my lips are sealed. As my reward, he says, I will be the first to hear it, though Norman, unaware, has been listening to bits and pieces of it and has asked Clem what he keeps writing in his notebook. I have told him he still needs to get outside more often because he looks pale to me and doesn't seem to have time for play, which all boys his age should have. He admits that he hears music when he is on the beach and the clouds are scudding by while the waves crash against the shore. But he says he can never be far away from the piano or else what he hears disappears between the strand and the front door of the cottage.

As for Norman, he has helped Mr. Garson find a very rare butterfly, which is a real boon to his budding naturalist's reputation. Mr. Garson tells me Norman is quite a special boy with unusual qualities that allow him to rise above the limits of ordinary science and see not only the insect but its place in the larger scheme of things. In God's scheme, I am certain, and wonder briefly if Norman's true calling might not be to follow his father and Ernest on their spiritual quests. Thomas has told me that Norman compares butterflies to angels but confuses nature in the field with the nature of eternity. Well, that will straighten out in time.

Lettie has been transformed by something. She will not tell me when I ask her why she is so happy these days and looks so healthy, her face wind-burned from all her walks along the coast. She does go off for hours at a time, and I am often tempted to follow her, though I know I could never keep up. It may be that as much as she seems to love this place she knows we have only a few weeks left here, and so is simply determined to look positively on every moment and live each one to the fullest. Whatever it is, she will have many good memories to carry home with her. I only hope when we do return to Yorkshire she can present a warm and loving demeanour to the world there, and especially to any prospective suitors who happen along.

Bertie

I went to see Jamie MacBride and repeated to him what Alice had told me about Roger Nicholas's advances. When I had finished, he simply turned away and stared out the barred window of his cell.

'Your continued silence will do neither of you any good,' I remonstrated. 'Alice…your wife is determined the truth will out, but her word alone will not be accepted by the court. You must speak up in her defence and your own. Surely you cannot wish Mr. Nicholas to triumph.'

His gaze swung slowly back to meet mine. While I did see sadness there, I thought I could also detect some measure of acceptance of my words and perhaps the slight stirrings of a fire in his glance.

'I had hoped to preserve her honour,' he said.

'Her reputation is not at stake if you support her claims against Mr. Nicholas. It is his character that will be tested. Tell me your version of events.'

His description of what had occurred upheld hers, though he could only speak directly to the aftermath of the assault when she had appeared tearfully before him and he set off to confront her assailant. It is well that he stumbled a little in his account of what she said had happened in the barn and could barely bring himself to mention the distasteful kiss applied to his wife's lips because the court will be suspicious of any glib replication of events. He delivered that part of the story in subdued tones, but when it came to his beating of her attacker, he became more animated and concentrated on the physical details.

'When he laughed at me, and at her, saying she had led him on if I knew the half of it, I swung my fist as hard as I could and caught him on the cheek. He raised his own fist as if to reply so I hit him again, this time on his nose which bled abundantly. He fell to his knees, cursing all the while. I pushed him over into the straw and left him there, but not before I gathered up the lambs, one under each arm.'

'Then you took them home and cooked and ate them.'

'Yes. They were owed us, but I could never keep them.'

'What you say, then, is the ticket to your freedom. There will be no stain on your wife, and the court may well charge Mr. Nicholas for his attack on her.'

'But she will still have to speak?'

'Certainly. It cannot be only your word against his.'

Now that I had the whole truth, I thought of how difficult it would be for Alice to testify. Nicholas's barrister would not make it easy for her, and I myself would have to make sure there was nothing in her past behaviour towards the guilty man that would compromise her honest account of the incident in the barn.

'You must think very hard,' I told her. 'Is there anything at all Mr. Nicholas can bring forward that will cast doubt on your evidence?'

We were sitting in her tiny fenced garden with scattered bluish-purple wildflowers in the grass she identified for me as Scottish Primrose.

'They grow only here and on the north coast opposite the islands,' she said. 'Hardy little things that bloom twice, once in the spring and then again in summer.'

'Alice, please pay attention to what I am saying. Roger Nicholas will do everything he can to besmirch your name and your husband's. Mr. Campbell and I must be sure any such assertions are false. Is there anything you have not told me?'

She shifted uncomfortably in her seat then smoothed her skirt. 'There may be a letter still,' she said quietly.

I could feel my heart racing and had to grip the arms of my chair to keep myself steady. 'What letter?' Though I was afraid she could mean only one thing.

'Everything I have told you is true. I did step out with Roger all those years ago, but then I met Jaimie and knew I would marry him. When I tried to break off, as I said, Roger could not accept it.'

'Break off?' My pulse had settled and I became the assistant barrister again. 'If he paid you only pleasant attention, as you said before, why would you have to break anything off? Before you met Jamie did you make any promise to Roger or provide him with any expectations?'

She began to cry, and I offered her my handkerchief to wipe her eyes. 'We cannot go back now, Alice,' I said softly. 'Tell me what happened.'

I will not soon forget how she looked up to the sky as if in the cloud formations some kind of protective figure were dwelling there, and then, not finding it, across at me as I were a substitute knight-in-armour come to her rescue. It was at that moment that I knew I loved her and almost knelt at her feet to declare my undying fealty. Every English schoolboy knows of Lancelot's passion for Guinevere, but I was not so besotted that I could forget how their actions brought down the Round Table. Besides, this queen would never return my affections, loyal as she was to her Arthur languishing in a Kirkwall cell. It was all mixed up, the kiss that I wished I had the courage to emulate, though with tender feeling rather than grotesque force; the combat that had already been fought over her that I could only aspire to join; the unbearable feeling that I might have played Roger Nicolas's role in the drama if I had known and lost her as he had done. Such a vision overcame me that it wasn't a matter of kneeling but of falling forward in a swoon with which I had to contend. Thank God she spoke again at that moment.

'It was after a dance,' she said. 'Jamie had not yet arrived from Westray. I was with a group of girls in a barn used for such occasions. There were fiddlers and pipers too. We had a good time and I took the floor with a few boys, Roger more than once. When the music was done, Roger asked if he could escort me home. There was much laughter and teasing from the girls, but I agreed. As I told you, he was older and a handsome man to boot, and I felt flattered at his singling me out. We walked along the paths, not so much as holding hands, chatting about the dance and when the next one might be. All was normal until we came to our cottage gate and I thanked him and said good night. Then to my surprise he drew me to him and kissed me hard.'

'Just as in his barn.' I murmured.

'No, not at all. I was young and it was a pleasure to be kissed like that instead of having a silly peck from one of the younger boys. I returned his affection but pushed him off when he tried again. 'You're not my sweetheart yet,' I told him laughingly and went inside. When I peeped out through my bedroom curtains, he was still standing there in the moonlight.'

'What happened after that?'

'The next morning I was still a bit giddy with the excitement of it all and foolishly wrote him a letter saying that he should be careful because I didn't know what I would do if he should kiss me again. I can see now, of course, he might take it as an invitation, but on my part it was only a playful effort to keep his attentions. Jamie appeared before the next dance so nothing more happened between us.'

Struggling to keep my jealousy at bay, though of what or whom I couldn't clearly say, I tried to focus on what this meant for her husband's case.

'Whatever I may have said back then, he still shouldn't have taken advantage of me after I had married Jamie,' she said. 'And I a mother, as well.'

That was true enough, but I knew the court would see a history where she saw only a passing moment in time. Meanwhile, the crucial question remained. Did he still possess that letter?

The Frame

While I wouldn't say yet it's a family on the cusp of exploding, there are certainly indications of a looming crisis of sorts for Thomas and Elizabeth as the scions of order and respectability. Thomas himself, of course, is at the head of the line when we consider the reasons behind possible calamity. As his wife suspects, his position as Methodist minister, while enabling his sympathies for the working-man, will not protect him from the full force of the law should he continue to aid Rory Parker. I'm sure there was a 19th-century statute against the harbouring of those accused of criminal acts, and decisions as to Mr. Parker's guilt will rest as much on the long history of clashes between his ancestors and those serving the Crown as on his more immediate grabbing of an M.P.'s ankle.

Elizabeth aids and abets her husband with the fugitive in the Chapel loft, but she does not want to deal with the legal consequences should her Thomas arrange the smuggling of Mr. Parker out of town. The authorities might be satisfied with scolding and fining two ordained Methodist activists for briefly hiding a man on the run in their Chapel, but they will deal more harshly with any long-term threat to class-based stabilities such as arranging an escape to an unknown spot from where the accused can always return. Meanwhile, the proud mother lauds Clem's composing and Ernest's preaching and is sanguine about what she sees as her youngest son's spiritual journey. Troubled by Arthur's wayward secularism and Lettie's inexplicable behaviour, she will not let herself stoop to interfering with the former, but indicates that her daughter's future is predictably foretold whatever the reasons for her 'transformation.' Outside the family borders, she seems to assume everything with the MacBrides is about to settle down nicely and anticipates a friendly correspondence as the natural outcome.

We haven't heard from Ernest directly since his return from the southern islands, but from what Arthur and Clem have to say, he's a changed man. Launched by his experiences on South Ronaldsay and Hoy, and especially his insight into the earthly origins of sainthood and accompanying faith, he does appear on his way to an independence of mind that will ultimately challenge Thomas outright. It's already a giant step to inform his father he wants to visit the Cathedral and learn as much as he can about the Viking-Christian connection, but I wonder if he's telling the whole truth here. Thomas's surprising agreement with his plans provides him with access to the ancient stronghold but also encourages him to bring in Clem as an ally. I'm not sure Thomas wants his child prodigy expanding his repertoire through the St. Magnus pipes or listening to Presbyterian orations.

Bertie's increasing involvement with Alice MacBride, while tame enough by today's standards, is causing a confusion between his defence of her husband and his desire for her free of consequence. As the layers of her involvement with Roger Nicholas unfold, he is losing his aspiring barrister's objectivity, and I suspect he wants to read that letter because he wishes it had been written to him, just like he has imagined kissing her in sudden – if not equally aggressive – fashion as Roger has apparently twice done. I like to think the court will take care of the business entirely, but there's something about Alice that the witness box can't entirely contain.

Horace is another one who is growing apace in his capacity to absorb new experience. He wouldn't see his thoughts about the feathers of death as metaphorical, but they have led him nonetheless to an expanded vision of his father's faith and his own creed of self-sufficiency. Perhaps he will return to Yorkshire as Thomas has decided, but Mr. Spence has become another kind of father-figure to him now with his slain 'child' at his feet, and Horace is bound to that image as well as to the heavenly herd as pure emblems of reckoning.

Arthur's and Clem's respective creative surges represent how they deal with complexities of character and event in the family, but the results are not the same. Arthur's poems emerge from his questioning of what goes on around as well as within him and are charged, or so he intends, with resistance to the commonplace acceptance of things, while Clem's musical notations are an attempt to capture and fix what he sees and hears without much interrogative purpose. The poems unsettle Elizabeth while the proposed piano arrangement brings her pleasure. The irony, if we're looking at the efficacies of art, is that Arthur's vision is far greater than his talent, and his earnest, rather staid work hasn't much chance of publication by John Murray or anyone else, while Clem's incurious efforts might well receive public attention one day.

Norman may be about to descend into mythical territory armed only with a butterfly net and child-like optimism. Mr. Garson supposedly tells his romantic tale to teach his acolyte a lesson, but in the end he leaves the romance intact, and, unlike his naturalist mentor, Norman is a city boy with no local background to provide distinctions between seals and selkies and little knowledge of island topography. His image of the Tortoiseshell's angel wings is a saving grace, but whether it has any connection to a gray bull seal or an Orkney mermaid remains to be seen.

As for Lettie, her reference to a vanishing is the biggest clue of all as to where she may be headed. On the one hand, she is becoming firmly grounded in the demands of sailing a small craft on a capricious sea and in the history of a female ancestor who dodged many dangers and made a lasting mark on the world. On the other, she has been hooked by Margaret's lure and is calculatingly controlling her mother's concerns while dreaming of a voyage to Shapinsay. Once the original cargoes we carry with us become the flotsam and jetsam she has described, they are endless drifters on the current and never return to land.

The figures in the photograph stare back at my glance, astonished at the divergence between their reality they cannot share with me and the imagined figures they have become. Of course, it is fancy in the first place that they can see me, let alone express any incredulity as to my writing them down. But, for better or worse, they have dug themselves into a story, whether I articulate my narrative frame or not, as characters and voices that refuse to abandon our mutual need.

9. Coming About

Elizabeth

Today I followed Lettie when she set off earlier than usual. At breakfast she told me as the weather was so favourable and there was a northeast wind she would be gone until tea. I asked her what the wind had to do with it, and she replied it made for a pleasant outing. Immediately after she left the house, carrying her canvas bag and wearing, as was her habit these days, only a kerchief on her head, I put on my stoutest boots and took one of Thomas's walking sticks from the hallway. It seemed foolish following my own daughter through the streets of the town and waiting behind the corner of a building until she had descended to the beach, but I was determined to discover what she was up to. I knew she was making extra efforts to help around the house and not setting off on her almost daily jaunts until late morning or noon-time, but I was also aware that her rapid completion of tasks was designed to free up hours for something more preferable.

As time went by, I couldn't help but wonder if a young man was involved but tried to assure myself Lettie had no reason to deceive us in that way. I was hard pressed to consider what else it could be, though. She never talked about her days away except in the vaguest fashion and seemed happier than I had ever known her to be. I was willing to forgive any deception in the short-term because, if she was in love, it was doing her a great deal of good. Her skin glowed with the effects of sun and wind and, as I struggled along the beach in her wake, her legs carried her at a surprising pace towards her destination. I had not told Thomas of my intended sleuthing. For now, this was still a mother-daughter affair that could perhaps be simply resolved without worrying him. If I found her walking out with a young man, I would approach as if having come upon them by chance. We would be introduced, and, as long as he was a suitable sort with his own plot of land or business in town, perhaps, no harm would have been done. I still preferred that Lettie be married at home, but she had made herself so difficult a catch that I was beginning to bend on where she might live.

Eventually she climbed off the sands and took a stony inland track roughly parallel to the coast. I was huffing and puffing as I laboured uphill and wished I had brought an umbrella to shield me from the almost oppressive light and heat. Far at sea there was a haze that hid the other islands. The heel of one boot felt loose, and more than once, while trying to keep her in sight, I sat down on flat-topped rocks and tried to push it back into place. As I was doing so for the third or fourth time, she suddenly dropped down the far side of a rise and disappeared. I hurried on, and when I arrived at the spot where she had vanished found myself standing at the top of a narrow vale that descended in bumps and hollows to the shore. At the bottom I could see a wharf jutting out from the rocks and a small boat tied to it. That view occupied me for only a few seconds as I was more concerned with Lettie's whereabouts. Gazing across the slanted ground I saw a thatched cottage with smoke rising from its chimney. There she was in the garden with another young woman pointing up at the roof as if there were a curiosity there, a bird's nest perhaps or some damage from a storm. She has a friend, I thought, and clapped my hands together silently at the lack of any complication in our lives. Then I recognized my exposed position. Had they turned around I would have been visible as the spy I was, so I stepped quickly back and down until hidden by the slope.

On my homeward trek, I made plans to walk back out later that afternoon and meet her and her friend with the same facade of coincidence I had reserved for the imagined young man. She was always home for tea, and it had taken her nearly an hour to reach the cottage, so if I set off around two o'clock there would be plenty of time for the encounter and an invitation to her companion. I wanted everything to be quite natural and without suspicion as all three of us arrived at the house, so in the meantime I planned to say nothing to Thomas who, although at the Kirkwall Chapel for the morning, would likely be present for tea since he had announced no plans for Stromness that day.

More tired from my secret journey that I realized, I fell asleep in my parlour chair after lunch and woke to hear the mantel clock chime twice. Fortunately, I had had the foresight to stop at the shoemaker's shop on my way back for the repair of my boot heel so I could now hurry down the beach and up into the stony country without worry. As I went along, though, I couldn't help but wonder why Lettie had kept private her new relationship. Surely she and the young woman had been to town for shopping – that is what girls did together, after all. But if so, why hadn't anyone in the family seen them on the high street, and why on earth hadn't she brought her new friend to the house? Whatever her proclivities for argument and prospects for spinsterhood because of these, I had to admit she showed great loyalty and affection to her parents and brothers, so perhaps I shouldn't begrudge her this independence. Once we returned to Yorkshire, she would have to settle in her ways and accept that the world makes certain demands of young women none can deny. My concern about an Orkney suitor mollified, I entertained comfortable visions of an appropriate petitioner closer to home.

This time I had come prepared and, after peering over the top of the rise before the cottage and seeing no one about, I stepped back and down to sit in the shade of my umbrella and await my opportunity for advance. I would hear their voices as they came out the door, stand up, and walk unconcernedly towards them, appearing as if by magic or at least honest happenstance. There had been no smoke from the chimney so they must be out walking, and for a moment I was afraid they had gone into town while I slept and one or both would soon approach me from behind. If they were together my plans would not be thwarted just fulfilled from another direction. If her friend was alone, so much the better. Travelling the same path we could not help but introduce ourselves, and once my name was given all would be revealed.

An hour passed, however, and there was still no sign of them. I had peeked across at the cottage to no avail and was beginning to accept they were in town and I would meet them on my return journey. Perhaps that was the least suspicious way to bump into them, I realized, so I stood up for one last look at the pleasant thatched abode. There was still no smoke or other sign of habitation, but out of the corner of my eye I glimpsed a flash of colour below and, turning, saw a blue sailboat approaching the wharf with two figures in it. Peals of their laughter carried up the vale and then fragments of their voices, and I knew one of the happy couple was Lettie. My shock overwhelmed me, and I sat abruptly down on the path barely noticing the bramble's tear to the edge of my hem as I did so. My heart was beating far too quickly as I tried to comprehend what I had seen. My daughter, who couldn't swim a stroke, indeed had never ventured into Cleethorpes waters beyond her knees, had been sailing in a small craft on the open sea with no seasoned captain but only another woman! I thought such astonishment could not be surpassed, but when I half-stood and stared down at them on the wharf securing their vessel I almost fainted dead away. Lettie, who was lowering the sail, was clad in pants and knee-high boots like a fisherman! Perhaps I did lose my senses for a short time because suddenly their voices were much closer and I realized they must be nearing the cottage. As I could hardly approach them with my nerves so upset and my thoughts racing, I turned into a rising wind and made my way in the direction of the town, praying that my trousered daughter would not catch up.

It was well Thomas was still out when I arrived home out of breath. The others were away, too, except for Clem and Norman who were too young to notice any distress, though Clem did ask if I had stumbled and fallen because there were patches of dirt on my dress.

'No,' I told him and went on in a formal tone that was meant to disguise my distress at any attention to my state. 'Long skirts, while proper for a woman, do not allow free passage on difficult ground, that is all.'

'What difficult ground?' my youngest male asked, for whom all physical territory was accessible without question.

My reply must have surprised him as much as it did me. 'That is what I will find out,' I said.

Lettie

For the first time in my life I feel I am looking through an open door to the future. Margaret and Mrs. Secole have turned the knob. Mary remained an independent woman all her life, ministering to cholera victims in Jamaica and Panama, and then tending to soldiers' needs in the Crimea. She never married again, but it seems had lovers and perhaps even a child born out of wedlock. Everywhere she went government and military officials tried to place restrictions on her, but she would not be turned away from her service to others and the satisfaction it gave her. Even if I lack her talents and goodness, she makes me feel I can do anything I want to and should not be discouraged by my present lot in life. She overcame attacks against her race and sex, and though the colour of my skin plays no role in my minor adversities, I am determined to combat, like her, assaults on my female mind and heart.

As for Margaret, her example is that much stronger because I am at her side and can see not only her skills on the open water that must match those of any sailor, but also how she carries and presents herself from moment to moment with a quiet strength and dignity no one can dismiss, whatever *his* power or station. I should like to be a fly on the wall if father tried to overwhelm her with his learning and sheer force of character. The look of consternation on his face when she answered him on equal terms would be worth my own silence. However, if I am to go off with her to Shapinsay I must either introduce her to the family or concoct a story so monstrous in its fiction it would make George Eliot blush. Since I am neither Maggie Tulliver nor Dorothea Brooke and refuse to suffer their fates (yes, I know Dorothea wins Will Ladislaw in the end, but he's not my idea of a great reward for her awful time with Casaubon), I will have to bring Margaret to the house.

For some days now mother and I have not been on speaking terms except in the most minimal fashion in regard to the preparation of meals and the barest of exchanges in the mornings and before one of us goes up to bed. She has admitted to following me to Margaret's cottage and spying on us there. I am betrayed beyond my wildest imaginings and will never forgive her. Father and the boys know something is amiss but dare not intrude on unfamiliar territory. How could she do such a thing? I know I was disappearing for hours on end, but I always returned for tea, and the bloom on my cheeks and lightness in my step should have told her all was well. Instead, as she informed me, it was her motherly concerns that prevailed, and she was witness not only to Margaret and me talking in the garden but also our landing of the boat. It was the latter, of course, that made her apoplectic. Had she discovered the reason for my absences was just a new friendship with a young Orkney woman, I am sure she would have found a way to extend an invitation to tea or supper without revealing that she had engaged in secret scrutiny of her daughter. But the sailboat went beyond the pale. That and my wearing of pants while aboard.

'How could you do such a thing, Lettie?'

'Do what, mother?' I would not give her an inch.

'Endanger your life in such a manner, of course. You've never been in a small boat before nor in such wild waters.'

'Margaret is an expert sailor. Her father was a fisherman and taught her well.'

'I don't give a farthing for her abilities. It is you I fear for. You can't even swim!'

'You say I have deceived you, and you're right. I am sorry for that, but what of your own deceit, pursuing and spying on me as if I were an enemy stranger who had broken the rules and not your own daughter whom you had raised to trust you?'

This gave her some pause, but she offered no apology.

'It is my duty to look out for your safety until another is in a position to do so.'

'A man, you mean.'

'Yes, a man. A husband to take care of you.'

'To wear the pants, you mean. That's what's bothering you just as much as the boat, isn't it?'

She pressed her handkerchief to her lips and spoke in a muffled voice through the linen. 'It isn't proper, Lettie, and I was ashamed to see you so. If you insist on meeting that woman again, I shall inform your father of your behaviour.'

'Her name is Margaret, mother, Margaret Muir.'

'Whatever she is called, Lettie, she is in the wrong to have exposed you so to danger.'

That marked the end of our altercation and I left the parlour for my room. She did not know how her intransigence simply spurred me on, and that father's inevitable disapproval would just propel me deeper into my voyaging than I had been thus far. I sent Margaret a note explaining the situation and saying we might have to postpone our plans for Shapinsay. She replied that I was of age and, if matters came to a head, I should take refuge at the cottage for as long as I liked.

Arthur returns tomorrow. He is the only one I can talk to about all this. I shall take him to meet Margaret and there will be three of us against two. I do not count Ernest and Bertie who will toe the parental line when it comes to their sister's conduct. Confronted by father's wrath I shall claim that, whatever my love for my family, my happiness is more important. I know it will anger and dismay them, but I have no alternative. I will not stop seeing Margaret, and I will take the tiller from her warm hand again and again. I am coming about in my life, and those who stay on dry land will have to accept my new direction.

But in my turmoil, I must not ignore my younger brothers. Horace has told me he is helping Mr. Peverel, the local veterinarian, who says he will write on his behalf to a Yorkshire colleague. While he may never have a business of his own because of the exams that must be passed, Horace could certainly become an assistant to make us all proud. His determination matches my own in that he is resolved to return here once he is sixteen and has some treatment experience under his belt.

'Father will object,' he admits. 'But it is what I want to do.'

'I think you must show him what you are capable of, Horace.' I will not call him 'little brother' again. He deserves more than that.

There is no need to worry about Clem. I can tell he is working on something and not to be interrupted. But I haven't heard him play in a long time. When I mention this, he smiles and says mysteriously, 'Would you prefer the small or large concert hall.'

He's talking about Mrs. Drever's, but can he also mean the cathedral where father has lately allowed him to meet the organist? Surely anything he does with those keys is in private? The main point is he has permission to expand his horizons along with Ernest, Bertie, and Arthur. Horace will soon follow them. Only Norman and I, the true children of the family, are supposed to remain within bounds. As for Norman, I watched him march off this morning with his rucksack over one shoulder and a coiled length of rope on the other. What could he be up to?

Thomas

Lying lips are an abomination to the Lord: Proverbs 12:22.

I cannot escape what I have done despite Mr. Taggart's support. There is a little comfort perhaps in some earlier lines from the same chapter: *The lip of truth shall be established forever, but a lying tongue is but for a moment.* I hope the Lord will forgive one moment's dissembling for the sake of the larger truth it saved.

Yesterday evening, a Saturday, we had just watched the hatch close down after Taggart had handed some food and drink to Rory Parker when there was a knock at the locked Chapel door. Ordinarily we would not have turned the key, but under the circumstances we had put caution before routine ways. Mr. Taggart swept his eye over the pristine ceiling, and we could only hope the bid for entrance had been heard in the loft as well. When he opened the door there stood the Chief Constable of the islands, Mr. Colin Andrews. I knew who he was because fishermen had pointed him out to me at the meeting-hall and I had recognized him as a uniformed figure of authority at the docks before that. A burly man, he squeezed his heft sideways through the opening Mr. Taggart allowed, took off his cap, and shook my hand as we introduced ourselves. His grip was firm and dry, but I could feel the clamminess of my own palm against his. He surveyed the room and apologized for interrupting any Chapel business.

'Not at all,' Mr. Taggart said coolly. 'We were just making some arrangements for tomorrow's sermon.'

'Ah yes,' he replied, and I won't keep you from that. I'm here, as you must suspect, on the matter of Rory Parker.'

I had on my face what I hoped was a calm and interested look, as if I couldn't wait to hear what he had to say. But inwardly I was grateful we had provided Rory Parker with only bread, cheese, and a bottle of water so there was no odour from warm food to twitch the Chief Constable's nostrils. I pictured him chewing quietly overhead and prayed the bottle was securely in his hand.

'I take it you have not yet discovered his whereabouts?' Taggart said.

'That we haven't, sir, and I am here to ask if you are privy to such information. I do so because your sympathy and that of your church for his cause are well-known.'

Taggart's response cleverly avoided the directness of this query and surely kept him spotless in the eyes of the Lord. 'Should I come across

Mr. Parker, I promise to inform him of your vigilance, though I am sure, wherever he may be, he is bound to observe it without my assistance.'

The Chief Constable took out a large handkerchief and sneezed loudly into its folds. 'Excuse me,' he said. 'It is the time of year when the hay-fever is upon me.'

If this action and remark were meant to lull us into acceptance of him as an ordinary, harmless fellow, his next remark set us straight. His eyes swivelled to lock with mine as he lowered the handkerchief.

'And you, sir. Have you seen Mr. Parker recently?'

Had he asked if I knew Rory Parker's immediate whereabouts, I doubt whether I could have avoided the truth and so established his imprisonment, if not forever then for a long time. But because Taggart had been the one to hand up the food and drink, I had heard only a muffled 'Thanks' and the scraping of a leg across the loft floor after the hatch was closed. I had not actually laid eyes on our fugitive since the day before.

'No,' I told him as resolutely as I could, choosing to interpret 'recently' in a liberal manner. 'I have not.'

Mr. Andrews sniffed, though whether it was from some dust affecting his condition or because there was tang of cheddar in the air, I couldn't tell. I hoped only that further deception would not be necessary.

'Very well, I will take your word for it, gentlemen. But rest assured, I will be asking a number of your congregation the same questions, and surely one of them will have something worthwhile to offer. Rory will be caught eventually, make no mistake.'

'I cannot say I wish you well in your quest, Colin,' Taggart told him, as if reminding him with such first-name address, that they went back a long way together before their professional lives had taken them in different directions. 'But I will pray for everyone involved.'

'Aye, John,' he said. 'I know prayer helps to ease the difficulties, but in the end it will make no difference.'

He left after shaking my hand again. I watched him through a window as he moved off down the street then nodded at Taggart who thumped on the ceiling with a broom-handle. Rory Parker's head appeared in the hatchway.

'Did you hear all that, Rory.'

'Aye, I did, and I'm grateful again for your protection.'

'I think we'll have to move you as soon as possible. Knowing Colin Andrews, he'll be back, and not least because he might be right, I'm sorry to say, about some hangers-on in the congregation. You keep still up there while we pay a visit to your friends at the harbour.'

We took up our coats against the chill night air and locked the door behind us. As we walked along, neither too quickly nor too slowly as to draw the attention of any watchful eyes, I tried to explain my evasion in response to the Chief Constable's questions.

'If I am guilty in the Lord's eyes,' I said, 'then I can only plead the rightness of the cause.'

He stopped and placed his hand on my shoulder.'I think the Lord showed you the way to tell the truth without being deceitful. Remember Psalms 119:29 – *Remove me from the way of lying and grant me thy law graciously.* His law, I believe, is based on faith and justice, and that is what he has given us to work with as best we can.' He drew his collar tight against a wind from the water. 'Come, we must find a boat this night.'

Bertie

Should Jamie MacBride be acquitted as expected, it will mean the end of my relationship with Alice. Of course, since I will be returning to Yorkshire within the next few weeks, there has never been any prospect of continuance except by letter. I suppose I had hoped a correspondence would lead…would lead where, Bertram, you foolish man? How can you work in earnest for a client's release when you are in love with his wife? For that is the true case before a court of no appeal, as I have known for some time. Each minute I am with her my heart beats faster, my cheeks are burning, and it is all I can do to keep my mind on business rather than take her in my arms and hold her until she surrenders and returns my passion. I cannot explain these feelings except to say, apart from her beauty, which is without question, the combination of strength and vulnerability in her character leaves me lost in admiration. It is not that I am without words when with her but that I cannot possibly offer up the ones that come to mind, so inadequate would they be in expressing my emotions. I know she is aware of my plight for she will not meet my eye when there are any pauses in our conversations about Jamie, and our personal exchanges are stilted and without their earlier warmth and ease. Though she calls me 'Bertie' I can almost hear her crossing out such personal address and replacing it with 'Mr. Larsen,' very much as she would speak to me in court. The case will be heard the day after tomorrow, and I dread having to watch her on the stand as it will be difficult for her to speak of the assault on her person and hell for me not to be able to protect her from prying eyes and ears.

126

Mr. Campbell has been informed by Mr. Gordon, the barrister for Roger Nicholas, that a compromising piece of evidence is in his possession and will be used, if necessary, as a crucial part of Mr. Nicholas's defence. It is most certainly Alice's letter to which he refers. If it is introduced, our response will be that it is the scribbling of a girl not yet married and has no bearing on what occurred in the barn. But Mr. Campbell has told me once the judge hears this evidence of previous feelings between accuser and accused, it is bound to affect his decision. We have asked Alice more than once if she has told us everything that she wrote to Mr. Nicholas the morning after the dance, and her position has remained firm. It was a brief and giddy note that suggested she didn't mind that he had kissed her, that was all. Besides, it was years ago, and how could anyone believe it had any significance today?

Mr. Campbell shakes his head as he wonders aloud whether we should bring up the letter in her testimony or wait to see how Nicholas's barrister presents it and then respond.

'If we get her to speak of it first it could take the wind out of their sails. On the other hand, once the judge's ears prick up at its mention, how much does it interfere with her description of the assault? But if we wait, then the letter becomes a sudden weapon for the defence that can be wielded with great effect.'

'Or else her evidence is powerful enough from the outset to render her own youthful words obsolete whenever they are introduced,' I reply.

'Yes, perhaps, but I am inclined to raise the matter in the beginning and catch the other side by surprise. We shall have Mrs. MacBride express regret that she was once so young and foolish then ask the court why she should be held to account years later when so much had obviously changed between her and Mr. Nicholas.'

'Jamie has finally agreed to testify and will do so first, will he not?'

'Yes, I pressed him with how vital it is that he confirm his wife's evidence. If he remained silent, I emphasized, he would be doomed and, along with this tragedy, would not have prevented her from revealing what happened in the barn. She was determined to tell the truth, I said. But it wasn't until I told him about the letter that he broke out of that calm shell and swore he would not allow such further besmirching of her character. I could see then something of the man who went after Roger Nicholas. When I indicated we will ask him if at any time Mr. Nicholas's name has come up between them or if he had any reason to suspect she was unfaithful to him, if only in her heart, he became quite angry.'

'Never!' he declared, and no judge could reject the truth of his tone.

This morning the case of the Her Majesty the Queen versus Jamie MacBride was heard in the Kirkwall assizes, Judge Murray residing. The charges: common assault against the person of Roger Nicholas and the stealing of two lambs owned by Mr. Nicholas. Mr. MacBride had pleaded not guilty and evidence would be presented by both sides.

Jamie McBride retained his composure as Mr. Campbell took him through his paces. He had discovered his wife distraught, and when she told him of Mr. Nicholas's trickery and assault on her person, he set off to call him to account. He had meant only to dress him down and warn him never to repeat his behaviour, but when Nicholas laughed at him and defamed his wife's reputation, 'I could do naught but teach him a lesson, your Honour.'

'And the lambs?' Mr. Campbell inquired, not wanting him to dwell on any details of the fisticuffs.

'I took those because they had been promised.' He stared across the room at Roger Nicholas who to my eye appeared rather too comfortable and smug beside his barrister. 'No less was owed.'

'Mr. MacBride, I have one final question, and you will forgive my asking it, sir, but it is to settle one important issue for the court, once and for all. Have you ever in your married life had any reason to suspect your wife of infidelity in any way whatsoever?'

He looked directly at Alice and smiled at her in a manner that broke my heart, so full of love was it, and trust. 'No,' he said. 'I have not.'

Mr. Gordon then put it to him that either he was lying in defence of his wife's unseemly conduct or had been duped by her. It was clear the defence mean to claim the man had been charged but it was the woman who was guilty, and I shuddered to think of how he would deal with Alice. Jamie's calm demeanour stood him in good stead against such onslaught and he simply repeated what he had already told Mr. Campbell. When Mr. Gordon tried to trip him up on details of their violent exchange in the barn, the judge interrupted him and said that since no one was contesting the fact there had been an assault by Mr. MacBride, this line of questioning was without merit. Mr. Gordon said he was finished with the witness for now but reserved the right to recall him later on. The judge agreed then called a short recess during which everyone except Jamie and his guard drifted into the hall outside the courtroom. There I tried to concentrate on what Alice would have to say and not on its immediate consequences for her husband and inevitable impact on myself.

When we all returned, she took the stand.

Arthur

When butterflies are angels we see plain
And touch the sky in sun and rain

When fields in spring are all ablaze
Colours descend beneath their gaze

When world's a flower in which we live
All tongued petals theirs to give

Then boys have wings to tell us true
They are so many, we so few

Norman has told me Mr. Garson's story of the selkie, and I see how poetry follows in the wake of creatures he admires rather than summons them from the heights and depths. It is inevitable I will write some words about this mythical mermaid, but they will pale beside my brother's already eloquent vision.

Something extraordinary has happened! Father mentioned to Mr. Taggart my interest in Shelley, no doubt in disparaging tones to indicate his disapproval, and Mr. Taggart has told me privately that he knows of an old Orkney man who met Shelley when he stayed in Edinburgh for several weeks in 1813. He is Daniel Brechin born in Kirkwall and resident for more than fifty years of Papa Westray, one of the outermost islands to the north.

'Please don't inform your father from whom you learned this. Like him, I have grave concerns about your poet's atheism, but must admit a soft spot for his shorter poems about nature and his great tribute to Keats – *till the Future dares/ Forget the Past, his fate and fame shall be/ an echo and a light unto eternity!*

'You have read *Adonais*!'

'Yes, but it is not something I share with my congregation,' he replied. 'Or my fellow ministers,' he added.

I thanked him for his information and added my assurances that I would not betray his confidence. Indeed, I did not know in my excitement whether I would tell father the news even if I managed to disguise the source. There would have to be an approved reason for my

129

wanting to be away for a few days, let alone journey to another island. Ernest had been sent off with father's blessing, but the Word I would carry with me, as Mr. Taggart had suggested, would not ever be heard in a Methodist chapel or sermon even though *The soul of Adonais, like a star,/Beacons from the abode where the eternal are.* A different kind of immortality and very different kind of heaven would be my companions.

I wrote to Mr. Brechin and received a prompt reply at the Kirkwall post office in which he said he would be happy to meet with me and discuss his 'brief encounter with fame, such as my memory will allow.' I did a quick calculation. Even if he had been just a boy in 1813, he would now be in his early nineties. Unless someone else had written his letter to me, the steadiness of his script and clarity of his expression indicated he was still of sound body and mind and my trip was not to be a waste of time.

I asked father if I might speak with him in the small room beside the parlour he used as a study, thinking it would be better not to involve my siblings in the discussion as their own desires to travel about would become involved and influence his decision. I could just hear Clem and Norman shouting for a family outing to other islands, and my inclusion would be a matter of course.

'Ernest has had the opportunity to visit the south,' I said, and I would like to take a short voyage into the northern regions, just for a few days.'

'Ernest has been serving the Lord, Arthur.' He was sitting at his desk, pen in hand, preparing what was undoubtedly his next sermon.

It was here I felt my success depended on slight prevarication without which father would see no reason to grant my request. My proposed sojourn would be for pleasure only, and that was not sufficient for any man of the cloth, let alone one who had six sons and a slightly errant daughter to keep in line. So I took a chance and went right to the heart of our concerns about one another. He suspected me because of Shelley and I could never trust him entirely because of such unwarranted qualms.

'I am spending too much time with my books and poetry. Perhaps I have become just a man of ideas and fail to understand the ways and beliefs of people not as fortunate as myself.'

He peered up at me over the top of his spectacles, seemingly interested in my *mea culpa*.

'And how would a few days' journey help you out in that respect?'

'Well, for one thing, I am determined not to take any books along, except for my Bible. I want to discover the world afresh and look for correspondence between it and the Lord's Word that I have ignored for so long.' This wasn't slight prevarication, but outright deceit since I would take my copy of Shelley's poems as my guidebook and had no intention of letting the Lord interfere with my reading of whatever I would find out there. Father smiled, obviously pleased with my intentions, and though I was sorry to betray his belief in my apparent conversion I could not be disloyal to my own convictions.

'Where will you go?'

I had done my homework in the guidebook of the Orkneys we had purchased on our arrival, and told him Westray, in particular, where there was a great castle built by a member of Mary Queen of Scots' household.

'And how will the battlements of a Catholic monarch serve your newly-minted Methodist cause?'

He was sharp, but on this day I was sharper. 'I must learn what I must reject, father. After all, Ernest has been to the cathedral here and spoken with the minister. Surely it is to strengthen not weaken his own faith?'

He pursed his lips and tapped his nib on the desktop. I knew, whatever his expectations of us, he wanted to be fair to all his children, even the wayward ones like Lettie and me. Perhaps he was also thinking of Horace and how my request was a small one in comparison he could afford to grant.

'Very well,' he said finally. 'You may go, but I shall want a definite return date so your mother will not worry.'

The ferry went to Shapinsay, then Eday, and on to Westray where I did disembark and visit Noltland Castle, which, despite the remains of some impressive ramparts, is basically a ruin, having been burnt by Royalists during their war with Cromwell and not repaired since. After a fishing smack delivered me to Papa Westray, I found Mr. Brechin in the only village of a few dozen souls, his house a small cottage with thick stone walls that kept it snug, he said, in the fierce winter tempests I could only imagine.

Given his advanced age, he was an impressive specimen with a shock of white hair and a tall frame that did not slouch as he sat before his fire and told me his tale, but not before offering me a 'wee dram o' the malt for your health.' I felt I couldn't refuse, though I had never had anything stronger than glasses of watered-down wine on special occasions at home. I sipped the golden liquid very carefully from the small square tumbler he had given me and felt a burning on my tongue and in my throat that was at first harsh and then strangely pleasant after it had gone down.

'Ye did not cough, which is a good sign,' he said. 'It is God's amber you have taken, and ye'll never be the same again for it.'

'So you met Percy Shelley,' I declared, fortified by another sip.

'Aye, I did, and only a lad of eighteen at the time.'

I gasped. That made him ninety-nine, born just three years after Shelley and a contemporary of Keats.

'I was working for Mr. Dumbreck, a coach-maker in Edinburgh where my father had sent me to learn the trade. He was a good man, Dumbreck, even-handed and honest with us all, though we had to work hard for our keep. Six in the morning I was there, every day but Sunday and often 'til supper time mending wheels and frames for the wealthy as well as smaller carriages for doctors and the like.'

If I had worried about his lapses in memory, my concern was soon put to rest. He seemed to have an exact recollection of what had occurred over eighty years previously and was eager to share his 'acquaintance with Mr. Shelley' as if it were a bit of excitement in his life that had occurred only yesterday.

'He came roaring into town in a coach-and-four I had never seen so battered. All the way from London, I heard him tell Mr. Dumbreck, in sixteen days, though they had stopped in the Lake District in an unsuccessful search for a house there. I was put in charge of fixing the damage. Broken under-plates, springs, and two lamps shattered. It was as if he'd driven it through hell and back under a heavy load.'

O that a chariot of cloud were mine, I thought but did not say.

'I had no knowledge of who he was, o'course, none of us did back then, except he was a poet about to become notorious for something he'd just written. His companion, Mr. Peacock, told us so. I can't recall the name of the work.'

'Queen Mab,' I said.

'Aye, that could be the one,' he replied. 'Was it any good?'

'It is, Mr. Brechin, a very great work that attacks tyranny wherever it can be found, but especially in the monarchy.' I decided not to mention his bouts with religion in the poem, but I needn't have worried.

'Then it is after my own heart, for I despise what the English kings and queens have done to my country and those in other high places like the nobles and men of the cloth.'

'Did you have a chance to talk with him, Mr. Shelley, I mean?'

'Did I not? He was in daily to ask about the progress of our work and how much it would cost. Always carping on what we would charge him. In the end it came to just over eight pounds, a small price, I should think, for the son of a baronet as I had by then found out he was. When I left Mr. Dumbrack's employ five years later, he was still trying to collect the money.'

Disappointed to have come all this way only to hear of Shelley's miserly ways, I pressed him. Did you speak of anything else?' I asked. 'Of his poetry or personal life, I mean?'

Clem

Arthur has gone off on a trip to the northern islands and will be away for a few days. I asked if he'd take me with him, but he said father would never approve, and I suppose he was right. Still, it's a surprise he'd be allowed to go off on his own just like that. I'll have to build this bolt from the blue into his section of my work.

But what of the Arthur I've known up until now? Well, he takes his poetry very seriously, though I've never read anything he's written and can only guess at the kinds of things that inspire him. Arthur's not sensible like Ernest or mostly straight ahead like Bertie, but more unpredictable and willing to take chances. Oh, I don't mean he'd do anything foolish, but there's a spontaneous side to him that's both attractive and infuriating. I remember when I was eight or nine and father and mother had stepped next door for a visit, taking Norman with them and leaving me in Arthur's charge. I wasn't too happy about this arrangement, thinking he'd just bully me around for the hour or two they'd be gone. But instead he invented a game we played for the entire time, and he made up the rules as we went along. First he found one of mother's old hatboxes, carried it outside, then set it on an angle against the garden wall. He picked up Bertie's cricket ball by the edge of the shed and tossed it to me.

'Stand here, Clem,' he told me, indicating a spot several feet away from the box. 'You must toss the ball in, and it must stay in, mind, and then I have to do the same. Once we're successful we'll step back three paces and try again.

'What happens if I miss?'

'Then you'll stay there and I'll march backward to victory.'

'How do we know when someone wins?'

He looked behind him. 'Tell you what. The first one of us to get to the end of the path and throw it in from there is the winner.'

That was twenty feet or more from the box, and I wasn't sure I could make the throw with any accuracy. He sensed my anxiety and introduced a new rule right away.

'One bounce is allowed for each player at each distance,' he assured me.

I was much more competitive than him, determined to beat my older brother at his own game, but that just made my muscles tighten up while he remained carefree about the results. We both got back to the end of the path on even terms, though he was putting the ball in the box without the aid of the bounce I needed by then. I remember watching his arm effortlessly rise toward the target while mine felt more like a weight I had to lift and swing awkwardly with each toss.

'This is it, Clem,' he announced as we made ready for our longest attempts. 'Winner takes all.'

I was first up and stood for a few moments staring fiercely at the halfway spot where I had to place my bounce. Just as I was about to throw he interrupted my attentiveness by saying I could have two bounces if I wished. If it had been anyone else, one of my schoolmates for instance, I would have been certain the remark was intended to break my concentration, but I knew it was just Arthur speaking what had just come to mind, and no malice was involved. The outcome was maddening, though, as my toss missed the halfway mark by at least a foot and came nowhere near the box.

'Bad luck, old man,' he said, as he retrieved the ball and arced it perfectly into the centre of the target.

That must be the musical key to Arthur – seemingly casual phrases held together by an underlying order that never quite takes control, much like those off-hand rules of his game. Chopin is like that with his *rubato* in his etudes and mazurkas, straying from the strict rhythms that are anticipated. But even this intentional wandering is unpredictable and depends for its effect on whoever is at the keyboard. I must ask him if he will let me see one of his poems or, better still, if he will read one of them to me. There will be melodies and harmonies there to draw on, I am sure.

He promised to send us picture-postcards from the north, which he must have purchased before he left. They all arrived yesterday. I didn't read anyone else's but Norman's, which has a mermaid lying on a rock with her tailfin in the air. 'Haven't found her yet!' was all he said. As for me, he chose a giant wave breaking over rocks on the coast, the spray jumping towards the viewer and threatening to soak him. 'Dear Clem,' he wrote, 'this is what your music will do to us all one day.' I am pleased by the image of a moving ocean of sound but remind myself I haven't yet learned to swim.

Ernest has introduced me to the cathedral organist, Mr. Berry. With father's permission I am allowed to go to St. Magnus weekday mornings and listen to him practise the hymns for the upcoming service. He knows most of them by heart though the sheet music with accompanying words rests above the console, so when he invites me to play 'Rejoice, rejoice, believers!' I have no difficulty. Perhaps he was expecting a Methodist boy with ordinary skills, but I can see from his wide-open eyes that I have far surpassed his expectations. *See that your lamps are burning, replenish them with oil/Look now for your salvation, the end of sin and toil*. I turn the page and launch into *Lo! He comes with clouds descending*, transfixed by the size of the sounds reverberating off the walls and arches. When I have finished, silence descends like a warm blanket of air. Mr. Berry takes out a handkerchief and wipes his brow.

'You say your father lets you play the organ in your chapel?'

'Yes, but not a lot. I mostly play the piano at home.'

'Well, you have a great deal of ability, young man, a great deal.' He taps the middle C with a fingernail. 'Since I must be away Sunday next on family business, perhaps you would like to sit down in my place. We can work up the hymns beforehand.'

I am so grateful for the offer that I cannot speak and am about to replace my knotted tongue with a delighted nod of acceptance when I hear father's voice booming like a mighty wind through the pipes. 'Play at a Presbyterian mass! You had best remember who you are and to which faith you belong, Clement!'

I find sufficient voice to thank Mr. Berry and tell him I don't think it will be possible as I must attend Chapel at the time of the cathedral service.

'It's a pity,' he tells me. 'I am no mere journeyman on this instrument, but the congregation deserves to hear what you can do with it. If you change your mind, you must let me know.'

At first, as I walk back to the house, father's reproach rings in my ears, but gradually it fades and only temptation remains.

Horace

Mr. Spence knew I wasn't myself.

'You've been stumbling about the past few days like a lost calf,' he said. 'What's wrong?'

Ever since he had to put Bess down, I've felt sad. I know there was nothing to be done, that she could never stand on that leg again, but I felt so helpless when the gun was the only tool to end her pain. I'd thought about it since that feather touched the ground, and I'd made up my mind.

'I'd like to work with Mr. Peverel,' I told him. 'Not every day, but enough to learn how to help animals in their sickness and when they've injured themselves.' I was worried he'd think me ungrateful, but instead his face lit up and he smiled.

'You'd like to be a veterinarian, then?'

I knew men like Mr. Peverel had been to school for a long time, and none of my teachers ever thought I'd amount to much. 'Leave Horace outside in the wind and rain and he'll manage but put a pen or book in his hand and he's lost,' one of them told another when I was standing nearby.

'It's a lot of study, isn't it?' I asked.

'Yes, if you want to have your own practice. But to be a vet's assistant and learn on the job, now that's another matter.' He wiped some dirt from his hands and looked out across the field where we were picking rocks from the soil and piling them on the wooden sled.

'I'll tell Mr. Peverel you wish to speak with him. I should hate to lose you, Horace, but perhaps something can be arranged so that doesn't happen altogether.'

He had spoken as if I was staying on the island, and I didn't know how to reply. Father had already made himself clear on that score. But even if I could be an assistant in Yorkshire I would want to return and help Mr. Spence and others on the island as well with my training. It's not just what I might be able to do but where I want to do it.

A few days later he told me I should pay a visit to Mr. Peverel. The vet's office was above a shed at the edge of the town where he saw to the smaller creatures brought to him and the larger ones he couldn't treat in the field. I had been to the shed with a stallion that had caught its hindquarters on a broken piece of wire fencing. The wire had gone in deep and Mr. Peverel had to tie him tight and give him a draught of medicine to make him sleepy before he could twist it out. I liked the way his hands and fingers moved like they always knew exactly where they were going and never stopped until the task was done.

He was upstairs just finishing with a spaniel's injured paw. The dog was lying on its side held down by its owner, a farmer I recognized from the sales, and those busy fingers were dabbing ointment between its claws.

'Come in, Horace, come in,' he said. 'I'm almost done and then we'll see to Mr. Spence's latest concern.'

After a few minutes, the grateful owner gathered up the dog in his arms, told Mr. Mr. Peverel he'd settle with him at the end of the week, and clumped down the stairs.

'What is it this time, then?' he said loudly. He was washing his hands in the sink, and the running water sounded like the beck in springtime that rushed beyond our garden wall at home. 'Horse or cow?'

Since Mr. Spence had spoken with him, I knew he was teasing, but my tongue was suddenly tied in knots. I had been foolish in coming to him. How could I ever hope to learn what he knew or find out the secret paths his fingers followed so surely? Then his voice softened.

'It's neither, is it?'

I don't know why, but I suddenly heard Lettie's voice in my head telling me we all had to find our own bit of heaven here on earth. That's what I was trying to do, wasn't it, find whatever it was made me happy and stick to it? I had thought working for Mr. Spence would be enough, but now I realized that healing animals was better than just leading them about, grooming them, and mucking out their stalls. Better for me, that is. I did not want to put myself over the men who took care of the livestock on any farm.

'I want to do what you do,' I burst out. 'I don't want to stand by while horses are shot, even though I know they sometimes have to be. I want to be trying to save them, at least. And then there are all the others that I can sew up or mend so they won't have to die until they're old.'

He shook the water from his hands and turned towards me, rubbing his palms against his shirt-front. 'That's quite a mouthful of 'wants,' Horace. When did you make up your mind about this?'

'After Mr. Spence had to shoot Bess,' I said. 'I know that's all there was in the end, but I started to think about how I didn't want to stand around anymore and watch creatures suffer.'

'You know there's often not much you can do, don't you? That dog that was here, if I'd seen him tomorrow he'd be dead of infection. I can't go out looking for troubles. People have the responsibility to bring them to me, and it doesn't always happen.'

'Yes, but if you had the time wouldn't you travel about trying to find those troubles before they got too bad?' I said.

'There's not that much time in the world, Horace.' He was putting his instruments in a small cabinet. 'But it's a nice idea.'

'If I knew what you do, I'd never stop trying.'

'Mr. Spence suggests you'd like to do some work for me, is that it? And perhaps I'll send you out to the farms and villages here and on the other islands, looking for troubles as you put it?'

He wasn't laughing at me, but there was a testing in his words. 'Yes,' I said, with as much conviction as I could muster.

'And what about your family? Mr. Spence told me your father turned down his offer of employment and schooling for you here?'

The wind went out of my Orkney sails. Father would not let me stay, I knew that. But even so, if Mr. Peverel let me help him for the next few weeks and I did a good job, perhaps he'd write a letter for me to a vet near home and father would not object as long as I finished my schooling in the next year. I said all this to him in a rush.

'I promise to come back here and work for you if I can learn things at home. But maybe you could teach me some things now,' I added hopefully.

There was a knock at the door.

'Another bit of trouble,' he said. 'Why don't you stay and watch.'

Norman

I asked Horace if he would bring me a length of rope from Mr. Spence's farm. 'What do you need rope for?'

I had my answer ready. 'Clem and I have found an old wagon and we want to pull each other around in it.'

This was only partly true. It was a dilapidated old thing with one cracked wheel, and Clem and I hadn't talked of riding in it at all.

'Like horses.'

'Yes, like horses. I'll give it back,' I said.

He did as I asked. 'It's hemp,' he said, tossing a light-brown coil at my feet that evening and laughing. 'Good and strong for stallions.'

It was thick and rough against my palms when I picked it up but looked long enough for my purpose.

I packed my small rucksack, in which I usually carried my specimen jars, with some biscuits mother had baked, a pockmarked apple, and a bottle of water. I stuffed my mackintosh in as well since there were low clouds on the horizon though the sun was brilliant over the town. After breakfast I told mother I was meeting some other boys down at the beach and wouldn't be back until late afternoon. I'd done this before and she was pleased I'd found some friends. There were none of them I wanted to take along this day.

I was sorry about fooling her, but she'd only worry if I said where I was going or tell me I wasn't allowed. As I rounded the corner of the house, I picked up the pile of rope I'd left beneath a window and slung it over my shoulder.

'Don't forget your hay,' I heard Horace shout behind me as he headed in the opposite direction to the farm. Clem was already at Mrs. Drever's house so no one would be checking up on my horse-and-wagon story for a few hours at least.

I hadn't been beyond the far side of the bay before where Mr. Garson said the sea-caves were, but it was a long tramp, and I stopped more than once for a mouthful from my bottle. The sand ended in a pile-up of big boulders and a high cliff that stopped me in my tracks. I couldn't see around the base of the cliff but thought I could hear a distant booming sound that I told myself was from the waves crashing into the hollows of the rock I was seeking. Since I couldn't get any farther straight ahead, I turned and walked back to find if there was a way inland through the blowing grass that was as high as my waist. It was when I started to climb upwards alongside the cliff's edge that I saw the path. It was very narrow, and as I left the grass below me it became harder to keep my footing. Bits of stone crumbled under my boots which kept sliding sideways. I couldn't hold on to the rock that rose up beside me but leaned into it for the comfort of something solid close by. It was scary, and I was thinking about going back even though my rucksack on my shoulders meant I couldn't turn around very easily. There was nothing to tie the rope to either if I wanted to drop straight down. Just go slowly, I told myself, slip-sliding my boots through the scree. Then I turned a corner and the path opened onto a steep, wide slope leading to the top of the cliff.

From up there I could look north to Shapinsay where Arthur had gone on the ferry and back at the town at the far end of the curving beach. The air was so sharp and clear I could see wisps of chimney smoke behind me and glints of buildings on the distant island shore, but I didn't stop long for the view because I had a task at hand. I was searching for that break in the rock Mr. Garson had told me about. I also listened for a closer booming sound that would tell me the caves were below, but the wind was swirling in my ears and the only thing I could hear was the cry of birds sweeping across the sky. Mr. Garson hadn't said how long he had walked along the cliff-top before he found the break, but because of the sun's height I knew I must have struggled for an hour or more over uneven ground before I collapsed and ate three of my biscuits, washed down with the last drops of water from the bottle. I decided to save the moistness of the apple for later.

I was after the selkie. Mr. Garson had warned me off, and I was more than a bit frightened by his counsel not because of what I might discover but because of the danger along the way. It wasn't like going after a butterfly in the smooth safety of the fields, and I couldn't put her in a jar and carry her home to study. Then I was mad at myself and said a bad word out loud that I hoped father couldn't hear even if he was miles away. I should have brought a camera but had no idea where I would have found one or how I could have ever carried it with me. Barring that, I should have had a pencil and paper in my knapsack so I could draw what I found. It was true I could do this from memory when I got home, but what if something happened to me and nobody knew what I was doing out here? I remembered I had told Arthur of Mr. Garson's adventure, but what if I did get down to the shore and couldn't get back up and nobody ever found me? The picture wouldn't matter then, would it? I couldn't stop my thoughts from smashing into one another and one of them was of a selkie swimming through my head and trying to confuse me with her magic. I stood up and yelled out to her that I was a naturalist not a collector and let all my butterflies go, but the wind snatched the words from my mouth and spit them into the sky. It wasn't true, of course. I had helped Mr. Garson find the Tortoiseshell and now it was on his board. Maybe the selkie knew that and was waiting to pin me in a sea-cave forever.

I picked up the rope and rucksack, pushed my glasses against the bridge of my nose, and stumbled on a few yards, almost ready to give up, but kept myself going by wanting to tell her I was sorry about her butterfly and that I'd never put one in a jar again. It wasn't any use. The cliff was going to keep its secret and there would only be seals in the world. That should be enough, I thought, but I knew it wasn't.

I don't know how long I staggered on before I heard the waves' rumble like a dull thump from the depths of the earth. Out at sea the whitecaps were churning toward me and the caves that were swallowing them whole. I lowered my eyes to shut out their fury at being trapped and saw a crevice cut into the top of the cliff as if a giant finger had pushed itself into the rock and pulled downward in a single stroke. Not a gift but a warning, I heard Mr. Garson say, but I was already uncoiling the rope.

Ernest

How did the Vikings, at least those in Britain, become Christian? Were I at home the Leeds library would provide me with some answers, but here there is only word of mouth for satisfaction. Despite his differences with father over the fishermen's protest, I have visited on several occasions with the minister of the cathedral, Mr. Scott, and he has told me an interesting tale. It seems after they had raided and pillaged England and Scotland, some of the warriors chose to stay behind when their dragon-ships left the coast and settled down alongside those they had defeated to become members of a permanent community. While it is difficult to imagine these stalwart figures of legend more than history turning into farmers and raising families rather than roaming and fighting, it is even more difficult to conceive of them giving up Odin, Thor, and that host of gods who inhabited Valhalla. But there was little chance of dying in combat on tilled land in Ayrshire, so once you stopped your warfare you presumably lost your chance of residing in that post-battle paradise.

Mr. Scott says that it was through living side-by-side with Christians for a very long time that the descendants of the original invaders came to accept their neighbours' faith. As Roddy Erlendsson informed me, somewhere around a thousand years after the birth of our Lord, the Norwegian king ordered all his subjects to convert on pain of death, so any stragglers leapt into the fold without much ado. In other words, it all seems a matter of a gradual wearing-down of old habits and an ultimate threat rather than any leap of faith or embrace of Our Lord through the undeniable power of His Word. I know we are all born into circumstance as I was into my family with a Methodist minister at its head who has reminded me of Mark 16:16 often enough – *Whoever believes and is baptised will be saved, but whoever does not believe will be condemned* – but I have to wonder, if I were not my father's son but a stranger raised to trust in Valhalla or another heavenly alternative, would the strength of a neighbour's conviction be sufficient to convert me to his cause?

Then there is the matter of my own possible descent from the Vikings and, naturally, father's as well. If this is true, as Roddy suggests, my role as a Christian has troubling origins in a pagan past and the absorption of creed almost by habit. I am a Methodist through deliberate choices made by my immediate ancestors who preferred Mr. Wesley's interpretations of Holy Scripture to those of other clerics, but it is hard to deny I am a Christian through accidents of fate that have little to do with learnedness and more with casual conversations across medieval property lines. There he is, Eric Larsen, broadsword laid aside for a hoe, listening day after day to his fellow citizen extol Jehovah as they tend the rough Scottish earth together. Finally he or one of his sons says, 'Enough is enough,' and joins the congregation of the local church. All these centuries later, my entire life seems based on such circumstance, and I put this to Mr. Scott.

'You make it sound as if we are all bits of leaf blowing in the wind,' he replied, rather than sturdy trees that have grown up according to God's plan.'

'It is the roots of those trees I am questioning not least because they offer me some explanation for my ability to sit comfortably here with you in an edifice that my father abjures as housing...I won't say a false faith but a misguided one. It is those roots that draw me to the cathedral's protective power and to the statues of saints bound up in papal edicts whose authority I cannot accept.'

'In other words, given those roots, it is apparent contradictions amongst faiths and their representations here on earth that disturb you?'

'Yes, and what to do about them.'

'Why do you have to do anything?'

'Because I should be supporting my father without question in the Chapel and village streets and not be distracted by all this.' I raised both hands, palms upward, and looked about me to include stained glass and stone alike, as well as Clem's organ and pipes.

'I think, Ernest, you are just discovering the truth of Christ's words to Simon Peter, *In my father's house there are many mansions: if it were not so I would have told you. I go to prepare a place for you.* The Lord houses all contradictions above us. Therefore, we should not be troubled by their appearances here below. Indeed, we should include them in our approaches to His realm.'

I did not say that one of the most difficult aspects of such inclusion was that I could speak to him about my concerns but not to father, and that signalled to me a weakness not only in myself but in the Methodist path that brooked no oppositions as it led straightforwardly to the door of God. Was this unassuming Presbyterian minister, sitting beside me in a pew beneath his beloved Romanesque arches, a wiser man than the one who had schooled me in every facet of my existence? Or was I, despite that education, which I could not help but honour, simply being tempted by golden calves out of the first barns and churches of heathen conversion? Whatever the answers to such questions, there is no doubt the Orkneys have changed me. Whether I am a better man remains to be seen.

Mother is greatly disturbed by something she will not speak of. I have caught her weeping more than once, though she insists it is nothing at all and will not divulge any reasons for such misery. Meanwhile her nerves are frayed and she goes about the house pushing things and people out of her way. When I mention it to Bertie he tells me it must be women's trouble and she will come through it, though his response to the opposite sex is coloured, no doubt, by his preoccupation with Mrs. MacBride. I don't think he realizes how often he mentions her name or celebrates her virtues. Arthur says he is besotted, though that is surely going too far. She is a married woman, after all. As for mother, I have my suspicions Lettie is involved. At times, her gestures and lamentations leave one little space for private reflection. The other night I was leafing through Proverbs and found a suitable text —*It is better to dwell in the corner of the housetop, than with a brawling woman in a wide house.* 21:9.

10. Crossing the Bar

Thomas

It was nip and tuck getting Rory Parker away. When the boat had disappeared into the darkness beyond the mole, Mr. Taggart turned to me and said, 'We've done what we can, and the rest is up to the Lord.'

We hadn't been back in the Chapel for more than five minutes when the Chief Constable burst in with five men and arrested us. The charge was harbouring a known fugitive, someone having seen us outside of the building with Parker just a half hour before. It was fortunate we had made all the arrangements for a quick boarding and departure or they might have caught him on the wharf. We were taken to the gaol, but because of Mr. Taggart's position and our word that we would not leave the island, we were released pending a hearing before the Stromness magistrate three days hence. Since the Sabbath intervened, Taggart would be allowed to preach at Kirkwall Chapel. Other than that we were told to observe the boundaries of the town during the day and our own homes at night. As we drove our carriage north and east to that loose confinement, we discussed the situation.

'I believe they will assume Rory has gone to the mainland,' he said. There are many fishermen's groups there that would give him shelter and many routes of further escape if necessary. But since he's heading north he might not stop at Papa Westray or North Ronaldsay and go on to the Shetlands. I'd keep moving for awhile if I were him.'

'Doesn't he stand more chance of being discovered in a smaller community?'

'Aye, there's that possibility, but the smaller the island the more close-mouthed the folk. There's informants in any place looking for the Queen's coin, to be sure, but those who would betray Rory would be lucky to escape with their lives.'

I shook my head at such a picture. 'They'd resort to such violence?'

'This is a rough country, and rough justice is what it breeds at times, but it's mainly officials with their silver-tongued application of the laws that we must fear.'

I tried to clear off any doubts. If they caught him, Rory Parker would suffer harshly and not just because he had grabbed the ankle of a government member. Those in charge had a great deal to protect and would click those silver tongues in the strongest disapproval possible. For my own part, I assured myself there was no true danger of imprisonment. Surely we would get off with a lecture and a fine, good Methodist men of the cloth as we were. However, there was always the chance we would be made an example as well, especially since we had brazenly played the tune of resistance by being in his company outside the Chapel. We had got him off safely, but now the piper must be paid. Before I could pursue the consequences further in my mind Taggart spoke up again, his voice charged with resolve.

'I have had enough of cat and mouse games. This Sunday I will accuse the authorities of hounding Rory into exile and call people into the open to support the fishermen's cause. I will demand that businesses shut their doors to Her Majesty's servants until Rory is allowed home and the matter of a fair fish price is settled.'

'But they will accuse you in return of fostering rebellion. They will take away your pulpit, Taggart and …'

'Then you must step in the next week and do the same. There are enough stout men in the congregation to carry on for as long as it takes.'

'What if they shut down the Chapel? Have you thought of that?'

'Aye, but there are other places, aren't there? They can't close up all the fields and byways, can they?'

It was dangerous ground he was asking all of us to tread. Despite my concerns, my commitment to the cause was still strong in principle, but we were due to leave for Yorkshire in less than three weeks. If I refused to participate in this insurgence, how could I hold my head up in our remaining time in the Orkneys? But if I did take part then rode away to the south when the struggle was at its height, how could I escape the brand of traitor? That night I informed Elizabeth of what had happened in Stromness. It wasn't that I expected her to tell me what to do. The decision was my own and the Lord would be my final counsel. But the family was involved, and she deserved a voice in my deliberations.

'You're sure at this point you won't be gaoled?'

'They cannot prove we directly aided Mr. Parker in his flight. That is the more serious charge. Nor can the witness testify that he saw anything more than that we were in the company of a fugitive. It's a long jump from there to our having sheltered him and arranged his escape. We can always stand behind our word given to the Chief Constable that …' I paused and realized that if asked under oath whether we had given Rory Parker sanctuary in the Chapel, I could not lie. I knew Taggart could not as well. And they would surely ask. I was caught up in the open rebellion whether I wanted to be or not.

'Elizabeth,' I said, 'you must take the children and return to Yorkshire. I must do my duty here whatever it entails for me, but there is no need for my family to bear my cross.'

She understood that my own conscience was going to aid the law's prosecution, and imprisonment might well be the result. Her hand came up to stroke my cheek and I felt the lace at her wrist.

'We must tell the children,' she answered. 'Then we will decide.'

Arthur was due back the next day. In the morning we would let everyone know they should be present at tea.

'I shall inform Mr. Campbell. I am sure he will come to your defence.' We were gathered in the parlour, all except Norman who had not returned from his beach games with friends on the beach. I would deal with him later.

'I don't think that will be necessary, Bertie, at least not yet. Mr. Taggart and I have agreed to pay any fine in regard to our association with Mr. Parker.'

'And if a fine does not satisfy the magistrate?'

'Then we shall undoubtedly be discussing matters with Mr. Campbell in our cells.'

'Surely it will not come to that,' Ernest said.

'Not initially, I believe. But when Taggart gets up, then others along with myself, to criticize the treatment of Rory Parker and call for demonstrations of support for the fishermen, then gaol is a very real possibility.'

'*I met murder on the way – / He had a mask like Castlereagh.*' Arthur had walked in the door but an hour ago, the most political of my sons who, I knew, would be firmly in my corner. His poet was too extreme in so many ways, but his truth about the slaughter of innocents at Peterloo over seventy years ago was undeniable.

'Arthur…' Ernest began, but I interrupted him.

'I agree there are things to proclaim, but we shall have to be careful. While Mr. Gladstone cannot have me transported, libel and sedition are still charges to be feared.'

Horace and Clem said nothing, but I could see that fear reflected in their young faces even if they did not fully understand the nature of those crimes I mentioned. I had always preached to them the supremacy of the law – the Lord's first and then the Queen's – and here I was about to break one if not the other. I had to assure them all that the higher precept was unassailable.

'Let us all depend on the Good Book for guidance. In *Matthew* the Pharisees are condemned as hypocrites. While teaching the law they neglected justice, mercy, and faithfulness. We will not do the same.'

Lettie had been silent thus far, but I knew she would have something to offer. My only daughter and oldest child had no pretty tongue, and on this occasion I was glad of it. She spoke her mind after I had indicated everyone might have to return to Yorkshire.

'We can hardly leave you behind, father. It would not become us as a family to retreat, hiding behind mother's skirts when that is never the kind of shelter they are meant to provide.' She looked around at the faces of her siblings and each of them nodded in agreement.

'Perhaps not right away, then,' I responded. 'But if worse comes to worst and Mr. Taggart and I are gaoled, you will all go home' – they interrupted protesting, and I put up my hand to hush them – 'with the exception of Ernest who will have to take over our Chapel responsibilities here.' There was a reluctant murmur of assent and Ernest looked very pleased.

Elizabeth

When Thomas told me of his arrest I was very upset, however much he tried to convince me a fine was the most likely outcome. That he had seen the inside of a gaol was bad enough, but the prospect of lengthy imprisonment began to weigh on my mind when he later admitted to me his deception regarding Mr. Parker's whereabouts. Surely the law was bound to punish such a transgression, I said, and perhaps with a heavier hand when a man of the cloth had crossed the line. We had come north because of his inheritance, but everything could have been settled by documents and the post, and now our presence here had led to this perilous entanglement with authority that did not answer to God.

Thomas is my husband, and my support for him is unwavering, but even so I cannot understand why he had to become directly involved in smuggling Mr. Parker off the island. It was one thing to give him shelter in the Chapel, a kind of sanctuary, I suppose, but quite another to help arrange his escape that should have been left to other men. Of course, we will do as he says and return to Yorkshire, though all the children are grumbling about it except for Ernest. Their loyalty I never doubted, and I am especially proud of Lettie whose words were supported by everyone.

Nonetheless, I had planned to speak to Thomas about her behaviour with Miss Muir before the Parker matter intervened. I have had tried to keep my lamentations over her obstinacy to myself, but Ernest has noticed my distress as he came across me in the kitchen wiping away some tears. Now doesn't seem the right time to bring up my concerns, however, and I shall wait a day or two to see if she has settled down and accepted my decree. If so, I will let her wayward activities recede into the past; if not, then Thomas will have to step in. It will not only be her disobedience but also her foolishness in the face of real danger to her person that will prompt me to act.

We sit over our tea and crumpets, speaking of other things. Arthur's trip to Westray diverts our attention from threats to the family, and we listen with great interest to his description of Noltland Castle and the surrounding landscape.

'Did you meet anyone along the way?' I ask.

He replies only the crew of the ferries and his hosts in the small inn where he stayed two nights. 'They didn't have much to say except the almanac promises an early onset of winter this year.' He hesitates, then goes on. 'I took a fishing smack across the channel to Papa Westray just to say I'd been to the outermost island. There was a very old man there who regaled me with tales of the Napoleonic era.'

'He was *that* old?' Ernest said.

'Yes, in his late-nineties, but still spry.'

'North Ronaldsay is northernmost,' Clem says rather primly, then asks in a more curious tone, 'What did he say about Napoleon?'

'He was living in Edinburgh at the time and said everyone feared invasion. The question wasn't whether the French would land but where.'

Bertie is visibly distracted. I know the trial of Jamie MacBride is nearing its end. Mrs. MacBride has testified with scandalous results, and Mr. Nicholas's testimony was damning to her reputation. The judge's verdict is expected any day now. What she said when questioned by Mr. Nicholas's barrister has been chronicled in the Kirkwall paper, but it is not a suitable topic for our family gathering, so, after repeating that he will seek Mr. Campbell's advice on father's behalf, Bertie has lapsed into silence, his mind undoubtedly elsewhere.

There is so much going on, I find our situation overwhelming. Horace has told me he's helping Mr. Peverel and wants to learn as much as he can at home about animal medicine so he can assist a veterinarian there and come back to the Orkneys once he is sixteen to do the same.

As usual I am to be his ally and convince his father of the rightness of his cause. This I can certainly do because it will provide him with a far firmer position in life than would a career as a farm-hand. I know he would likely not succeed at college, but anything practical he can master, and I am sure there are apprenticeships he can take up at home that will help him advance.

I watch Ernest out of the corner of my eye. His father's confidence in him has clearly had an effect. Naturally he doesn't want to see Thomas imprisoned, but he will be ready to take over if necessary and do a proper job. And if we are all able to go home together, then his future in the service of the Church is not in doubt. I feel sure with Thomas's help the path to his own pulpit will be as smooth as possible.

My consideration of the children has been beneficial and taken my mind off the Parker affair, but even deep in my thoughts I am aware something is wrong. As I look across the room at Thomas and the window beyond his shoulder I am shocked at the lateness of the day. Where on earth is Norman, and why haven't any of us remarked on his continued absence? Though I do not hear my own voice, I must murmur something of this aloud because Thomas puts down his cup of tea and stands up as if to face an advancing foe.

'It will be getting dark soon,' Lettie says. 'He should have been home by now.'

Ernest

When your father is charged with a serious crime, you are different. Perhaps not overall, but in some undeniable, significant way you are not the same. He took me aside a short while before speaking to the rest of the family. Mother already knew what had happened in Stromness, of course, but no one else.

'I have a feeling things will go badly,' he said.

'But surely they will not deal too harshly with an ordained minister!' While I have harboured doubts as to his unquestioning support of the fishermen's cause, I have never believed the authorities have had right entirely on their side. Surely a compromise is the best solution. Fine father and Mr. Taggart and give them severe warnings, but do not humiliate them with a gaol sentence.

'As I have said, Ernest, if Mr. Taggart and I are prevented from performing our duties you must take over services in the Chapel. I am confident you are well on your way to becoming a minister yourself, but I must warn you that down the road of righteousness difficult choices must be made that are not always settled by simple divisions between black and white. I have always known so but have only lately discovered the costs.'

Despite my excitement at the prospect of my own pulpit, what I saw and heard was not just my father but a careworn man in his fifties who was trying to gather strength from complete honesty with his eldest son. I welcomed but feared such candour at the same time.

'When I was asked by the Chief Constable of Stromness if I had seen Mr. Parker recently, I clung to his fortunate adverb and said I had not.'

'But...'

'Mr. Parker was, at that moment, hiding in the Chapel loft immediately above my head. Taggart had just handed him up his dinner, and I, standing to the side, caught no sight of him. The last time our eyes had met had been that morning. Strictly speaking, then, I was not lying to Mr. Andrews, but it was a truth I bent around a larger lie.'

I did not know what to say. Father was clearly affected, but he was reporting his deed not seeking to excuse it. Regardless, I was deeply moved by his trust in me, which was furthered by his certainty that I could readily step into the breach should he and Mr. Taggart be absent.

'I must emphasize, Ernest, that a minister's lot is not always smoothly governed by those lines from the Good Book that we employ so unhesitatingly in the higher education of ourselves and others. We must be careful not to twist the name of the Lord to meet our own demands. Psalms and Proverbs, as you will become aware, can be made to say quite different things when one's soul is troubled.'

I wanted to discuss this very point with him concerning Methodist and Presbyterian readings of the Bible and Mr. Scott's assertion about 'many mansions,' but felt this was not the time. I could never shake father's faith, but I might trouble him unnecessarily now if he had to cope with my disquiets. I was already thinking of ways to express them from the pulpit that would not be personal in nature but address the question of doubt in a more general sense. One verse in particular has come to mind that illustrates father's point about readings by the troubled soul. In Matthew 14:31 Christ grasps Peter's hand after He has walked on the waters of the sea and says to him, '*O thou of little faith, wherefore didst thou doubt?*' The miracle is meant to banish fear and misgiving, but at the same time it is irrefutable that these feelings exist and even hold sway. Since we are not privy to miracles on a daily basis then belief and doubt must be in constant opposition. It will be my job to insist that belief wins out in the long run and to find other verses to support this claim, but it will not be easy to overcome my own qualms.

What father did not say to me in private was that he planned to send the rest of the family home immediately if he were sentenced to prison. Their subsequent resistance, led by Lettie, was very potent, and he seems to have given in for the time being. I am not sure how he foresees the funding of a continued stay in Scotland. While on leave from his Yorkshire pulpit he receives his usual pay since it is understood he is carrying out his duties with another congregation, but once those duties are terminated the Chapel elders at home will surely have questions about his position. Indeed, even if mother and the others were in residence there, there would still be a stand-in minister to pay for a longer term than just the two months we will have been away. While I might be able to perform his duties in this outpost of Methodism, I would not be an acceptable replacement in Yorkshire. Matters will come to a head quite soon as he is due to appear before the Stromness magistrate early next week, and, from what I can tell, this Sunday he and Mr. Taggart plan to foment open rebellion. He will expect me by his side, and there will be little if any room for disavowal of the cause.

Bertie is concerned that anything tantamount to an uprising by the populace, however peaceful, will condemn father to a long gaol term. He has been to Mr. Campbell who certainly concurs. Father and Mr. Taggart should lie low until their hearing and if they must preach in the interim say only innocuous things. 'The Lord does not move in innocuous ways!' father declared in response to such pleadings.

Arthur and Lettie have had their heads together and have come up with a strategy. Rather than father speaking out, Arthur should do so in the tradition of Shelley and other *provocateurs*, thus distancing him and the Chapel from any rabble-rousing but accomplishing the intended aim. I was surprised at how tolerantly father took this absurd suggestion. Arthur knows no restraints when it comes to Shelley and his anarchistic cohorts and would do far more damage than good with any fiery orations. But father thanked him, saying that while he appreciated the concerns for his and the Chapel's reputations, this was precisely the kind of issue that true Methodists could not shrink from.

'I could not forgive myself, having come this far, if I stepped back now,' he told them.

I knew part of him was thinking of his dissembling before the Chief Constable and that he was determined not to place himself in any position but one that would allow him to speak only the truth. He would admit to helping Mr. Parker escape, and he would not turn from the reasons why and what they now demanded – communal not individual action.

Mother's face is drawn but her eyes remain bright. She has not had much to say other than that Lettie is right – her skirts are not for hiding behind. When I ask her how we will manage if father is gaoled, she offers a tight smile. 'Like the fishermen and their families, I suppose. There is no manna from Heaven for them either.'

In the midst of all this Norman was in grave danger.

Bertie

Her face was tired and pinched as if she had lacked sleep for several nights. But she sat up tall and proud in the witness box, and I was ready for her to sweep Mr. Nicholas into the bins of disgrace and perhaps even eventual banishment from the community. Mr. Campbell took her through the story of the assault first, establishing that she had entered his barn willingly because she accepted his goodwill but was then taken advantage of in no uncertain terms. She told the court how she pushed him away and ran home where her husband learned what had happened. He strode off immediately to Nicholas's place to set things right. She did not falter at any point, and it was a strong and believable woman whom Mr. Campbell led towards her letter. Yes, long ago before she was married, she had written Roger Nicholas a foolish but harmless letter teasing him about their embrace after a dance. Soon after that she had met Jamie and her attempted friendship with Roger had failed because of his disappointment in her choice of a suitor.

'Did Roger Nicholas have any reason to doubt your loyalty to the man who was to become your husband?' Here Campbell turned to point at Jamie MacBride sitting in the prisoner's chair.

Without hesitation she replied that he had not. 'I have loved my Jamie faithfully all these years.'

Satisfied, Campbell took his seat and it was Mr. Gordon's turn to question her. From the beginning it was clear he had something up his sleeve.

'You admit you wrote Mr. Nicholas a letter after a certain dance?'

'Yes, but as I said…'

'Can you tell us exactly what you said in that letter?'

She glanced over at her husband and then at me.

'It's so long ago, I can't remember, just that I teased him a little.'

'Oh, I'd put it a little more strongly than that, Mrs. MacBride. I'd say, in fact, that you provoked him and drew him on.'

I heard a sharp intake of breath as if the crowd behind me was breathing as one.

'Let me refresh that faulty memory of yours,' he said, picking up an ink-covered sheet of paper from his table and flourishing it like a flag.

'Here is what you said in your 'teasing' letter to Roger Nicholas.' He began to read quietly and without emphasis, letting the words speak for themselves.

My Lovely Roger,

You took advantage of me last night, but what's a girl to do when swept up in the arms of so handsome a man? I am giddy with it but will protest should you presume any further intimacy is permitted between us. Of course, you can always ignore any objections my head is bound to make even though my heart might be willing. Who knows where it will end? Until the next time, your

Alice

It was worse than could be imagined. She had been brazen in her invitation, even if nothing had come of it because Jamie MacBride had arrived on the scene. I saw Campbell rub his eyes then blink several times as if to clear away a film upon them. Alice sat stock-still, her own eyes staring at the floor as if the letter were printed there and held her gaze mercilessly with its devastating revelation.

Mr. Gordon milked the silence for a few moments more then broke it harshly.

'*Who knows where it will end?* Well, Mrs. MacBride, do you still find 'teasing' an adequate term?'

She did not reply until the judge finally told her she was obliged to answer the question.

'I was young and foolish, that is all.'

This whispered reply was barely perceptible. Still, I thought, we can weather the storm unless Nicholas portrays her as equally brazen in his barn. That is what I would do if I were him, I knew, and wondered if Campbell might ask for a brief recess so as to prepare Alice for such testimony. Her word against his would have meant a stand-off, but his word and the letter against her might tip the scales. Gordon was not quite done with her, however.

'Mrs. MacBride, I have one further question, and I advise you to consider it very carefully. Was there any, as you put it, 'further intimacy' between you and Roger Nicholas before you told your husband of his supposed assault against your person?'

I knew what he was doing. No matter her forthcoming denial, her own words from the letter were being used against her and placed solidly in the judge's mind, not to mention the thoughts of the gossipy crowd in attendance.

I could see her knuckles white against the rail in front of her and hear the quaver in her voice as she tried to keep her balance. Jamie MacBride waited with the rest of us, his own body slumped forward as if he might topple from his chair with the weight of her past on his shoulders. When she answered I heard his stifled groan.

'Not that I can remember,' she murmured.

'Speak up, please, Mrs. MacBride, so the court can hear you,' Gordon demanded.

'I cannot remember,' she said, and was damned beyond rescue.

Campbell was clearly stunned by this course of events and waved me off when I advised him to ask for a recess. 'It's no use,' he told me. 'Nicholas doesn't even have to exaggerate now.'

Alice stepped down from the box, tears streaking her cheeks, and walked past our table without a glance.

'Alice!' Jamie MacBride called after her, his own voice trembling with shock and, dare I say it, shame arising from what could only be natural suspicions.

'Silence!' the judge commanded, and we heard the courtroom door close behind her.

Roger Nicholas's testimony was unfaltering. He described how she had come to his barn where he had planned to make a gift to her of the two lambs, one for each of her children. Her gratitude was not becoming and quite unexpected in its effusion, he said. She had thrown her arms around his neck and told him her affections for him had never disappeared. Then she had kissed him passionately. Yes, he had responded initially as any man would have, but soon pushed her off and told her to be off home, he would bring the lambs another day. When she saw that her warmth was not to be returned, her manner became hard and she warned him not to speak of their embrace.

'I had no intention of doing so,' he said when pressed by Mr. Gordon. 'You can imagine my surprise when Jamie turned up and assaulted me for attacking his wife.'

I believed none of it. Neither would the judge or anyone else in the court if not for that damned letter and Alice's refusal to answer directly Gordon's insinuations of an unseemly familiarity. Campbell never broke broke Nicholas's line of defence with his subsequent questions, though I must say his efforts were not very effective.

When the debacle was over, I went immediately to Alice's cottage, but she was not there. Thank God she had not had to listen to Nicholas's besmirching accusations. I had listened, though, and wanted to tell her they made no difference to me. She had been caught by her unfortunate choice of words years before and by the fact they had been written down for a posterity without sympathy for her age or circumstance. She was guilty of indiscretion then, and that clouded judgment of her now. I wondered how Jamie would respond and whether her long-ago imprudence would result in his present imprisonment or release.

I have just come from the courtroom where the decision has been rendered. The judge has found Jamie Campbell not guilty of the assault against Roger Nicholas. Given the deception of his wife he acted as any man would have when honour appeared at stake. However, the lambs were not his to take, even if they had been promised, and the sentence for this theft is one month in goal and a fine of twenty pounds. I want to discuss the injustice with everyone, but my duty to Norman and father's own legal predicament are more important for the moment.

Horace

Today Mr. Peverel dissected an old dead tabby cat he found behind the fishmonger's shop.

'It's like a graveyard out there in that back lane,' he said. 'Old cats have one last feast and then expire. I've even found some birds as well.'

I knew this was a test of sorts for me. I needed to learn about the insides of animals, and the drawings in the books Mr. Peverel had shown me weren't enough. But the question was how would I react to the innards the scalpel would reveal?

'Some swallow hard and keep everything down,' he told me, 'Others are sick right away and then quite fine. Very few have an affliction for life, Horace, and I don't expect you'll be one of those.'

I nodded and hoped he was right. What good was a vet's assistant who couldn't stand the sight of blood and guts?

He lay the cat on its back. 'How many years would you say this old fellow had?'

I looked at the grey whiskers and sagging skin around the eyes. There were scabs on its legs and tufts of hair missing from its sides as if plucked out by a ravenous foe. 'He's been in lots of fights,' I said.

'He has that. I'd say he was twelve or thirteen, at least.' He drew a line with the blade from the throat to the bottom of the stomach. A thin line of blood grew into a red stain that he staunched with a cloth. 'There's less than you think unless you nip an artery,' he said. Then he used both hands to draw back the skin and pull apart the rib-cage, exposing all the organs inside. 'There's the heart,' he told me, pointing with the scalpel.'

It was its stillness that made me sad. I had seen dead creatures before and knew their hearts had stopped, but it's different when you can reach out and touch the silence. The lungs were like two little scraps of tissue paper, and Mr. Peverel showed me how the throat passage divided so that air went down into them while food and drink went lower into the stomach where we found some tiny pieces of fish-bone and a bit of gristle.

'He didn't die hungry, you can see.'

Everything was so small, and he gave me a magnifying glass to study the kidneys and liver. 'You can't do much if something goes wrong with any of these, just hope they heal on their own, but you need to know where they are so you can tell what's injured and what is not. There are medicines to ease their pain, of course. As for the testicles...' He touched the two grey sacs gently as if they were made of glass. 'They can be ruptured occasionally and of course removed if the tom-cat takes over the parlour when his blood is up.'

I wanted to help injured animals even if I couldn't fix them up like new. The bones of smaller ones could be set, and I'd already seen Mr. Peverel do that with the broken hind leg of a border collie who'd been snagged by a hole. But the larger ones like Bess the mare just had to be put down. I wondered if they knew when the bone snapped and there was no hope.

Father had assured me horses galloped in heaven, but were any old tabby cats mentioned in Revelations? I didn't think so, but I said something to Mr. Peverel to help me think it might be so. 'They're just like us, aren't they?'

'How do you mean, Horace?'

'Their insides are just the same, and even if there's fur or hair on the outside, they've got skin like ours.'

'That's so, but what they lack is a brain like ours.' He picked up a small hammer and chisel and split the cat's skull with one quick blow. Then he reached into the cavity and lifted out the wrinkled mound and put it in my hands. It wasn't at all heavy and felt soft and smooth as I closed my fingers and thumbs around it.

'And that's all there is to being a cat,' he said. 'You're holding just over an ounce of matter, I'd guess. Whereas if I was to pluck out your brain it would weigh almost three pounds.'

I'd always thought cats and dogs were as smart as us and still thought so whatever Mr. Peverel said. Maybe they couldn't read or write, but there were lots of things they could do that we couldn't match. I'd watched a cat stalk a squirrel with a patience no hunters possess and seen that border collie's cousins round up sheep more skilfully than any shepherd could do.

'Are our brains the biggest?' I asked him.

'Not nearly,' he replied. 'Whales have the biggest, then elephants.'

'What about horses?'

'They're about half the size of ours, which means they're not dumb. But we train them, remember, not the other way around.'

'Does that mean we're not as smart as whales and elephants?'

He chuckled. 'You're after some answers I haven't got, Horace. Let's just say there are different kinds of intelligence.'

'I wonder what whales think of when they're swimming along?'

'How to avoid the next harpoon, I should think. There's too much killing of that sort goes on, whatever livelihood it provides.'

But I knew they dreamt of heaven just like us. And anything with a brain, no matter the size, did too.

'Watch carefully,' he said. 'I'm going to sew him back up.'

After a few pulls of the needle and thread he gave them to me. 'Do a neat job, mind, as if it were alive and dependent on your skilled efforts.'

The tabby's eyes were watching me as I worked, and I told myself he would live forever.

Father has gathered us all in the parlour and informed us of his arrest. He might go to gaol, and if he does we are to return home except for Ernest. But I think the family will need some money if father can't preach anymore. Mr. Peverel has said if I stay here he'll pay me ten shillings a week while he trains me. Later on I'll make more. Even if father only has to pay a fine, I can help.

Mother wants to know where Norman is. I mention the rope.

Arthur

'Mr. Shelley would come into the shop every afternoon to check on my work with the coach. 'I might be returning south sooner than expected,' he told me, though why he would have driven all this way only to turn around before the winter was out was a puzzle to me. The wealthy have different ideas from our own, of course, and can spend half their lives moving around from fancy house to fancy house. Some of us are meant to drive and some to mend the damage done. I accept that, but I've never liked time-wasting in any man.'

'He wasn't well-off,' I told Brechin. 'Though his father was a baronet, they weren't on good terms. He would have inherited quite a lot had he outlived Sir Timothy, but, alas, he did not.'

'Aye, I could see his cuffs and collars were a bit thread-worn, but he wore knee-boots of good leather and always gave the impression he had just come from a place of importance or was going there. Not by bragging, mind, but through the confident air he had about him and the way he talked about things in general. I've never heard a voice like his before or since. Musical it was, but played on strings of steel, make no mistake.'

Brechin held up the bottle of amber liquid and raised his eyebrows, but I shook my head politely. I was still feeling the effects of that first dram and wanted a clear head to absorb his recollections. He poured himself another libation, though.

'It's very medicinal, isn't it?'

'Aye,' he replied. 'It comes from the Isle of Skye where the spring water courses over the rocks and peat to rest on your tongue as it does.' He sipped his dram slowly. 'And it warms your stomach like no other.'

'You suggested Shelley was an idler,' I ventured, not wanting him to stray.

'Och, that was the whisky not making myself clear. Ye don't have to be rich to be shiftless, and I could tell his mind was always busy however much he travelled hither and yon.'

'So he revealed a little of himself?'

'He did that, though I still don't understand why. I didn't read books and was as far from poetry as Hoy is from Heaven, but I was a good listener and perhaps that's why he took to me and talked about his situation – why he'd come north, how what others expected of him compared with what he expected of himself, and that he wanted to travel to the continent where he could be free of cursed English ways and manners. 'You're free of them here,' I said, and he laughed. He'd sit on an upturned cask and talk while I hammered the hinges or wheel hubs.'

'Did he seem happy?'

'He was concerned about his young daughter and caring for her properly, but I couldn't help notice he barely mentioned his wife.'

'Harriet.'

'It must be her. He said a man can be trapped in a marriage no matter how fond he might be of his partner and urged me to choose mine carefully when the time came. It was good advice as I was with my Annie for nigh on fifty years.' He took another sip and clicked his tongue against his teeth. 'What happened to them after they left Scotland?'

'He was fated to love another, a woman whose way of seeing things was closer to his vision of the world. He left Harriet though she was carrying his second child. Just over two years later, that dream of gaining the continent came true and he never returned to England.'

'He died over there. I heard. Mr. Dumbreck read the London papers and asked me one morning if I remembered the English poet with the badly-damaged coach. Well, he'd drowned in Italy, he said, and now he'd never get his money from him. It was ten years or more after I'd made those repairs and I was manager of the firm and doing very well. Not only did I remember him, I said, but I'd read a poem of his about a great king buried by the desert sands.'

'*Ozymandias*,' I said.

'Aye, he's the one. 'Look around ye mighty and despair.' I'd always liked that line, and when I finally left Mr. Dumbreck and tried to make a go with my own shop, I imagined a change in my prospects that meant the overthrow of the mighty in charge. The ones who'd bring me their vehicles but never their friendship.'

'You're more like Shelley than you might think, Mr. Brechin.'

He smiled at this. 'It's good of ye to say so, but I'd rather have lived this long and be talking to ye now than die so young and such a long way from home.'

'I can't say I disagree, but he does live on in his work, of course. That will never die.'

He grew silent, seeming to take in my claim for such immortality. Stuffing some pungent tobacco into a corncob pipe and bringing a match to the bowl, he spoke through clenched teeth and I wasn't sure at first if I'd heard him correctly.

'He told me he wanted to be at sea when death came for him.'

159

I was shocked by the prescience almost a decade before Spezia. 'What on earth prompted him to say that?'

'He'd asked me about my own family and I told him my father and older brother had been lost when I was just a boy. Fishing, they were, and ignored the weather warnings.'

'I'm sorry to hear it.'

'So was he, but I could see a sparkle in his eyes as he told me of his wish.'

He puffed on his pipe until wreathed in a plume of smoke that slowly rose towards the rafters. 'I didn't put it right. He wasn't going to wait on death's storm, he said, but would seize it by the throat and go down singing. Aye, that's how he put it on the same day I told him the bill was eight pounds.'

Long and light the schooner limns
The wave-torn sea with crowded sails
As vision breaks on farther shore

In his pocket Keats' poems swim
And in his eyes approaching gale
The opening of a greater door

Choice is made when sky grows dim
When thunder lightning and the hail
Consign the craft to godless lore

On the beach at fire's rim
Trelawney Byron Leigh Hunt pale
Against the flames' consuming roar

It was getting dark as father finished his story about Mr. Parker and his own arrest. Mother is always worried about Norman, but this time none of us had any idea where he could be. It was only when Horace and Lettie mentioned the rope that I remembered Garson's story. *Long hair and arms like a girl's above its grey coat and tail fin.*

'I know where he's gone,' I said.

160

Clem

I hadn't been feeling well for several days so my excuse for not attending Chapel was accepted by father and mother without much question. Mother brought me some warm milk as I lay in bed and said they would likely be delayed after the service because some of the ladies were having tea and scones in celebration of an elder's birthday. That suited me perfectly. As soon as she was gone with the rest of the family, I leapt up despite my aching bones, put on my shirt, tie, and pressed trousers, and headed for St. Magnus. Fortunately, the church was on the far side of town, so all but the most lagging of Methodists would be out of my way, and any of those would likely avoid the Presbyterian crowds. Mr. Berry had been very pleased when I told him I would play the organ even if only for two or three hymns. He hadn't asked me if I'd obtained permission, and I didn't volunteer any information on the subject. I hadn't really lied because I truly wasn't feeling well and might have stayed home as it was, but of course I knew I was deceiving father and mother and that they would be appalled by my reasons for doing so. While it was difficult to accept that my musical inclinations were responsible for such betrayal, at the same time I was overjoyed at the opportunity to fill that array of cathedral pipes with glorious sound. Yes, I was bound to feel guilty later on, especially when mother's ministrations followed her return from Chapel, but as I hurried up the stone steps and through the great oaken doors, my fingers twitched with anticipation and my thoughts had nothing to do with family.

There had been no time for rehearsal, though Mr. Berry had given me sheets with the musical score to three hymns – *Now that daylight fills the sky*, *Not here for high and holy things*, and *Awake, my soul, and with the sun* – so I had been able to practice on Mrs. Drever's piano when she and Norman weren't about. While not in perfect form, I was fairly confident I could carry things off. He was waiting for me as I slipped in behind the curtain and took my seat. I hadn't paid much attention to the congregation as I'd passed down the side aisle, but now I could hear their coughs and muffled whispers as they waited for their minister to take the pulpit.

'All set, then, Clement?'

'Yes,' I said in a quiet voice that still sounded a little too high and squeaky for my liking. I was nervous, as I always was before a performance, but not frightened of failure. This was what I was born to do – not to hide behind a cathedral curtain while my parents assumed I lay out of sorts beneath the blankets of my bed but to *play music* in waves

161

that rolled up the shores of faith for whoever it was sang words to accompany me.

Mr. Berry had pulled the edge of the curtain aside and was peeking out. 'Just so you know,' he whispered loudly, 'the service begins with a hymn, followed by a prayer and another hymn. Afterwards there are readings from the Old and New Testaments by members of the congregation. The choir will sing a Psalm, but you needn't worry about that. Then there will be a third hymn leading into a Gospel reading before Reverend Scott delivers the sermon. When he is done everyone together recites the Nicene Creed.'

'Yes, *We believe in one God, the Father, the Almighty.*'

'I'm not sure you go as far as us with our prayers for the well-being of the Church, the nation, and the world. Very ambitious, we Presbyterians! We also include the needy and the dear departed. We subsequently make a general confession of sin and shake hands with our neighbours.'

'I'll have to go home then.' I was somewhat overwhelmed by all these details and worried about how long everything would take. Despite the tea and biscuits, I knew father and mother would be back by noontime and it must have been half ten now.

'Oh, no, Clement. You can't miss communion!'

I was about to ask what that involved here when I heard a noisy shuffling of feet as everyone stood up, followed by more coughing which I recognized as the like signal in Chapel that a hymn was in the offing.

'Now!' Mr. Berry said, touching my shoulder lightly, and I launched into *Now that daylight fills the sky* as the chorus beyond my sight rose and swelled with conviction, a strength and sweetness of common voice you could not label with creed or denomination.

'Excellent,' he said when we had finished, patting my shoulder now. 'You are a natural indeed, Clement,' he told me with an enthusiasm I was sure rippled through the nearest pews. I listened to the prayer, played my second hymn, and heard individuals in the congregation read from the Bible. Then it was time for my finale, and as I played the last line of the score and *'praise Father, Son, and Holy Ghost'* reverberated from the surrounding stone I was already planning another Sunday escape from the house. How long I could keep such subterfuge up I didn't know, but I felt charged with a creative spirit that demanded loyalty to those keys and stops.

I was in a bit of a reverie, I must admit, and barely took in the sermon, something to do with serving the Lord and not straying into sin.

All I know is the minister's voice droned on somewhat and was sometimes interrupted by babies' cries, though, as in Chapel, everyone pretended not to notice. I was preparing my exit but was suddenly aware at how awkward it would be for me to emerge from my sanctuary, retreat down the side aisle, and push open one of the heavy doors. Surely there must be a side exit I could quietly employ. I was about to ask Mr. Berry for help when I realized he wasn't there. Outside the curtain there were more prayers I didn't recognize, then an unaccompanied hymn that sounded like our own Sanctus, followed by the Lord's Prayer. Mr. Berry's head suddenly appeared around the edge of the curtain like the Cheshire Cat in *Alice in Wonderland*. 'You're welcome to join us in communion, Clement.' And just like the cat's, his smiling face disappeared, and I was left to contemplate his invitation.

Father had told us often enough about the Church of Rome's belief that worshippers actually become one with Christ by drinking his blood and eating his crucified body though a sip of wine and bite of bread. Were Presbyterians the same? After all, this had once been a Catholic cathedral. It was one thing to play hymns that weren't much different from those in Chapel, but quite another to partake in something entirely foreign to Methodists who believed that communion simply brought the living spirit of Christ among us. Yet I was curious and couldn't help peering out at the lines of people waiting patiently for their encounter with the priest, grown-ups mostly though there were some boys and girls around my age. When I looked across the pews I could see older brothers and sisters tending to their younger siblings and even holding babies in their arms. From my angle I could see tongues outstretched to receive the little square of bread and lips waiting for the sip of real wine (not grape-juice!) from the cup the priest wiped each time with a cloth. It all seemed so down-to-earth yet strangely powerful as if the pretense of becoming one with Jesus became, for that instant of reception, real and undeniable.

Still in my trance and drawn by this communal force I stepped out into the open and immediately became part of a line inching its way forward. I had no intention of opening my mouth but just wanted to get closer to the source of the belief I could feel holding sway in the building. Just in front was Mr. Berry, the bald spot on the back of his head shining in the light that slanted in from the stained glass windows. As I neared the rail that separated the altar from the front row of pews, I saw a door in the side off to my left, a clear route of escape, but somehow my feet kept shuffling in time with the others and I was pulled closer to the point of no return. Mr. Berry had vanished, and then I saw him just a few feet away, kneeling before the priest, tongue extended, the whiteness of the bread like a tiny beacon of light blinding me with its intensity, and I too was down and waiting for the Body of Christ. All around me organ music was whipping the air into a frenzy and I wondered who was playing with such passion, indeed fury, as I looked up into the priest's eyes and saw father robed in splendour gazing down at me, in his hands a dried piece of crust a bird might have spurned.

'What are you doing here, Clement?' he asked me not unkindly.

I could not bring my tongue back into my mouth to answer him. The organ crashed on, and I could feel the anxious press of people beside and behind me as if the crust were a prized part of Christ's anatomy desired by the multitude.

I watched father raise his arms above my head as he declared to all who could hear, *'Truly, truly, I say unto you, one of you will betray me.'* Then I came awake in the middle of the night, sweating and tangled in my sheets, crying out *'I don't know the man,'* Against the opposite wall, Norman's bed was empty.

Norman

When I open my eyes I am lying on my back on the beach, my right leg twisted beneath me. I remember how halfway down the rope ran out and I couldn't hold on any longer and my hands were burning and then my forehead and knees were banging against the rock. I think I was screaming or yelling. All I know is my mouth was wide open and I couldn't get enough air. Then there was no more rope and I hit the ground hard and everything went black. I don't know how long I have lain here before waking, but the sun is right above me in the sky so it must have been a long while as I left the house at half eight. Somehow I am still wearing my glasses though one of the lens is cracked. No one will be worried about me until tea-time because I often disappear down the beach or into the fields for the day. Sometimes Clem goes with me, but mostly I am alone. Mother and father don't mind as long as I promise to stay clear of any big breakers if the wind is up. I don't have to make any promises about cliffs because they never think I'd go near them or take any foolish chances.

I wish I could straighten my leg, but every time I try a pain shoots up my shinbone and through my knee. It's better if I lie here and rest until someone comes. But how will they know where to find me? The only person I told about the selkie was Arthur. He sent me a post card with a mermaid picture so maybe he'll know where to look. He'll bring Mr. Garson and everything will be fine. But I'm cold even though the sun is hot on my face, and the wind mother and father were worried about is picking up. I'm too far from the shore to worry about breakers. At least I think I am. When I turn my head I can see a pile of kelp a few feet off and hear the booming of the swells hitting the cave walls. A fleck of spray hits my cheek and I tell myself it must have been carried a long way by the wind. Then another lands on my lips and I can taste the closeness of the sea. The sun goes away behind a cloud and stays there until I count to ten. Another, bigger cloud comes along, and I reach twenty-five before the yellow ball peeks out from behind the ragged curtain. If it rains I'll have to keep my mouth shut or I'll drown before the breakers have a chance to reach me. If I bend my neck back and look up I can see the top of the cliff. I think it's where I tied the rope because it's a long way up, but it might just be a bump in the rock so anyone standing on the real top won't be able to see me. Did I find the place where Mr. Garson climbed down or am I on another beach that nobody knows? I'm very thirsty but my pack with the bottle fell off and I can't see it anywhere. I had some biscuits and an apple too, though I'm feeling a bit sick and wouldn't be able to keep them down even if I found them.

I must have fallen asleep because the sky is darker now and the wind is blowing harder from the sea. My leg hurts a lot and I wish I could turn on my side. I wish all the butterflies I had ever caught and set free would come along and lift me from my bed of seaweed and stone, carrying me in a cocoon to the summit. I'd gladly lie there and wait for rescue. Arthur and Mr. Garson would come along and ask me why I was being so lazy, and I'd laugh and tell them this was the best way to see a selkie because she'd think you didn't have the strength to run after her. They'd unfold my leg gently and carry me home where mother would bring me hot milk and scones piled with jam. She'd be angry that I'd gone off without telling her where I was bound, but she'd protect me from father whose punishment would be harsh. I start to cry because I don't care what the punishment will be and there are no butterflies down here and Arthur and Mr. Garson are far away. It's not a drop of spray this time but a whole splash that comes down hard on my face, and I can hear the waves hitting the pebbles on the shoreline and sliding away with a scary hissing sound. I put my hand out after another salty blow and feel the cold water trickle between my fingers. In another few minutes I will be soaked through. Now I am really scared the waves will drag me under so no one will ever know what happened.

Slowly, slowly I try to turn over so I can get away. But each time I start to roll the pain shoots so sharply through my knee and shinbone that I cry out and have to settle in my old position. It's not the spray now but the tips of the waves themselves that are upon me, so I have to try again. If I do it all at once I will burst through the pain and be all right.

Then I can haul myself along to shelter. 'One, two, three,' I say out loud, rocking slowly back and forth, but count again and again so it won't hurt until I am almost too tired to care about the water churning over my boots. Finally, using my last bit of strength, I twist onto my stomach, but my knee does not come around as quickly as the rest of me and stays locked in its old position. I can hear myself screaming as my fingers scrabble uselessly at the stones, trying to hang on, and then there is only blackness.

In my dark sleep I see nothing at all, but I can hear the wind and the water shrieking together in mockery of my pain and feel myself moving dreamily as if pulled by an invisible force towards the back of the beach. My body bumps and scrapes over obstacles, and the salt tang in my nose mingles with the sweeter scent of something familiar that I cannot place. My fingers are bleeding and I know it is not my own strength pulling me to safety but a strange kind of faith that while the natural world may hurt me and make me cry it will not kill me. All I have to do is reach the bottom of the cliff and all will be well. Then the retreating hiss is prolonged beyond measure and I hear the huge wave gathering to destroy that faith. Although I cannot see the curl, I know its height and weight will crush my puny body and pull it into the depths offshore without a trace. The wind stops and the watery curve is overhead. Even in the darkness I close my eyes, and that is when I see her long hair cascading over her shoulders and feel her hands grasping mine as the thunder crashes down on us both and I am a sea-creature being born.

When I open my eyes again I am sitting with my back against the cliff and my legs straight in front of me. The pain is gone. Somewhere a voice is calling my name.

Lettie

Arthur looked at me as he told Mr. Garson's story of the selkie, perhaps because he knew I wouldn't dismiss such a magical quest even if it had lured our youngest brother into danger.

'Filling a child's head with stuff and nonsense,' mother cried, 'the very nerve.'

'If anything has happened to Norman, I'll have him up before the magistrate,' Bertie stated firmly.

Father and Ernest looked vexed but said nothing for the moment. Out of the corner of my eye I saw Horace and Clem with heads together and four hands flying in all directions as if they were trying to grasp

Norman's wildest expectations. It was mother who, despite her emotions, pressed us into action.

'He's out there lost! We have to find him!'

'Yes, Elizabeth,' father replied, his tone suggesting he'd been in control all along. 'But let's be organized about it. Arthur and Lettie, you've been out along the cliffs, haven't you? Do you know exactly where these sea-caves are?'

'More or less,' Arthur said. 'There's an easier approach than the tricky footing above the end of the beach where it's hard to climb without putting oneself at risk. Once you get above the caves, of course, there's the matter of climbing down. I don't see how he could do it by himself.'

'He had a rope,' Horace said. 'He told me he wanted it to pull an old wagon around.'

'I saw him with it this morning, and he had a rucksack,' I add.

'How much rope?' Arthur asked.

'Thirty foot maybe.'

'It wouldn't be enough. You'd need twice that, at least.'

'Ernest,' father said, 'go to the constable's office and tell him we need his help. Your mother will stay here in case Norman turns up. The rest of us will set out for these cliffs though we'll need the Lord's aid to find him in all that wilderness.'

'Margaret will know what to do,' I said.

'Who?' Father had discarded his good shoes and was pulling on his walking boots. Mother looked at me reprovingly, but I knew I was right. 'She's a friend who lives in a cottage beyond the cliffs and knows the coastline like the back of her hand.'

'Good, then. See if you can rouse her and say we'd be most grateful for her advice. Bertie, and Arthur come with me. Horace, you get more rope from Mr. Spence and follow on. Clem, stay with your mother.' He really was in charge, and I thought how well he'd done with Rory Parker.

'Oh, father, I can help!'

'I don't want my two youngest on the loose. And I won't have your mother left alone at a time like this.'

'But...'

Father raised his hand. 'I'll hear no more, Clement.'

I put on my own boots and wrapped a shawl around my shoulders. There was a crisp wind as I stepped out the door, and the afternoon sun was low in the sky, obscured from time to time by scudding lines of cloud. Arthur was there beside me.

'I should find Mr. Garson,' he said.

'Of course! Why didn't we think of that?'

'He's getting on in years now. I just don't see how any of us will be able to get down to the shore if that's where Norman is.'

'He'll know someone, a fisherman perhaps, who's young and strong enough. Meanwhile, there's Margaret's expertise.'

'Who is she, Lettie?'

'I was going to introduce you anyway,' I told him as I made to set off for her cottage. 'You'll like her. She reads for one thing, and for another she's a wonderful sailor.' But he'd already turned in the direction of town, and my last words disappeared into the wind.

Even hurrying, it took me nearly an hour in the coming dark to reach the cottage, and I was greatly relieved to see a column of smoke from the chimney as I approached, signalling she was likely inside. There wasn't much daylight left, and as happened most clear evenings, the wind had dropped and the previously-cresting seas had settled into long rolling swells from the north-east. When she opened the door, the alarm on my face must have been evident.

'What on earth is the matter, Lettie?'

Standing on the stoop I told her as best and briefly as I could of Norman's inspiration by Mr. Garson, of the thirty feet of rope, and that a search party had been organized with, I hoped, the town constable at its head.

'I know those caves,' she said. 'It's a dangerous spot.' She pulled me inside. 'Put your trousers on,' she ordered, already unbuttoning her dress. 'Even if he managed to make it safely to the beach, they'll have a devil of a time hauling him back up. But it may be that he's injured himself, in which case a rescue from the cliff will prove impossible.'

'What shall we do?' I trusted her judgment implicitly, but we were two women in trousers, nothing more.

'We'll take the *Tom Paine*, of course.'

Down at the wharf the water slapped roughly against the sloop's hull, and although there were no white-caps out at sea, the swells seemed gigantic, obscuring Shapinsay's coast not so many miles away.

'Store this,' she said, handing me a lantern. 'It will be dark by the time we get there, though the skies are clearing and we'll have some starlight to aid us. I just pray that's where he is and not on some other bit of coast I can't get near.' She threw a canvas bag into the stern.

For the first time, I allowed myself to wonder whether Norman was alive and, even so, if he could be found with the night falling and visibility from the cliff-top all but gone. If he was injured and unconscious then the search party would have no way of tracking him in the dark, their calls ringing uselessly on deaf ears. We hauled up the mainsail and Margaret guided the boat into deeper water. Because of the wind's direction, we had to do what she called 'tacking,' which meant cutting back and forth at angles in order to advance down the coast. It was effective but took a lot of time, and when we finally rounded the dim outline of a headland and she pointed us into shore the only difference between the black sheets of sea and sky were the steady pinpricks of starlight above and the ceaseless undulations beneath our hull. I lit the lantern and held it firmly on the edge of the bow.

Caught by the narrowness of the cove and the rebounding surges from the caves, the swells twisted and turned on themselves, and *Tom Paine* pitched from side to side as we rode at alarming speed towards the beach. Margaret yelled at me to let down the sail. My fingers found the rope-end on the cleat and the canvas slid down the mast, the metal rings clanging into one another as it collapsed, and I bound it raggedly to the boom. Rocks jutted up everywhere like sentinels, and I waited for a fatal ripping sound as she manoeuvred us around and through their gauntlet, the shore agonizingly close but revealing no secrets whatsoever.

'Norman,' I called, cupping my free hand at the side of my mouth and holding up the lantern with the other. Once I thought I heard someone else calling his name, but it could have been an echo of my own voice, desperate now for some reply. Scraping over an underwater shelf, we lurched forward onto the strand and leapt out into frigid, knee-deep water, hauling the sloop up as high as our strength would allow. There was nothing on which to secure the line so Margaret lifted out the anchor and carried it up the incline to the end of its rope, shoving it down hard into the pebbles and sand beneath.

'It's not much, but it will slow things down a little,' she said.'

My boots and pants to the knee were soaked through, but I paid no heed. Holding up the lantern I walked unsteadily toward the cliff shouting his name again and again. This time we heard no echo just muffled cries from above, though the protruding rock prevented us from glimpsing any lights at the top. Enormous piles of kelp indicated how far in the waves had carried. Was Norman beneath one of these tangles or trapped in one of the caves off to the side where the hollow booms sounded like cannon-fire? In the dark it would be too dangerous to attempt an entry, though I knew we might have to try. Then, stumbling along the line between stone and sand, I saw a movement at the base of the cliff and heard my name softly spoken.

He was sitting up with a pile of dried kelp over his legs like a blanket.

'Are you hurt?' I cried.

In the low light, he gave me a big smile and shook his head. 'I saw her, Lettie. She pulled me back here and made my leg better.'

I hardly remember how we got him to the boat. His one leg was injured and he had to drag it along through the loose stones as we supported him under each shoulder and tried to keep our own footing. Before we started out I shouted as loudly as I could to the cliff-top that we had him safe and they should meet us at Margaret's wharf. But the wind was blowing again and we could hear nothing in reply. It was no easy task getting him over the gunwale, but I foolishly felt we were home-free once we had done so and he was propped securely between the seat-board and the stern, covered in a blanket Margaret had shoved into her canvas bag.

'It's not going to be easy,' she said quietly, and when I turned and looked at the sea I saw what she meant. The cove was boiling with cross-currents and the wind had come up so strongly there were white-caps now on the crests of the swells. The explosions from the caves were unending, and I was terrified of our being dragged inside.

'We'll have to row out, Lettie. It's our only chance.'

In all our days on the water I had never picked up an oar, so skilfully did Margaret handle the tiller and sails. Now we shoved our craft down the slope and fought to turn it in the shallows. Halfway around it suddenly lurched up against me and I went under its solid curve, submerged to my neck in the unforgiving cold. Just as quickly it went the other way and I jumped up sputtering and angry at my rag-doll condition. Margaret laughed, but I could hear the tightness in her voice.

'You'll soon be warm enough. Get in!'

She set the oars in their locks, told me to watch her and keep in time with her pulls. 'Put your back into it, Lettie!' she shouted. 'It's the only way.'

Norman's eyes were closed, but I could see his lips moving as if he was trying to tell us a story. It was going to be quite a tale if we could all live to hear it. Not only did he think he'd seen the selkie, but apparently she'd saved him as well. I hoped this was true, but I didn't have time to dwell on miracles now. We were tossed like a cork but somehow kept the bow pointed to the mouth of the cove. The water poured over the sides as we rose and fell and the danger of sinking before we capsized was real enough. My arms ached terribly and I could feel the skin ripping from my fingers and palms, but I dared not let up and concentrated on Margaret's repeated lifting and dropping of her oar, pulling against an unrelenting force that seemed intent on our demise. I thought of father praying that we'd survive and gave him credit for entering my mind at such a precarious time. Then I remembered Arthur's rendition of Shelley's last moments. He went down with a friend and a cabin-boy. There was a boy at my feet but no friend in sight, just my captain and beloved.

The Frame

There's a great deal of withholding and outright evasion by my ancestors, however justifiable at times, which makes them no different from members of many families, past or present. The photograph in the garden that started everything off is meant to suggest otherwise, but then all such recorded gatherings contain a high quotient of disguise, protection, or deflection in one way or another.

First and foremost is Thomas the patriarch and public defender of a faith that seems to have compromised him. I'm on his side when he uses the Bible to justify his misleading of officialdom in the Rory Parker case. He knows a material wrong when he sees one, and if the words that he has depended on for so many years cannot sustain him in his dance around secular authority what good are they? There are holy verses for every situation as long as you ultimately believe you are acting in good faith, which is why fundamentalists of all persuasions can convince themselves of their righteousness and contradict one another at every turn. Hypocrisy is one of the worst personal results of such unacknowledged relativism, but I don't believe Thomas has been insincere in his statements and actions. He questions what he is doing even as he is being driven to an extreme he would rather avoid. 'Being driven,' of course, suggests a combination of external events and psychological pressures that did not fit well together in the early 1890s and do not fare much better as partners today. When he gets up in that pulpit Sunday next, he'll be faced with a crisis of conscience that can't be quietly resolved with biblical platitudes, and I'm not sure what he can reach for to ease his troubled mind and soul.

Elizabeth is caught between a rock and a hard place – her husband and her children. She wants to defend both simultaneously, but when that's not possible she usually chooses a waiting game of sorts, telling herself a little time is all that's needed. Hence her defence, up to a point, of Horace's wishes to remain in the Orkneys and her rather reportorial take on the MacBride trial, though motherly intuition should tell her something of the basis for Bertie's 'distraction'. As to the issue of Lettie and Margaret Muir, Elizabeth has no suspicions at the moment of any forbidden feelings on her daughter's part but is simply and understandably anxious about her safety – a female sailor after all! She has delayed telling Thomas of this worry because his precarious legal situation is paramount, an interesting judgment call considering her qualms about Lettie's life being at risk. Perhaps with her primary loyalty to her husband she is simply choosing to walk conventional matrimonial lines. Since she was born in the middle of the 19th century and is the wife of a Methodist minister with all the accompanying external, not to mention interior, baggage, the assigning of blame on my part is questionable.

Then there's Ernest grappling in secret with his own doubts. Well, not in secret, entirely, since he's shared them somewhat with Reverend Scott. The key is, he hasn't revealed any of his religious misgivings to his father who has been his spiritual guide all his life. Thomas would likely be appalled that his eldest son, heading directly for a Methodist pulpit, is conversing about the contradictions inherent in Christianity with a Presbyterian minister. And if 'appalled' is too strong a term, then 'deeply distressed' is undoubtedly apt. Ernest didn't come clean, as well, about his exchanges with Roddy Erlendsson and the curiously smooth road to Viking sainthood. This has bound guilt up with doubt, and it will be interesting to see the result if he has the chance to take over from a gaoled Thomas and Mr. Taggart.

Bertie appears to have no doubts, at least about his own feelings. He has admitted his love for Alice MacBride, even though it is unrequited. But has he really accepted the inevitable dead-end of his passion? Jamie will be imprisoned for a month, and it's difficult to imagine Bertie staying away from the lonely spouse. Not only that, his father's own possible incarceration provides potential grounds for his remaining in the Orkneys. Oh, I know Thomas has ordered everyone home, except Ernest, should he be gaoled, but won't Bertie feel a legal as well as a filial responsibility to remain on the island and defend the accused, with Mr. Campbell's help, of course? After all, there's a third modifier of that sense of responsibility that he will hold himself to – 'heartfelt.'

Horace is the one flaw in the prevarication thesis I'm trying to promote here. He comes from the 'honest-as-the-day-is-long' school without being at all aware of his status as an upstanding character in the eyes of everyone he encounters. It is hardly his fault he lacks the intellectual acuity to see patterns and connections in his thoughts and feelings or to follow them to some satisfactory end or at least resting place – hence the unresolved tension between his desire that the dead tabby live forever and the fact such feline immortality isn't mentioned in *Revelations*. But that 'lack' doesn't prevent special insights. Remember his recognition of a barn as no different from a church or chapel and his certainty at finding the Lord's presence in the eyes of dumb animals. Now that I think of it, Horace keeps a great deal from the rest of the family because he articulates such awareness only to himself, content to sit at his book-like window and read the fields, rivers, and mountains that transcend anything he can say aloud.

Arthur is a poet so he's bound to dissemble. Shelley lied in his personal life all the time, but he wrote verses for the ages. Arthur's not on that creative level, but aspiration and allegiance to it can go a long way in alleviating minor transgressions. If he can't tell his father that he wants to visit a man who knew Shelley, who is more at fault? After all, would any of us, whatever the parental barriers, turn down such an opportunity (select your favourite historical figure)? He's there when it matters, listening to Lettie and Norman with respect, neither dismissing the former as a flighty female nor the latter as a child taken in by a romantic tale. Although Lettie's desire to disclose to him something of her relationship with Margaret has been interrupted by the search for their selkie-seeking brother, there's little doubt Arthur's the one member of her family who would sympathize with her feelings. Meanwhile, all those private poetic imaginings are becoming visible marks on the page that he wants to publish, despite his knowing that parents and siblings will make of them what they must.

Clem is my grandfather and a more gifted artist than his elder brother, yet he lacks Arthur's humanity. Certainly he's not revealing his covert desires to anyone except, in limited fashion, to strangers like the cathedral organist, Mr. Berry. His dream of communion and participation in a Presbyterian service suggest an unconscious longing to join the wider community and how far from his father's faith his creative urges have taken him. But the dream also suggests that his guilt about his deceit is stronger than Ernest's who tends to focus on his father's struggles in the outer world where, as a result, he might gain his own pulpit. Clem sees his father as high priest usurping the Catholic-like communion with his power that becomes quite god-like in nature when it shapes him into a betraying Judas and denying Peter combined. There is the saving grace of his piano variations either as a simple diversion or to the extent music is a religion for composer as well as listener. You can't help notice Clem has found melodic form for his siblings but not yet creatively captured the figures of his parents.

The only thing Norman might be guilty of is realizing he'd have no chance of meeting a selkie if he told anyone else of his plans or took anyone else along, even Arthur (who was away). Yes, he put others in danger when they tried to rescue him, but that was never his intention or even in his wildest thoughts as he gathered his gear and set off. His attachment to the natural world is at the heart of his quest, and we have seen his innocence and integrity in his treatment of the butterflies and interactions with Mr. Garson. Indeed, so strong and unsullied is his connection to creatures and their territories that his pursuit of the selkie might be deemed spiritual in its intensity, especially given his ultimate vision on the beach. Thomas and Ernest could learn something from him by reversing their application of faith to earthly experience, and Arthur has already used him as a source for poetic expression. How the years will treat Norman, I don't know yet. I hope he has the chance to gain some formal knowledge to augment his uncontrived response to life.

Lettie could well appropriate the male-centered cry from *Song of Solomon* and speak it to the world (and more specifically, her family) about a woman: '*This is my beloved, and this is my friend, O daughters of Jerusalem.*' Indeed, given the same-sex nature of her burgeoning passion for Margaret, an initial introduction to a band of sisters would be most suitable. But given the time and place will she let herself follow her yearnings to their unsanctified ends, let alone be allowed to do so? She has been an outsider from the beginning of this story, clearly searching for some alternative to the life set out for her by parents who, whatever their personal tendencies, have been shaped inexorably by public heritage. She can talk to Arthur about many things and offer some guidance to Horace whom she admires for his ability to be himself. But, ultimately, she is alone in the family and in a larger society that presses in on her with its rigid rules and expectations for one particular kind of marriage. Margaret, on the other hand, has grown up relatively free of such demands and has had the open spaces of island and sea to expand her sense of a world, often dangerous, of unregulated harmony and flux. The sheer physicality of their experience together has lifted Lettie from the web of conventional mores long entangling the movements of her body and her cravings for something more than straight and narrow designs. Then, too, Margaret is a reader who knows the need for an inner life. There are many of us who would probably fall in love with her, she is that kind of figure. What does it matter if Lettie gets there first?

11. Remoter Worlds

Norman

When I open my eyes I am lying in a strange bed and staring at a ceiling that is much lower than the one in my room at home. Mother and father are sitting beside me, and Lettie is standing behind them. There is a woman I don't know next to Lettie who gives me a big smile when she sees I am looking at her. My leg hurts and the rest of me as well.

'Norman,' mother says. 'You've come back to us.'

Father reaches over and ruffles my hair. 'Quite an adventure, my son.' I'm frightened of his anger, but instead he laughs. 'Next time you'll have to take more rope.'

'There'll be no next time,' mother tells him, and I can see tears in the corners of her eyes.

'Did you see her, Lettie?' I ask.

'No, but you did,' she says. 'You were talking about her in the boat.'

'Hush, Lettie,' mother says. 'Don't encourage him when he's so weak.'

'You're a brave boy,' the strange woman tells me. I like her. She was in the boat telling Lettie to row hard. I didn't see them come ashore, but she and Lettie rescued me after the selkie pulled me away from the waves. My leg was bent backwards and then it was straight. I want to tell Mr. Garson what happened.

'The doctor is on his way,' father says.

'Is my leg broken?' I ask.

'No,' Lettie says. 'We couldn't have got you into the boat if it was. You dragged it along the beach without complaining too much.'

Mr. Garson will know how my leg got fixed. It must have been the same selkie for both of us, but she would be very old now and mine was young. Maybe they don't grow old like us or maybe there's more than one.

I am dreaming before I fall asleep in the middle of their talking, born again beneath that watery curve, a sea-creature swimming free.

Bertie

If only I could defend Norman's fate, and Lettie's, in a court of law the outcome would not be in doubt. The guilty person, Your Honour, is

Mr. Garson who should never have filled a young boy's head with such a story. If I were Norman's age I would have picked up a rope and gone selkie-hunting in a moment without understanding the peril. As for Lettie, if that is indeed her down in the boat, she is merely trying to right the wrong and possibly forfeit her life in doing so. Of course, you cannot put Garson in gaol for talking, but if Norman survives father should never allow him near the man again. As it is, there is only open air and a jury too emotional to listen to rational argument. I pace back and forth to keep my anger under control.

I was going to see Alice this evening and speak with her about her situation. Mr. Campbell has agreed to waive the usual fee for his services, well aware that it is their neighbours who will keep Jamie's wife and children fed during the next month. She would not accept any funds from me even if I had them to offer, but perhaps she will not shun my friendship for as long as I remain in the Orkneys. I must admit to being shocked by the letter she wrote to Roger Nicholas when it was read out in court, but I do not believe a person should be convicted for being someone different in the past. And that is the crux of the matter and the failure of justice. Oh, I know Jamie was convicted only of stealing the sheep, but Nicholas's testimony is what damned her and made the one-month sentence and twenty pounds irrelevant. She will not be able to hold her head up in the community, and I am afraid, despite her attachment to her parents, when Jamie is released they will have to leave the island.

There is Arthur crawling out to the edge of the cliff on his hands and knees. What is he up too? It's not as if being twenty feet closer to the beach will make his voice heard in this wind. Now there is Horace behind him, clasping his heels to keep yet another brother from being lost. Good old Horace! He acts without thought, just loyalty, whereas Arthur is always very aware of what he is doing and saying. For instance, right now I am sure he is telling himself, 'Someone has to try.' Still, even if his willing exposure to danger is not any more effective than my pacing, he is lending hope to our distressed mother by such action, whereas when she glances at me I can see the anguish in her eyes. I will be the one to pick up the pieces, though, should misfortune reign. The death of a son and daughter must be compensated especially if responsibility can be proven. Father would simply accept disaster, saying it is the Lord's will, but if Norman and Lettie go to Heaven, they will have died upon this earth, and it is here that accountability is paramount. We do not approve of Pilate washing his hands nor of Judas opening his palm for thirty pieces of silver even if Christ's crucifixion was inevitable. I don't know my Bible as well as father and Ernest, but I cannot recall any mere mortal forgiving the Roman prefect or the lost disciple.

Arthur turns his head and shouts, the wind carrying his words back to us unimpeded. 'There's the boat again!' We all gaze seaward, hands shielding our eyes from the blast. I see an outline on the water, the vague suggestion of a shape. 'They are blameless, Your Honour. I pray you, release them,' I say aloud. Then mother falls to the ground.

Ernest

Is this what it all comes down to, standing on a cliff-top powerless to effect any good? Perhaps Job said it best: *For he breaketh me with a tempest and multiplieth my wounds without cause.* No, I cannot believe that. But is it the Lord's plan to take Norman and Lettie from us so cruelly? Father and mother would never recover from such loss whatever the strength of their faith. To lose one child in a single blow would try any man or woman, but two? Even the Lord lost only one son, and He was redeemed. Yet this happens all the time, doesn't it? Fishermen drowned at sea, children dying from the croup and other illness, Viking warriors martyred by the sword. And each time a priest of some sort gets up before the survivors to explain the *peace of God which passeth all understanding*. I will have to do this, if not now then later in another parish where mortality springs suddenly like a wild beast or creeps slowly over the unsuspecting like a mist. In either case, the promise for those left behind is of calm and eventual comprehension in the face of their own inevitable deaths. Father's brow is furrowed as he gazes at the sea, and though I want to ask him to join me now in prayer, I cannot. It would be to interrupt his meditations that, for the first time, I see as his alone and not the minister's intercessions on behalf of his flock. All those contradictions of faith I have been contemplating matter little now. We pray according to our lights and share the beneficence or the silence that are answers of sorts. If my brother and sister are dead...

Suddenly Arthur cries, 'There's the boat again!' and I see it moving agonizingly slowly away from the shore though I cannot imagine how.

'*For thine is the power,*' I say to no one in particular, least of all the Lord.

Horace

When I see Arthur on his stomach and pulling himself forward, I think he's going after Norman. But why would he go frontwards, I wonder, because he can't lower himself down that way? Then he stops at the edge of the drop and yells something into the darkness in front of him, and I realize he's just trying to reach out to them with his voice because all our bellowing from farther back makes no difference. He's holding on with one hand and cupping the other around his mouth when a mighty gust nearly shakes him from his roost. Everyone else seems frozen in place except for Bertie who is marching back and forth to his own time. I lower myself to the ground and crawl after my brother. My hands grasp his ankles like plough handles, the bones digging into my palms as my fingers wrap themselves around. He doesn't turn but nods as if he knows it can only be me and that I will never let him go, however strong the wind. I cannot see the cliff-face but sense its steepness and wonder how Norman found the courage to descend. Then I remember Lettie is down below as well, if mother has not imagined her there. The woman who steered the boat, Margaret, mother called her, must be a great sailor to bring them into shore like that. But I don't think Lettie has ever been in a boat before. She would have told me if she had. They cannot sail out so they'll have to row. Maybe they'll be strong enough. When I lift my head starlight glints on the crest of the swells, and above the wind I can hear their hollow booming as they roll through the caves.

Arthur

The wind clears as much as it buffets the air, and I can make out two figures side-by-side in the middle of the boat, each holding an oar. If it is Lettie and her friend their skirts must get in the way and be soaked through. In the stern there is a dark shape that has to be Norman, though I can't be sure whatever my need for conviction. The craft rides up the face of a swell and is turned almost sideways because of currents or the lack of strength in one oar. Then it rests on the crest as if balanced between peril and safety, an equation lasting but a few seconds as the swell drops away beneath the hull and they vanish into a trough on the far side whose threatening depths I can only imagine. *Dreams of a remoter world visit the soul in sleep*, but we are all awake just as Shelley, his friend Williams, and that cabin boy must have been terribly so aboard the *Don Juan* as their storm drew them down. For what seems like hours my sister and her companion refuse to surrender, slipping and sliding their way always two strokes ahead and one back but finally out of the cove into open water where the swells are flattened by the wind's unhindered race across the channel between here and Shapinsay. For just a moment the craft is etched against the horizon line and I see the silhouette of a sail. No poem can do it justice, but I will have to try.

'It's mother,' Horace says and tugs at my heels.

Thomas

When we reach the cliff-top by the route Arthur advised, I am sure all is lost. It is nearly dark, and in the gloom I can barely make out the declivity in the rock pointed to by Mr. Garson.

'There's where I went down,' he shouts over the wind, pointing to a trough-shaped cut that slopes gently for several yards then disappears abruptly over the edge of the precipice. 'If he had only thirty feet of rope he's either clinging to the cliff or has fallen to the beach.'

Standing as close to me as he is, he must see my look of consternation. 'It's not all rock below,' he tells me. There's great piles of seaweed and kelp that could have cushioned him.'

'How do we know he's even down there?' The constable Ernest had fetched from his tea is a gruff individual who wants some proof that his time is being well-spent.

'There's nowhere else,' Garson replies. 'I told him my selkie story that he recounted to Arthur, and his other brother and sister saw him heading off down the beach with a coil of rope.'

Garson has his own coil slung over his shoulder, more than twice what Norman was carrying from the look of it, but I don't see how any one of us is going to lower himself into the darkness. In the illumination of the starlight I can make out the swells at the entrance to the cove, but below my feet very little is clear. Garson is older than me, and none of my sons, not even Horace, has the physical strength for the task, let alone the ability to bring Norman back up the cliff unharmed. I choke back my tears as I yell his name and the others call out as well, but our voices thin and strained as they leave our mouths are swept into oblivion by the unremitting gale. Then I see something beyond the tip of the headland where the swells are piling up, a shadow on the water a cloud might make, only there are no clouds, or perhaps a pack of seals clotted together, though that image makes little sense.

I clap Garson on the shoulder to gain his attention. 'What is that?' I ask, pointing seaward.

He leans forward as if to close the distance between himself and the shadow and rubs the back of his hand across his beard. 'It's a fishing smack,' he says, 'and he's very close to wrecking on the rocks.'

Suddenly Elizabeth is at my side, her hair undone and whipping about her cheeks. She grips my coat-sleeve so tightly, I can feel the tips of her nails dig into my skin. 'Thomas,' she cries. 'It must be Lettie and her friend!'

'Lettie? Don't be absurd!'

The craft is closer now though I can't tell if its course is intentional or it is just being sucked towards the land by the power of the swells. There are two figures aboard, one in the prow holding up a lantern and the other behind, but how can they be women in such a position and one of them my daughter? Are they really attempting a rescue from below? Then the boat is lifted and propelled forward with shocking speed and after a few short moments we lose sight of it beneath the projecting cliff. I wait for the sound of the crash against the waiting rocks but only the tempest roars in my ears.

'God save them!' Garson exclaims.

Arthur has crawled on his hands and knees to the edge of the abyss and is peering down at such an angle I am sure even a slight increase in the wind will blow him from his perch. Then I watch Horace inch out behind him and grasp his ankles, brave boys to expose themselves in that way for the sake of their brother.

'We'll lose them all!' Elizabeth shouts.

'*For He will give his angels charge concerning you. To guard you in all your ways,*' I murmur, but she does not hear.

We linger there uselessly for the longest time, battered and forlorn, waiting for something, a sign the boat has not been wrecked, or the coming of daylight, though it is many hours off, as if the morning light will provide a way on. I think of how we all journeyed to this island over a piece of property and where we find ourselves now. While I have been absorbed by the fishermen's cause, my youngest son has been bewitched by selkies and may be in mortal danger, and my only daughter may be sailing with another woman on waters rougher than any I have ever seen. What possible secrets dwell in the hearts of my wife and children, and after this night will any of us ever be the same?

Elizabeth

I pray for all our souls and have faith in the Lord. *Yea, though I walk through the valley of the shadow of death, I will fear no evil, for Thou art with me, Thy rod and Thy staff they comfort me.* It is well that I depend on Him so, for all of us on that cliff-top seem so apart from one another, lost in our own speculations of the probable and possible. I can see Thomas's lips moving and assume he is praying too. Ernest stands beside him, his features pale and immobile, and I feel this night is a true test of his own faith as yet untried. Bertie paces back and forth behind us, gesturing occasionally at the sea as if appearing before an assize to determine innocence and guilt in this matter, his own included. I am fearful but proud of Arthur and Horace as they lean like carved figures over the valley of the shadow, and prouder still of Lettie trying to save her brother though she and Margaret Muir have little chance against the wind and sea. With no sign of the vanished boat, it is likely there are three of them on the beach needing rescue. I won't let myself dwell on the image of wreckage and bodies flung like bits of flotsam at Norman's feet. Proud of Lettie, yes, but so troubled by her hidden ways. I resolve amidst the turmoil of my feelings never to let her from my sight again unless I know exactly what she is up to. We all need to get home to Yorkshire and begin again, away from this land of conflict and strange desires that have led Thomas to prison's door and our daughter to another way of life altogether, not to mention Norman and his wild imagination. I supposed I can depend on Bertie, despite his confusions about Alice MacBride, and most of all on Ernest whose feet, like those of his father, are firmly on the ground while his thoughts are of heaven. We shouldn't have left Clem at home by himself. His music won't help him at a time like this.

Clem

I am very upset at being told to stay at home – upset with father for his edict and, as time passes, with Norman for making my wait eternal. But, of course, I don't want anything bad to happen to him, and know when he doesn't turn up that he's out there somewhere, lost and possibly injured. Who would have guessed my little brother had such an imagination! No, that's not right. He hasn't imagined the selkie, he believes it exists because of Mr. Garson's story. If a grown-up tells you he's seen something magical, and you're only ten years old, it's real enough. Maybe if I'd heard the story first I'd be out there on the cliffs looking for…for what? Well, a lost chord of sorts, one needed to complete the score. I'm not making much sense, but one thing is sure – the only way I can deal with what had happened is to include it in my creation. If, before he went off, I'd considered how I would treat Norman musically, my thoughts hadn't been complicated. He's always been the young one, content with collecting insects, and full of questions that don't have any satisfactory answers – 'Why do you think God made butterflies, Clem?' (To give us dominion over them?) or 'Is the music in your fingers, Clem?' (Yes and no). But now he's shown more gumption than any of us and exposed himself to all sorts of dangers.

So I hear them. First the cliff – hard, bracing notes that will not relent, resounding against the entire body – and then the sea – wild and unpredictable plunging of the keys through the lower register that pummels the eardrum without mercy – but most of all, the creature who exists only to spirit him into the depths yet must not succeed. I must lure her instead into my music, finding a way to represent her unforgettably, yet never allowing her to become the dominant strain. I need to talk to Norman, and even Mr. Garson, not so their selkies will become my selkie but so my composition is true to the different forms she takes.

It is late when they arrive home – Ernest, Bertie, Horace, and Arthur. Norman is in bed at Miss Muir's cottage with father, mother, and Lettie watching over him. His leg is badly sprained and there are bruises everywhere, but otherwise he is alright.

'Won't shut up about the damned selkie, though,' Bertie says.

'He'll get over it,' Ernest replies. 'His mind is unsettled at present.'

'It must have already been unsettled to drive him out there in the first place!'

'*Something…has set me dreaming of the winds that play/ Past certain cliffs, along one certain beach/ And turn the topmost edge of waves to spray.*' Arthur is staring intensely at the fire as if these words are glowing in the embers there.

Bertie sniffs. 'You'll never get anywhere with such stuff.'

'It's not mine. Christina Rossetti wrote it, a very great poet.'

'A woman?'

'Yes, Bertie, a woman, and very interested in Catholicism to boot.'

'I'll bet that seal-woman is Papish as well.'

'I think if she exists she contains every religion at once.'

Arthur raises his eyebrows. It is Ernest who has surprised him with this last remark.

Lettie

My hands are blistered and my back is sore, but Norman is safe and so is Margaret and, for the moment, I am content with such blessing. The doctor has pronounced Norman fit under the circumstances, and he will send a cart in the morning. What is needed, he says, is a great deal of rest. The natural health of a young boy will have him on the mend very soon.

Mother and father are sleeping in the chairs by the bed and Margaret and I are dozing in the front room by the fire. My mind is surprisingly calm considering all the images racing through it – the rocks lurching toward us as we surge ahead on the final swell, Norman lying peacefully against the cliff while the wind tears our words from our mouths, our trek across the beach with his wounded weight in our arms, the *Tom Paine* nearly crushing me as we try to cast her off, and the desperate dragging of our oars through the heavy waters. Yes, we were lucky, but Margaret made our luck with her knowledge of the sea and how a boat should ride it. I love her for having shared this with me, but I know there is more to it than simple gratitude. Watching her now in the flickering light of the flames, head resting on a cupped palm, breath soft through parted lips, breasts rising and falling as her heart beats in time with my own, I realize I never want to leave her. The cost will be enormous, but if she will have me I will stay.

Somehow it helps that father and mother are here now as I make my decision because their distress will turn into a great distance and we will never be so close again. And the rest of my family? Until this day, I would have said Norman was too young to understand, but if I tell him Margaret is my selkie perhaps he might. Clem will keep on whatever my presence or absence because the music will always be his reward. Horace won't have much to say but will be pleased at my happiness. Arthur will be pleased as well, but he will have lots to say, most of it wise. I will depend on him as my voice to the world. Bertie will think me foolish. He would never stay here for Alice MacBride's sake but take her back to Yorkshire if he could. Finally, like father, Ernest will not forgive me, my love not so much the abomination as my breaking rules that maintain man's agreement between himself and the Lord.

Margaret stirs, and I cross over to her, kneeling at her feet and pressing my cheek to her thigh.

'Lettie' she says, lifting me up so our eyes meet on a level. When our lips touch, I let go of everything I have ever known.

12. A Distant Music

Thomas

Norman's return was a blessing, but it contained a warning as well. *The Lord giveth and the Lord taketh away*, and what is the life of one small boy in the grand and holy design? We should never be complacent about our earthly possessions even as we value them. Elizabeth and I must look more closely to our children, and our watch will be the easier when we return home. I have been taken up with the Rory Parker affair and missed the danger signs. It is all very well for Norman to pretend he is a naturalist. Perhaps he will be one day, but in the meantime, he must learn some alternatives to Mr. Garson' stories and that the butterflies of the field and the selkies of the sea can be known only to a certain degree. After that, they are part of God's mystery and best left alone. He is young and his body will heal, but his impressionable mind needs the direction I will provide from now on.

Then there is Lettie. Overwhelmed as I was by the dramatic actions taken by herself and Miss Muir, I did not consider how she came to be a sailor in the first place. I could not see or think clearly from the cliff-top, and when Elizabeth told me it was her in the rescue boat I dismissed such an idea and thought only of Norman's safety. The two shadowy figures were not real to me and the particulars of their coming and going remained obscure until after Elizabeth led us to the wharf with the help of Garson's lantern. There Horace and Bertie lifted Norman from the craft and bore him up the steep slope to the cottage. As she walked beside her friend, stepping ahead on the path with her own lantern to mark the way, I saw my daughter wearing men's trousers and heard her quiet laughter. How had she come to this masquerade and intimacy with someone I did not know at all? How had Elizabeth known where to go after the boat disappeared around the headland? Why was I a mere follower in a band of women and young men who seemed untroubled by such questions? It was evident that Miss Muir possessed some remarkable capabilities and we owed Norman's life to her, but Lettie, for all her courage, owed me an explanation.

After the doctor's visit, we sent the boys home and slept in our chairs beside the bed. In the morning, a cart arrived to convey the four of us back to Kirkwall. When I thanked Miss Muir she shook my hand with a surprisingly strong grip. I told her the Lord had been with her as the boat rode those swells, and she smiled and replied that while she had no doubt God had gathered the waters under heaven into one place, she wasn't sure he patrolled them as closely as we liked to believe. It was more likely he was testing us, she said, by leaving us to our own devices. 'It was Lettie I needed out there,' she asserted, and I was somewhat shaken by the thin line she walked between blasphemy and praise.

Norman was in good spirits on the way home, telling us how he'd lowered himself on the rope but couldn't hold on and had fallen onto some combination of seaweed and kelp with his leg bent out of shape. The waves were getting bigger, he said, and would have covered him had the selkie not appeared and pulled him higher up.

'She was beautiful, with long hair and white arms.'

'Did she speak to you?' Lettie asked.

He thought for a moment. 'No, I don't think so. Mr. Garson never said she spoke to him either.'

'Mr. Garson has much to answer for,' I said, and saw the puzzlement on his face.

'Father means, Norman, that Mr. Garson should not have told you that story. It put you and your sister in grave danger.'

'But mother, I'm alright, really.' I could see him looking to Lettie for support.

'I'm alright too,' she said, and there was that relaxed laughter again as if the entire experience had been child's play for which there need be no accountability.

'You should not be!' Elizabeth said sharply, but our recalcitrant daughter only shook her head slightly and reached out to pat her brother's shoulder.

When we were home and Norman tucked into bed after sipping on some broth Elizabeth heated over the fire, I gathered everyone in the parlour. First it was my duty to thank them, including Clement, for their participation in the rescue.

'We didn't do much, father, it was Lettie who led the way.' Arthur's commendation opened the floodgates.

'I'll say,' Bertie exclaimed. 'Where on earth did you learn to sail and row?'

'Lettie can do anything,' Horace said.

Even Ernest, whom I considered my closest ally after Elizabeth, offered his approval. 'You're living proof, Lettie, that *God helps those who help themselves.*'

I should have offered that as a rejoinder to Miss Muir's cavalier dismissal of the Lord's presence. Clem had opened his mouth to make the circle complete, but it was time to assert my authority.

'Certainly Lettie displayed selflessness and bravery, but there are several things I wish to emphasize to you all. As you know, I have been preoccupied with legal matters in Stromness and have not been home as much as usual.' I nodded at Elizabeth. 'Your mother has been my chief ally in this difficult period, managing the household while the rest of you have had a great deal of leeway to pursue your own interests – Ernest and Arthur on their trips to other islands, Bertie in the MacBride case, Horace with the animal doctor, Clem his music, and Lettie…well, whatever it is Lettie has been doing.' I saw a glint in her eye but continued despite. 'Meanwhile, who has been looking after their youngest brother?' There were murmurs of protest, but I carried on. 'I am at fault, but so are you all, with the exception of your tireless mother. 'When was the last time, any of you elder ones spent some time with Norman? You should not have expected your mother and Clem to carry the burden.' Clem smiled but I put him in his place. 'And as for you, young man, where were you when he was making his plans? Lost in your music, no doubt. Well, it's not good enough, and things will have to change. For our remaining stay on the island each of you will spend a good part of the day at home with the family, and especially with Norman who, whatever his outward appearance, will take some time to fully recover from his ordeal.'

There were sighs and shuffles, but no one spoke, and I assumed everything was under control as I wished. Then her voice cut like a blade through my delusion. 'Not I, father,' she said, and in her words I heard the Lord's own twisted by her conviction – *I came not to send peace, but a sword.*

I should have insisted our subsequent exchange occur in private so clear did its disturbing nature quickly become, but she was determined to have it out with us at once.

'What can you mean, Lettie?' Elizabeth cried.

There was no laughter now only a hard resolve in her tone. 'I mean, mother, I am leaving home. I will come to see Norman every day, but I will no longer live with you under this roof.'

I thought Elizabeth would faint and then, when Lettie spoke again, fought to catch my own breath.

'Neither will I return to Yorkshire with the family.'

'Explain yourself, young lady,' I demanded, shaking with anger and a fear that when she did so all would be lost.

'I will live with Margaret at her cottage.'

'But how will you live? You have no income and hers must be modest enough.'

'I don't know yet. Perhaps I will teach. We shall see.'

I looked around at the witnesses to this rebellion and betrayal. Ernest was clearly as shocked as I, his face pale and his hands clasped tightly as if ensuing prayer were the only solution. Bertie was watching from the courtroom of his mind, measuring the evidence, even if the ultimate verdict was not his to give. Horace was gazing at his sister with an affection I could only acknowledge, but I was sure he did not appreciate the inevitable consequences of her stand. Infuriatingly, Arthur was smiling, though I knew he did comprehend the cost if she did not back down. Clement's face was a closed book, but it was the thin volume of youth he was trying to hide. Elizabeth had lapsed into silence, and I was grateful I did not have to deal with two sets of emotions at once. Then, just as I was about to point out how thoughtless and selfish Lettie was being, she erupted.

'That wicked woman has blinded you to your upbringing! I will not have it!'

Lettie sighed. 'You cannot prevent it, mother. I am of age.'

'But how can you choose her over those who have raised you and loved you since you came into this world. What is she to you that you would break our hearts so cruelly?'

I was about to steer the conversation away from personal distress and onto the plane of duty where it belonged when her reply staggered us all.

'It is my own heart I must not break, and it belongs now to Margaret.'

Elizabeth

I watched her through the bedroom window as she walked away from the house that same afternoon. I had stayed upstairs since her appalling declaration, unable to summon up the least bit of sympathy in the face of such desertion. Though I was certain she would eventually return, she had to realize the deep tear she had made in our family fabric. Before she left, I heard her speak to Horace and then to Norman and Clem, their words muffled by the walls and their own subdued tones. What on earth she could say to them, I could not imagine, beyond excuses for her behaviour whose meaning and consequences they are far too young to appreciate. But Arthur is older and wiser, which is why I cannot approve his having met her at the garden gate and taken her valise in hand. They strolled off together as if on Saturday afternoon parade at Cleethorpes. I shall have a sharp word with him before tea.

What I don't understand is how she expects to live. It's all very well to speak of teaching, but there can't be many openings on all the islands put together. That Muir woman, Bertie says, has rent from some land she owns at the edge of Kirkwall, but is that supposed to do their every need? I blame her entirely. Wearing men's trousers and sailing on the open sea made my daughter into someone she is not. Well, the cuffs will begin to fray and the craft will spring a leak soon enough. I only hope Lettie keeps her skirts close by and is steering next to shore when the seams open. Of course, I will never bar her from our door, but she must repent of her wicked ways.

We are all at table with tea and scones on the damask cloth. Arthur appeared while the water was boiling and I was busy with preparations so there was no opportunity to speak. He is sitting back a little with his cup and saucer balanced on his knee while the others have drawn closer to the meal as if huddling up to the warmth of a familiar fire. I wait, as they do, for Thomas to take matters in hand. He butters his scone carefully, trying not to suggest there is any hurry or immediate cause for concern. But everyone knows our household is not the same without her.

'How are you feeling, Norman?' he asks.

We look at our youngest member whose near-loss and rescue, though only yesterday, belong to another time when Lettie was a daughter and sister still in our midst. He could say anything in reply, and we would not be shaken any more than we are. But he is a little boy whose leg doesn't hurt as much as it did and whose firm belief in the selkie's role in his deliverance outweighs any family disagreements. I wonder at Thomas's keeping him here, along with Clement, when there is so much of significance to discuss.

'I can't run yet, but Mr. Garson says it won't be long.'

Mr. Garson came by at noon for a quick visit. I would not have admitted him but heard Horace answer the door and invite him in. He spent just a few minutes with Norman and spoke briefly with Thomas before departing. Thomas told me it was not the proper time to share our concerns, and I suppose he's right. But I don't feel that man should be welcome in our house given his harmful influence on our son.

Thomas clears his throat, places his elbows on the table, and folds his hands in front of his chin. 'Let us pray.'

We bow our heads toward the purgatory, however brief it might be, of our new existence.

'Heavenly Father, we thank Thee for the safe return of our son and brother, Norman, and for renewing our faith in Thy mercy. He was a lost lamb who now is found and restored to his loving flock who promise to watch over him as we are watched over by Thee from above.'

He pauses, and I know he is struggling with what he feels necessary to say.

'We thank Thee as well for granting the strength to our daughter and sister, Lettie, and to her friend Miss Muir to rescue Norman from the beach as they did. Under your pity and guiding hand they overcame the angry waters and lifted Norman from his suffering. The lesson for us, O Lord, for which we are grateful, is that we recognize more than ever before how none of us must stray from the fold or else be lost.'

He is praising and admonishing her now, and while I do not like the inclusion of Miss Muir in our family service, I admit Lettie's courage without hesitation, even as her disobedience and disloyalty still rankles.

'We pray for the souls of all those who stray and ask that they follow Thy guidance to the righteous path. We ask this in Thy name and for Jesus's sake. Amen.'

'Amen,' we all say together. When I look up everyone seemed relieved that Lettie, despite her self-exile, is not to be banned from our hearts, but I am gravely mistaken if I believe any path to reconciliation will be straightforward.

'Now then, 'Thomas says. 'You all know that Lettie has gone off to Miss Muir's cottage. She seems to have the idea that she will have some personal freedom there she cannot find at home. That she is mistaken in this and will eventually see the light, I have no doubt, but meanwhile we must continue as we were and prepare ourselves for our return to Yorkshire. Mr. Taggart and I are to appear before the magistrate in Stromness Wednesday next. Before that he will have spoken out in the pulpit and call for open support for Mr. Parker and the fishermen. As we discussed previously, if we are convicted and gaoled, you will, except for Ernest, return home with your mother. I hope by that time your sister will realize the folly of her ways and be ready to assist with the move.'

There were nods all around. '*We* won't let you down,' Ernest says.

'Mr. Campbell is fairly confident the magistrate will not imprison you,' Bertie announces. 'They've gotten rid of Parker and don't want to give the crowd any new reason to stir.'

'Can I go and see Lettie?' Horace asks.

'Me too!' Norman cries.

'No, I think not,' Thomas answers. 'She must realize there is a cost to the choice she made, and it must not be an easy task for her to pay it off.'

'It is not a matter of holding the purse-strings to her emotions, father, but of Lettie finally discovering what she wants in life.' Arthur has spoken quietly but decisively, and I wonder what had been said between them as they walked away together a few hours before.

Thomas is unperturbed by this opposition between penalty and reward. 'And what is it she has discovered, Arthur?'

He leans forward and appears to sling rather than place his cup and saucer on the cloth, whose twill pattern, I know, is visible on both sides.

'How to love and be loved, father.'

'But that has always been the case at home. We have never withheld our affections from her. And she has always returned them in kind to her parents and brothers.'

'No, you don't understand,' Arthur says, and my world comes crashing down. 'She loves Margaret Muir as you love mother.'

Ernest

Paul said, speaking of the Romans, *For their women exchanged natural relations for those that are contrary to nature.* Arthur would have it our sister has become pagan and wholly aberrant in her behaviour. I cannot believe this is so and feel she has been blinded by the ridiculous idea that her freedom and future are to be found in a crofter's cottage – or a fisherman's, it hardly matters which. Lettie has always been a little too independently-minded for her own good. I have overheard some of her exchanges with mother on the subject of marriage. You would think from the way she goes on that parental expectations of a husband and a proper existence are a punishment akin to servitude under some callous regime or harsh expulsion to a foreign country. I can understand her not wanting to enter into a relationship devoid of affection, wedlock of pure convenience so to speak, but father and mother would never demand this. There are plenty of fine young men at home who hold down good positions and would provide for a minister's daughter as she is accustomed. But Lettie will have to make some effort with her appearance and much more with her attitude if they are to be encouraged as suitors.

Arthur has altogether too much imagination. Miss Muir undoubtedly lives a life untrammeled by the usual rules. I understand her mother died when she was quite young and her father not so long after that, leaving her without guidance and a sense of decorum. She cannot be blamed for such loss, but certainly she should be accountable for her adult actions and influence on others. If she wants to sail the high seas and carry on in dress and manner as if she were a man, all well and good, but to bring others under her sway is reprehensible. I do not believe she attends church regularly but has set herself up as priestess of her own domain. The true faith is larger than any she might feel she has constructed, so rather than proselytize her convictions I would rather she remember 1st Timothy – *Let the women learn in silence with all subjection.*

The trouble is, of course, I can be only grateful she and Lettie did not remain quiet in thought and deed else Norman would certainly have perished. And it does seem that Lettie played a necessary part in the rescue, trousers and all. If she had not met Miss Muir and become comfortable in the boat, we would have all stood helpless on the cliff-top while the wind and waves pummeled the thin strips of sand and flesh beneath. If my sister was clearly an instrument of the Lord in her efforts to save Norman, why must she not also be in the Lord's hands in her intimacy with Miss Muir? It is like those contradictions of faith I discussed with Mr. Scott – they all have to be held in the head at once and one is not to be touted at the expense of another. Or is it that she has simply surrendered to temptation and crossed a line of insubordination and infidelity of her own free will that Mr. Wesley tells us we all possess while the Lord looks on from afar? Mother is distraught, and father has the Parker case on his plate, so I am afraid Lettie is going to have to realize on her own, and without too much time wasted, what is the proper course. She will not listen to me or Bertie, but if Arthur is to be her only guide she may well be lost.

This Sunday I should like to preach in any village not too far from Miss Muir's cottage and take as my subject the parable of the prodigal son. Word might well make its way along the coast that redemption is possible through the return of the reckless to the fold. But everything is coming to a head here in Kirkwall. Mr. Taggart is to give his own sermon in Chapel in which he will call for a protest by all island citizens in support of Rory Parker and the fishermen. I cannot be absent for that. Three days later, he and father will appear before the magistrate and answer for their role in aiding Mr. Parker's escape. Who knows what role the response of the populace to the sermon will play in the court's decision? If it is a peaceful resistance, perhaps the magistrate will see no real harm done by Taggart's plea, and therefore mete out sufficient punishment in the form of a lecture and fine. But if things turn sour and even violent, then the connection between aiding Parker and the threat of larger unrest will be obvious to those in charge. I fear Taggart and father will be taken as the perpetrators of civil disobedience and strife, and the penalty will be shaped to fit the larger crime. If so, everyone must head for Yorkshire, Lettie or no Lettie, and I will become minister *pro tempore* here though I will have no authority but the pulpit. Perhaps then I can mention the prodigal son in an aside while giving my main attention to the true cause for which father is willing to sacrifice himself.

When I awoke this morning I was determined to take charge of my brothers and prompt them to consider what contribution they might make to the well-being of our family in such a difficult time. But father's directive was ignored after he left early to consult with Mr. Taggart. Bertie went off to meet with Mr. Campbell and Arthur strode out blatantly after breakfast to visit Lettie and Miss Muir despite my admonishments. Horace announced he had to go to work with Mr. Peverel and Clem that he would be at Mrs. Drever's playing the piano. That left me with Norman who is too young to expect much of, as especially evidenced by his recent quest and apparent failure to understand how he put the lives of others in danger. When I started to tell him of his sister's surrender of her own safety, prepared to create a parable on the subject, he replied that he knew she would come for him then offered up an image whose combination of blasphemy and beauty left me speechless, so worshipful was he and his words so filled with possibility.

'The selkie had Lettie's face, Ernest. I didn't know it before, but now I do.'

Bertie

Mr. Campbell says there is a possible way out for father and Mr. Taggart. While their case will not be helped if Taggart speaks out for justice in the pulpit, he will advise them to remain silent when asked in court about their aid to Rory Parker. British subjects have the right to do so even though a refusal to answer questions is generally taken as an admission of guilt. But since no one actually witnessed them helping Parker escape at the harbour, their involvement is not provable except by self-incrimination. Yes, a man saw them in Parker's company outside the Chapel in Stromness, but without their own testimony, or Parker's, there is nothing to say they were protecting him or to connect them to his flight.

When we had all gathered in his office, father told Campbell that he fudged the truth when the constable asked him if he had seen Parker 'recently' and the accused man was hiding only a few feet above his head.

'That is between you and your conscience, but I'd say essentially you told the truth,' Campbell replied. 'In the meantime, I shall ask the constable about his question and your response that night. It will be on the record even if I do not bring it up with you or Taggart.'

'I am uncomfortable about remaining silent,' father said.

'I understand. But there is a good chance it will keep you free to support Mr. Parker's cause, and I believe silence is not, to borrow your words, any fudging of the truth.'

'It is an avoidance of it, though.'

Campbell sighed heavily, clearly frustrated by his client's balking at likely salvation. It was then I took my own chance that would make or break us. That morning, expecting father's objection to Campbell's tactic, I had desperately asked Ernest if the Bible said anything about the value of keeping mum. He thought for a few moments.

'Is this to help father?'

'If he is willing to be helped.' I explained the situation.

He thought for a bit. 'Well then, Proverbs. I'd have to look up the exact chapter and verse, but I'm not sure he'll like it.'

'Tell me, Ernest.'

'Even a fool who keeps silent is considered wise; when he closes his lips he is deemed intelligent.'

'Yes, I see what you mean.' I did not relish the thought of associating father with a fool, but needs must I told myself.

Now in Campbell's office I summoned up my courage. 'Father, if I may…'

'What is it, Bertie?' His tone was gruff and impatient.

I was nervous and could not recall the exact quotation so I had to leave it in his hands. 'Well, I do not know the Bible as you and Ernest do, but aren't there some words in Proverbs about a man being considered wise when he decides not to speak?' At that moment I hoped the Lord was listening as I prayed He would jog father's scriptural memory.

Out of the corner of my eye I saw Mr. Taggart smile. 'He's hit on it, Thomas, you must admit!'

Father looked at me quizzically. 'I'm pleased that you know your Proverbs, Bertie,' he said. If he had any suspicions about brotherly collaboration, he was keeping them to himself for the moment. 'Though I trust you do not consider your father a fool.'

'Will someone please inform me,' Mr. Campbell pleaded.

Taggart gave him the quotation, and Campbell chuckled. 'The law couldn't say it any better. Well, sir, does that take care of your objection?'

I knew father would see no humour in any interpretation of the Good Book and hoped Campbell hadn't gone too far with his legal comparison.

'Not by itself, but as my learned son must know, there are other verses to add to our collection plate. Psalm 62:5, Bertie?'

'I…I cannot remember,' I stammered.

'No, I expect not. Perhaps I should ask Ernest.' He turned to Mr. Campbell. 'There is only one law, sir, for us all. *For God alone, O my soul, wait in silence, for my hope is from him.*'

Buoyed by the prospect of victory, I went to see Alice. I had no illusions there, but if Lettie was able to admit her feelings I would not be a man if I couldn't do the same, different though we were beyond the matter of our sex. My sister would have to come to her senses and realize that a giddy infatuation that crossed the bounds of decency could not last. My feelings, which were perfectly normal, were up against the bonds of marriage and equally doomed. Nonetheless, Lettie had made her declaration, and I was determined to do the same.

Alice had lost weight, and the rouge in her cheeks did not hide her pale complexion. For the first time I understood what the gaoling of her husband meant and the judgment upon her. When I said she should pay no attention to idle gossip, there was a flash of anger in her eyes.

'I know I damned him,' she said. 'But they paid attention only to what I had written as a girl and dismissed my loyalty to Jamie and the children. They are hypocrites, all of them. At least I did not deny who I was back then, silly as I might have been by putting pen to paper. I should like to read their private letters in public and pass sentence on their youthful follies!'

'How is Jamie?' I asked. I knew from Campbell he was holding up but had been remiss in not visiting him because of the business with father, Norman, and Lettie.

'Three weeks and he shall be home. I do not know if we shall stay here, though he insists we must hold our heads high. I think the mainland might prove better ground if I can convince my parents to travel with us.'

'We shall all be gone to Yorkshire by then,' I said. 'I am more hopeful than ever that my father and Mr. Taggart will be let off with a fine. My sister, however, is another matter.'

I told her about Lettie, including the story of Norman's rescue. She listened without interruption, her two girls amusing themselves at her feet with a ball of yarn as they tied knots on each other's fingers.

'She is very brave,' she declared when I had done.

'Well, I know my stomach would have been in my throat had I been in that boat with her.'

'Yes, but that's not all of it. She's gone on another voyage now, one of the heart, and will likely not return.'

'Of course she will. She must,' I said angrily.

'I've met Margaret Muir. 'She's an extraordinary woman.'

I was tired of other people, and this was the one opening I would have.

'You need someone to tell you, Alice, of your own remarkable qualities.' As good a man as Jamie MacBride was, I knew he could never praise her as she deserved. But before I could continue, she held up her hand.

'There is something I must tell you, and then we will say goodbye. Forever,' she added, as if to emphasize time and distance for us both.

'Alice,' I protested, but she would not be silenced.

'I did provoke Roger that day,' she said.

Why was she dwelling on the past? 'Yes, but you were still a schoolgirl.'

'No, I mean in his barn when he offered me the two lambs.'

Horace

I make my plans and take them to Lettie.

'Father would never let me stop here alone,' I tell her, 'but if you are staying then I will have someone to look after me properly. If Miss Muir allows it, I can build a little cottage next door before the winter. I will work for Mr. Peverel and that way I can give you money each week, but not be a bother to you or her.'

'It's a wonderful thought, Horace, but you will never gain father's permission.'

'Why not? He'll let you stay.'

'He's not letting me do anything. I'm of age so he can't prevent me leading my own life. And it's clear he's not at all happy about it.'

She must see my disappointment because she quickly comes up with a plan of her own.

'There's plenty of time' she says. 'Next year when you're sixteen you should insist on coming back up here for a holiday. Then we'll talk things over. Meanwhile, get some experience with a veterinarian at home and Mr. Peverel will hold a spot for you.'

I won't give up so easily. 'What if I just tell father I'm staying? How could he prevent it?'

'Listen to me, Horace. You can't add to the strife I've brought to the family. When you're older, you'll understand more completely, but right now you should be able to realize what it's like for a daughter to tell her parents she's going against their wishes, not for a short time but forever. They can't have a son do a similar thing, at least not so soon. You're the steady one, and they'd likely be more shocked that you left them than they are with me. And that shock would be worsened because they'd suspect it was me who influenced you.'

'Arthur says you love Miss Muir.'

'I do.'

'Like a man loves a woman. What does he mean?'

'Well, there's no man involved, is there? So I don't think he's quite accurate. But he is the one who best understands my feelings for Margaret, and I'd guess he means we'll be living together as if we were married.'

It doesn't make sense to me. Two mares in the same stall can't have children. It takes a stallion to do that. Isn't that why people get married, I ask her.

'Yes, most of the time. But often people just love one another and that's enough.'

'And it doesn't matter if they're two women?'

'It shouldn't matter, but it does to people like mother and father who've been raised in the Chapel and believe that scripture can say no wrong. You must realize they'll never forgive me because...well, because their God will never forgive me.' She reaches out and takes my hand. 'Promise me you'll never give them the opportunity to judge you that way.'

I am sad that it will be a long time before I see her again, and I wonder if father and mother will ever want me to see her. 'I promise,' I say. 'But do you think Miss Muir will let me build that cottage one day?'

'I'm sure she will.'

On the way back I walk up to the edge of the cliff where we had all been the night of Norman's rescue. In the sunlight everything looks normal, and I can see how he thought it was possible to get down. The swells haven't changed much, though, and I watch them roll towards the caves and hear their cannon fire as they collide with the rock inside. The entrance to the cove is more narrow than I remember, and I don't see how Lettie and Miss Muir sailed in safely through the darkness. Then, once they had Norman, how did they row out to the open sea, two women against all that power? There is a bond between them because they could have died. That is what father and mother should keep in mind.

As for Norman, I want to ask him and Mr. Garson more about the selkie. If they are like seals below and women above, how do they breath underwater? What would Mr. Peverel find if he opened one up? I'm glad no one has ever caught such a creature, but why is that? How do they escape all the nets or get away on the beaches when they must be so slow in movement? Why is it only some people see them through all the years, and why is one of those people Norman? I never asked such questions before I came to this island.

Arthur

If sea were land and land were sea
My sister here would wander free
Part the grasses of passion's earth
Sound the depths of passion's firth

But love is just a passing air
That haunts the breath of any pair
Blows a wind nor hot nor cold
Blowing still when love grows old.

Why have I written this? I believe in Lettie's feelings for Margaret Muir. That they should have found one another seems miraculous, and I use that term without hesitation. Father and mother should do the same instead of reserving their astonishment for loaves and fishes. That their relationship was forged in the fire of their rescue of Norman is undeniable. It is extraordinary that father can praise them for saving his youngest son but not allow that it was their love for one another that gave them the strength to do so. Why, then, the possibilities of human vision in my first stanza and the presumption in the second, as in Ecclesiastes, that it is always the earth that abideth forever under the aegis of heaven? All these biblical images have trapped me in father's web. Perhaps I should simply express my hope for their happiness with a different second stanza.

So love becomes a lasting air
That forms the breath of any pair
Warm wind of promise never cold
Nurtured love does not grow old.

I don't know what the reaction will be when the time comes to board the south-bound train and Lettie does not appear on the platform submissive and begging pardon. Whether or not father escapes the clutches of the law, her absence – and the reasons for it – will create a hole in the family heart that cannot be mended.

I can't help but compare Lettie and Norman and note the intersection of their particular quests. Margaret Muir is a sea-creature of sorts and has apparently transformed Lettie into a partner capable of making her own way through waters rough and smooth. Norman, if he but knew it, has a sister about to become more fabled than real in certain Yorkshire circles. What he does know is that she appeared from the sea to rescue him, and from what Ernest has told me he is now merging her with the selkie he says pulled him up on the shore. I think Norman will keep both females alive in his collector's mind, and he might eventually be the one –should he outlive us all, as expected – to tell the entire Orkney story without the fatal prejudices of his older brothers and parents. In the meantime, I am continuing to visit Lettie and Margaret every day, and after we return home I shall return as much as possible. Horace has told me he wants to come north again when he is sixteen and build a cottage beside theirs. Once he gets the bit between his teeth, he can prove quite stubborn, and I suspect father will not be able to hold him. What a great deal of change has occurred in the few weeks we have been here, and all, despite the pain, for the better.

We came in our disguise
To keep ourselves intact
And left with opened eyes
On myth as well as fact

No one who knew us well
Would recognize us now
We shift our shapes to tell
New stories and new vows

On cliff-tops we lack sight
With only dark below
Then storm gives way to light
Our boat kens where to go

The wounds may never heal
That bleed along the way
From out that battered hull
Whose wood-veins have their say

What marks where home is found
Or whether we are lost?
Once flat the world is round
Whatever seas are crossed

Clem

I hadn't given much thought to how Lettie would fit into my piece. Perhaps I was just putting it off for no reason, but she had always seemed to live in another world from me because she was so much older and my only sister, and that made capturing her in regular notes and chords very difficult to begin with. I can recognize the shared rhythms of my brothers as they walk and talk, and whatever the differences in our characters there has always been that familiarity to draw on. But Lettie is a world unto herself, closest to mother, I suppose, even though I can see her special fondness for Horace. Now she has suddenly left us behind and gone off to live with Margaret Muir. I have to deal with her break in my music and with the enormity of what she's done. It's not whether I agree or disagree with her decision, as I told Ernest when he warned me not to say anything vexatious, but that I have to try to fill the silence brought about by her going away.

First, there is the physical space she now occupies. I haven't been to Margaret Muir's cottage, but I can imagine it from what Norman has described. It sits on high ground and is visible, like so many dwellings on the island, from any passing ship. Inside is like being in a ship's cabin where everything is close together, but even so you don't feel crowded. There's a warm, safe feeling you get from the wind and rain being on the outside and the fire burning in the grate.

'How many chairs are there in front of the hearth?' I asked him.

'Why?'

'I just need to know.'

'There's two. I saw Lettie sitting on one side and Margaret on the other.'

'You call her Margaret, then?'

'She told me to.'

So there is peace in that front room and a good feeling throughout the rest of the cottage. I don't need to worry about Lettie, it seems. Yet I know the disruption she has caused to our family, and I must convey that with sharp cadences and quick, jarring tempos that signal her departure. Before that there is the rescue, which is really what started it all. The music must somehow call up the boat borne helplessly on the swells yet at the same time skilfully dancing around the rocks. They have control but no control as they make for the beach. Then there is the difficult conveyance of Norman into the boat, accompanied by the spirit of the selkie and followed by the strenuous pulling on the oars (to a steady count) out to sea. It will be the most difficult part to compose, but that's only fitting because Lettie's departure has changed everything. And maybe I should end the entire piece with this collision of tranquility and turmoil unresolved. If she should come home, as I know father and mother expect, then I can always add an extra phrase, though whether it would convey harmony or further discord remains to be seen. I must go to Mrs. Drever's to work all this out. It's a good thing Norman is confined to the house until his leg is completely better since he would just distract me from my task.

There's something else I have to consider. I started out by wanting to write the piece for Horace because he wasn't going to be allowed to stay here. But that's mixed-up because Lettie *is* staying. The original structure was made easy by having Horace at the centre and three of us on either side. I didn't think to include father and mother because, by the very nature of things, I can't possibly know them as well as I do my brothers and even Lettie. Besides, I had no thought of music when they made their decision to come here – which occurred in a previous time and belonged to the adult world that governs our own from on high with rules and reprimands.

Neither world is the same anymore. Lettie, one of their children, has changed the rules and shaken their perches. How can I not try to reveal this as honestly as possible? The problem will be how to fit them into the whole because, as I now realize, despite their roosts they are everywhere in our lives, and all I have composed about the others has been shaped by their influence on me and them. Maybe I should be writing a symphony or at the very least an octet that will take into account eight points of view (father's and mother's being the same, as they mostly are when it comes to us), but I don't know other instruments nearly as well as the piano. I'll ask Mr. Berry how best to proceed. Ever since that dream, though, I've been nervous about returning to the cathedral.

Norman

I would go back there if I could. That's what nobody seems to understand. Lettie would too, but she's not here anymore. Why was it her face I saw in the selkie's? How could she be there already when she had to land the boat with Margaret? But she was, so she rescued me twice. When Mr. Garson comes to visit I tell him this.

'Perhaps she did,' he says. 'The selkie is whoever we need her to be, after all.'

'What do you mean?'

'I mean I hadn't gone looking for the stuff of fishermen's tales, only for the seals I was sure lived in the caves. Remember I told you I thought I saw the top half of a seal change into the form of a woman. Unlike you, I didn't recognize her, but maybe she was there to remind me that we shouldn't take stories for granted.'

'Do you think I could find her again? I want to see if Lettie's face is still there.'

'I think you were given something on that beach, Norman,' he told me, 'something that only comes once, and it's bound up in the fact that nobody died when they so easily could have. Do you want to put things to the test again at the risk of those who love you losing their lives?'

I shook my head.

'Well then, think about how lucky you are to have escaped with your own life and with a memory that few people in this world ever have.'

Just then I heard mother cough outside my door, and Mr. Garson said it was time to for him to leave.

What I didn't tell him was that if Lettie was still in the selkie's face then maybe I could persuade her to come home with me. I like Margaret, and Arthur says Lettie loves her, but mother and father are very unhappy, and I am too because she's not here. Mother told me Lettie won't be allowed to visit me unless she decides to come home where she belongs. If she doesn't come before my leg is better and we go back to Yorkshire without her, I might never see her again. No, when I get bigger and father can't tell me what to do I'll get on the train and go to the cottage. I know Horace and Arthur aren't mad at her so maybe they'll come with me.

The only other person I told about Lettie's face is Ernest. When I did he looked down for a minute as if he was angry. He's going to give me a lecture, I thought. Then he lifted his head, and the warmth of his smile was like the sun on my face when I am chasing butterflies.

Lettie

So my new life begins. I regret the pain I have caused mother and father, but had I not chosen as I did I would have spent the rest of my days mourning my loss. It would have been bad enough for them if I had run off with a man, but they would have recovered as long as I married him. Arthur has told me he has left them with no illusions about my feelings for Margaret, and I am glad of that. But he also says they are expecting my repentance and return to Yorkshire with them. How can they think that I would reveal myself as I have only to admit the error of my ways and ask forgiveness a few days later?

I have known all my life that my family was a protective shield harbouring me until I could break free in some fashion and go my own way. Even as a little girl I felt there was another world for me to step into, like the mirror's reflection in Mr. Carroll's book that opens up for Alice so she can become a 'flower that moves about.' It wasn't something I could explain to anyone though I soon recognized Arthur as a kind of ally because of his imaginative flights and Horace as the dearest of my brothers because he doesn't have a dishonest or selfish bone in his body. There were others who stirred me, even if inadvertently. I remember one of my spinster schoolteachers, Miss Thain, introducing me to a female companion on the street one day and how I sensed something between them, a spark of sorts, and an undisguised happiness gained from one another's company such as I had never seen at home. That was my first real insight into distinctions in the adult world I had previously viewed as undivided. When I tried to write a note to Miss Thain to explain what she had given me, I couldn't find the right words because I was too young to understand the love I had witnessed.

Mother and father will think of Margaret and I as hiding our shame in this isolated spot and will forever associate such remoteness with our transgression of all the rules. But the truth is we will soon be exposed for who we are because the cottage sits in full view of any passer-by and everyone on the island talks to everyone else. At times we will become the subject of idle gossip and, at others, just a modest couple in the landscape not worth the bother. If the gossip becomes vicious we'll have to stand tall, and if we threaten to become too ordinary we'll have to keep each other on our toes. I spoke with Arthur about all this when he came by.

'I'll miss you, but I won't mourn for you,' he said.

I laughed. 'I know you won't. You'll be too busy becoming famous for your poems.'

He gave me a rueful smile. 'Do you really think so? Clem's much more likely to succeed. He's composing some big piano piece, Norman tells me. It's got us all in it, if you can imagine that.'

'Clem will do very well, but he's much too serious and possessive about everything. If he keeps going that way, I worry he'll settle for the solidity of a good job as church organist or choirmaster rather than step into the unknown as the musician he could really be. You on the other hand…'

'I on the other hand won't settle down at all, but I'm afraid I'll never meet the poet I could really be.'

'Why not?'

'I'm a great observer, Lettie. Like Wordsworth sometimes, seeing into the life of things. But I don't have his way with words to make me his equal.'

'But you won't stop trying?'

'No, I won't stop. I've been writing a lot here, and I will send you the poems after I get home and make some changes to them.'

I told him about Horace's wish to live by us.

'Having lost you to these islands, father will guard him all the more fiercely.'

'That's true, but Horace has a will of his own, and what he wants to do with his life falls completely within the usual sphere of things. Father can't object to that.'

'No, but it's your influence that will concern him.'

'I've gone over to the enemy, you mean.'

'Yes, given the enemy is anything of which the Good Book doesn't approve.'

'I don't feel heretical, Arthur. In fact, for the first time in my life I feel normal.'

'That's just the problem, isn't it, the definition of normal, I mean. Shelley faced the same ordeal.'

When I gave a little grimace at having the old example offered in my defence, he shrugged.

'Well, then, how about Mary who gave up so much to be with him? I think she must have written *Frankenstein* to question what normalcy is.' He clapped his hands. 'In the novel Victor Frankenstein creates a female creature in a laboratory on the Orkneys after the monster demands he be granted happiness like any ordinary human being. That's what you must do, Lettie, to show father you're not just a fallen woman who's but another kind of monster in his eyes. Write an island story in which an outcast and her mate live happily ever after!'

I laughed until I couldn't catch my breath. 'No one wants to read about the bliss of monsters,' I managed to say finally.

'No, I suppose not. But seriously, Lettie, you will be happy, won't you?'

'I *am* happy, Arthur, and grateful for that. What comes will come. That's what I tell myself, at least. I had a dream the other night that father confronted and condemned me with scripture. I felt like a heathen and thought of the Romans being preached to by St. Paul for purposes of conversion. When I woke up I knew I had to find an answer to his certainty, and where else to look but the Book of Romans in Margaret's Bible? Verse 12:2 – *Do not be conformed to this world, but be transformed by the renewal of your mind, that by testing you may discern what is the will of God, what is good and acceptable, and perfect.* If I ever meet him again in dreams or in the flesh that is what I will say.'

I asked after Norman, saying it was the saddest result of my actions that I could not visit him. When Arthur told me what Ernest had shared with him about my face intertwining with the selkie's own, I wept.

In our embrace that night Margaret and I swam as one in the sea where we had been born.

The Frame

Any nineteenth-century British family would be shaken by the choice Lettie has made. Thomas's belief in his role as patriarch and as the servant of his God has him convinced she must repent and return to his house. Failing that, his Yorkshire reputation would be severely undermined, especially since we know he will not lie about having seen her 'recently' with Margaret Muir. As for Elizabeth, it seems her sense of shame at her daughter's disgracing of all decent values will never be pardoned except by an abasement that renders Christian mercy unavoidable. She too expects atonement at the doorstep. For her and Thomas, although they can't admit it, the best option is forgiveness and reconciliation.

Ernest, because the Lord moves in mysterious ways, is torn between condemnation of his sister's immorality and an abiding recognition that without her affections for Margaret Muir the grace inherent in his youngest brother's vision of Lettie's face would never have surfaced.

Bertie's concerns are mostly for his father's legal predicament and Alice MacBride's well-being. While he is about to be disabused of his belief in Alice's perfection, he's never thought of Lettie as the ideal sister and will deal with her when all other appeals are lost.

Horace is puzzling out the complexities of sexual relations under Lettie's guidance and doesn't appear completely convinced by her arguments, though he is certainly sympathetic. Most important, mainly because of Norman's quest he senses that bodily dissection doesn't necessarily reveal all there is to know about cats, selkies, or human beings.

Unlike Horace, Arthur struggles self-consciously with his inner life or at least the articulation of it, and if you asked him would say that in all the family only he and Lettie are capable of such expression. Where it gets them remains to be seen.

Clem, as usual, has diverted strife and doubt into his music. His descriptions of his work suggest he's trying to represent real character and feeling, but his scored figures are simultaneously too precise and insubstantial to reveal the ragged edges of personality or ever fully materialize.

For Norman, the loss of Lettie when she so recently found *him* is alarming. Although the youngest and most naive, he's not so different from his father and eldest brother in his efforts to employ symbol to deal with the troubling spaces between myth and reality.

As for Lettie, she's finally going to try to live out her inner life in tangible fashion. Without intending it, she's become the catalyst for an enormous shifting of perception within the family, and I suspect the reverberations will ripple through subsequent generations.

I've gone over some of this before, but two of the ancestors in the 'origin' photograph lived and died in ways that eventually had their impact on me.

Letitia married and died in childbirth (her second pregnancy), but previously delivered a daughter, Enid, who was an aging lesbian when I met her in 1966, and not, in my youthful North American eyes, a happy one. She had a probing, intelligent mind but used it in rigid and even petty ways to take control of situations. My own youthful limitations, of course, determined my negative response to her, and my portrait of Lettie is a partial attempt to limn and expand the past that shaped us both. The portrait is intended, in its way, as homage to Enid's own grasp at freedom and to her partner whom I remember as a good-natured, kindly woman who didn't treat me as an inferior colonial specimen or long-haired reprobate.

Then there is my grandfather Clement who, as I've said, became a choirmaster and organist in a Lincolnshire church. I have a silver-mounted conductor's baton given him in 1922 by the Brighowgate Children's Home choir for his 'splendid and self-sacrificing work' voluntarily undertaken. A local councillor praised him for his role 'in fitting these boys and girls to be useful citizens of the Empire for the truest economy is a soul redeemed and a life saved.' There's an indisputably feeling of warm connection to this man I never met when I hold his embossed instrument, but I was raised by my mother to question the gap between his religious profession and his moral hypocrisy, a flaw, my agnostic biases say, possibly inherited from his Methodist minister father and shared with his ordained brother. He damned my mother to a distant purgatory by cutting off all ties with her when she married and left for Canada in 1946. Years later, she had her dream about him the night before he died 3500 miles away in which he looked at her but did not speak, and I suppose his revised presence in these pages is just another kind of dream in which dialogue between then and now has a role. I don't know whether Arthur really wrote and published poems as I eventually did, or admired Shelley like me, but my grandfather apparently did compose hymns (there are church records) so the creativity in one storied brother has some basis in fact.

When they gathered in the garden for the photograph, they were all participating, knowingly or not, in a ritual of projection – of themselves on their own present and of their images on the future of others not yet

206

born who might speak of an ancestral past. Undoubtedly, and primarily, they all believed in a greater preservation beyond that provided by the camera lens, and it may be they are now gazing down aghast at my presumptions yet filled with hope I will one day see the true light. If they do still yearn for some earthly remembrance of who they were, the lens I have fashioned reveals them in a different light as who they have become to me.

13. The Voyage Out

Elizabeth

I was very frightened when Thomas went before the magistrate. Shop-owners had followed Mr. Taggart's direction and had refused to serve officials of whatever stripe while people in general ignored any of their neighbours who did not support the fishermen and Rory Parker's safe return. The law had been powerless as it could not force good feeling in the populace, and I was afraid it would therefore seek to make an example of two Methodist ministers who had interfered with the course of justice, and especially of the ordained Englishman who would not deny he had helped a fugitive escape. I had been too upset to attend the proceedings, and before Thomas came home from the court, I feared the worst, that a heavy fine had been imposed and, as a lesson, some time in gaol. My relief was great when he arrived and told me of his contribution to the Stromness harbour fund.

'How did you ever get away with such a pittance?'

'Now my dear, five pounds is hardly a trifle.'

'Don't tease me at a time like this, Thomas. You know very well what I mean.'

'Why aren't you talking to an impoverished man through prison bars?'

'Yes, precisely.'

'Well, let's say that the magistrate was prepared to put Taggart away but not myself and an upright young man who aspires to be a minister and would speak like one from the Chapel pulpit.'

'Ernest! What has Ernest got to do with it?'

'I told his honour that I was prepared to repeat Taggart's message this coming Sunday and that if I were prevented from doing so again the following week my eldest son would speak out. Soon there would be three of us in gaol, the boats would remain in the harbour, and many angry people would further disrupt normal relations throughout the island.'

'But would you have let it go that far? To have Ernest imprisoned as well?'

'It would have been the only way. We could not have abandoned our principles or our actions based upon them.'

'Did you consult with Ernest beforehand?'

'I know my own son, Elizabeth, and you should too.'

It seemed as if my opinion in the matter was irrelevant. Of course, we had previously spoken about Ernest taking over preaching duties if Mr. Taggart and then Thomas were prevented from carrying on. But there had never been any talk of him putting himself at risk. Where would that have left us if he and his father were locked up? Bertie would be in charge of getting us home, and he would do a fine job with the tickets and transportation, but whom would I depend upon for true support with Lettie gone as well? Arthur and Horace wouldn't be much help, and Clement and Norman would be a handful without proper supervision. Nonetheless, I told myself I needn't worry, despite my relegation to the edges of great decision-making. The family that had arrived here almost two months ago could soon leave for Yorkshire intact. Surely, once our travel plans were in order, the prodigal would surely forsake her false idol and return to the path of righteousness.

I would not be put aside this time. 'When our daughter comes home,' I told him, 'we will both greet her at the door.'

He nodded, but for the first time in our marriage I felt a slight sliver of unease between us.

'And Thomas,' I added, 'what is to be said to her, before or after, we will say together.'

He looked surprised, perhaps because it was the first time I had ever asserted myself so directly. He ruled over six sons who never questioned his authority, but the perfection of his reign had not applied to Lettie, and what she had done had shaken *our* dominion. I would not let it happen again.

She was my first-born, and I have loved her all her life for that. For almost two years, before Ernest arrived, I had her to myself. She was a strong baby with never a moment of colic, who giggled and cooed much more than she made a sour face or let the tears flow. Her babbling turned very quickly into words, and she was very determined with her young talk, as if forceful sounds and limited vocabulary could successfully release her thoughts and feelings. But she was also loyal and affectionate, at least until her girlhood advanced and she became more independent and, at times, aloof. Before that we had many good hours together in the kitchen or reading and talking by the fire while the boys played their rough games outside. Sometimes she would sigh and turn her face from her book to the window. I never thought she really wanted to be with them, and only gradually realized their cries and commotions were signals of possibility she could not ignore. I remember the morning when I first thought she felt restricted in my company. Arthur, his cheeks glowing from the cold air sweeping down from the moors, had come running inside to tell us he'd beaten his two older brothers in a race and was the champion of the family. I congratulated him, then Lettie spoke up.

'How do you know that you're the champion.'

'Well, Ernest and Bertie are sitting on the ground with their tongues hanging out. That's after I left them behind in a run from the front door to the old beech tree and back. Horace is too slow, and Clem and Norman are just kids.'

He was all of ten or eleven himself.

'And that leaves…?

Arthur was confused for a moment. He looked at me and then at her and suddenly knew what she meant. He burst out laughing. 'Girls can't run.' he announced.

'Can't or don't?' she asked.

'Look at your skirts,' he said. 'You'd have to hold them with one hand. I'd be at the tree before you were halfway there.'

'What if I ran in my knickers?'

'Hush, Lettie,' I said.

It is only now I can see that's finally what she did with Margaret Muir when they won the race for Norman.

Bertie

'What barn?' I asked dully as if my tongue were frozen in opposition to my racing mind.

'You know very well what barn,' she said. 'Where else did I see those two lambs?'

The sharpness of her tone cut through my halting condition in no uncertain terms, leaving tiny shards of ice in its wake. I managed to push them aside. 'How do you mean you provoked him?'

'Honestly, Bertie, you'd think a barrister like yourself would put two and two together, or' – there was actually a twinkle in her eye – 'in this case one and one.'

I couldn't believe she was joking about so serious a matter. 'Then Roger Nicholas was telling the truth?'

We were standing in her living room a few feet apart, but now she drew closer as if to share a confidence. 'In a manner of speaking,' she said, 'or perhaps I'd best put it, only to a point.'

'You did kiss him, then?'

'Not as he described.'

'For God's sake, Alice!'

'Well, I was touched that he'd give me those two lambs for the girls, and I suppose that kindled memories of when we'd been on better terms. I thought his generosity meant he was forgiving me for abandoning him for Jamie so long ago, and, without thinking, I responded in kind.'

'In kind?'

'What else has a woman to offer except affection? I threw my arms around him and pecked him on the cheek, that's all.'

'But don't you see how he was bound to react?'

'You mean he was entitled to become overbearing and insist that he still loved me? If I had not fought him off who knows what would have happened?'

I was aghast at her duplicity. Nothing would have changed in court had her actions been known, but her reputation, damaged as it had been by that letter, would have been permanently broken. I began to see Roger Nicholas in a different light. Naturally, he should have held himself in check, but the intimacy, after so many years of distance, was fierce. She seemed incapable of recognizing the effect she had on people and would take little if any responsibility for what had occurred. There was always something she kept hidden then sprung upon you without warning. Likely my face revealed my thoughts for she soon took up her own defence.

'You're judging me, aren't you? And harshly, as well.'

'You never seem to quite tell the truth, Alice.'

'I'm telling you now.'

'But what else will there be to come out after this?'

I'll never forget the mocking sound of her voice as she leaned even closer until our faces were just a few inches apart. 'Do you mean did I ever take Roger Nicholas into my bed?'

I jumped back as if stung. 'How can you speak so?'

'That's what you were thinking, wasn't it? Come now, you insist you're after the truth.'

I was about to deny her accusation, as any gentleman would, but she was relentless. 'How long have *you* wanted to kiss me, Bertie?'

It was as if a strange woman had walked into my bedroom as I was undressing and I was helpless to conceal my exposure to her gaze. Even though she had not embraced me, I knew how Roger Nicholas had felt in the barn because, stranger or not, I wanted to take her in my arms and declare my devotion by pressing my lips to hers.

She put her hand on my sleeve and I felt the warmth of her touch for the first and last time.

'Do it now or be gone,' she said almost sadly.

My father's son to the end, I picked up my hat and left without another word.

There was no one to talk to. Campbell would be angry at her audacity but file it away for future legal reference. Father and mother would never condone our conversation, nor would Ernest who would see her as a woman without shame. Arthur would no doubt have some wise words, but they would be couched in such know-it-all fashion I would become vexed and forget my purpose. The others were too young, though for a moment I relished the idea of Horace's uncritical company as he explained how horses were social creatures that enjoyed one another's company or how the weather affected cows' moods. I was in despair with my own silence until I thought of Lettie. Selfishly, I hadn't given her situation much attention except as it caused difficulties for the family, but now, as I clung to a life-raft on different swells, I needed some of that courage Alice said she possessed. When I knocked on the door of their cottage, Miss Muir greeted me with a smile and led me into the front room. Lettie was sitting by the fire with a book on her lap. She looks happy, I thought. More than that, she looks content.

'What are you reading?' I said because I could think of nothing else to say.

'Miss Seacole's *Wonderful Adventures*.'

'I don't believe I've heard of it.'

She laughed, but gently, as did Miss Muir. 'No, Bertie, I don't imagine you have.'

'I need your advice, Lettie,' I told her. The surprise on her face emphasized that I had never asked her anything of the kind before, and I felt slightly ashamed.

It never occurred to me to ask Miss Muir to leave us alone, but after she had brought us some tea, she indicated she had to fetch something from the wharf. An image of her boat riding the dark water came to my mind.

'We weren't properly introduced the night of my brother's rescue,' I said, offering her my hand. 'I've never thanked you for your role in saving Norman, Miss Muir. I'm very grateful.'

212

Her grasp was warm and firm. 'Margaret,' she replied. 'And please remember I couldn't have done anything without your sister.' She walked to the door. 'I hope your parents understand that.'

When she had gone, I told Lettie the tale of Alice MacBride from beginning to end as I knew it. She listened without interrupting, her fingers stroking the leather binding of her book and occasionally straying to brush a strand of hair from her cheek. I didn't know what I wanted from her. I had called it 'advice' but realized it was more like counsel or guidance I was after. 'So,' I said, 'there you have it.'

'And what you'd like is that I suggest how you are to feel about this woman.'

'No, well, yes, actually.' My confusion was embarrassing, but she didn't seem to notice.

'I don't think she knows her own heart, Bertie, but she is hardly alone in that. The difference between you is that hers can beat for more than one, while yours throbs for her alone.'

The truth of it made me miserable. 'But where does that leave me?'

'It leaves you mourning a loss that is also a gain.'

'How is that?'

'She will never leave her husband for you or Roger Nicholas. To do so would leave her open to too many accusations and too much the prey of her own emotions.'

'Then it is a loss.'

'Yes, partly, but you have learned something about yourself, have you not?'

I pinched my moustache and felt the separation of tiny bristles, each one bending into a new shape then returning to its original condition, changed by such slight movement and forever the same.

'I suppose I've learned that you can't always have what you desire, especially when what you want isn't what you expected it to be.'

Margaret Muir came back into the room, her hair damp from exertion or the fog I could see pressing against the panes.

'This will eventually lift, but you'll have to stay for dinner,' she told me. She looked at Lettie and I saw the sparkle in her eyes.

'I envy you,' I declared to them both.

'O Bertie, you should just love us and forget about the rest,' Lettie said.

Horace

I had an argument with Ernest who told me I shouldn't be visiting Lettie. Father and mother don't know, but if they found out, he said, they'd be hurt and angry.

'You don't seem to understand, Horace, that in your own small way you're encouraging her.'

'Encouraging her to do what?'

He clicked his tongue. 'To do what she should not be doing.'

'You mean staying with Margaret.'

'It amazes me,' he said, 'how so many members of this family appear to be on a first-name basis with this woman. Yes, I mean staying with Miss Muir when it gives great pain to her parents and siblings.'

'I think you're the only one, Ernest.'

'Only one?'

'Only one of us besides father and mother who feel any pain. I'm happy for her, and I know Arthur is too. Bertie's been to see her as well.'

'Bertie!'

'Yes, he told me she's content and deserves to be so.'

'I don't believe it.'

'Well, it's true.'

He turned away from me and stared out the window, and I wondered if he was imagining the cottage beyond the cliff-top where he had been so briefly on the night of Norman's rescue.

'Don't you miss her, Ernest?' I asked him.

He gave no indication that he'd heard me except for a tightening of his fingers around the arms of his chair. The room was so quiet I could hear the gulls crying down by the harbour. He was still looking out the window when he finally answered, and his voice sounded tired. 'Of course I miss her,' he said. 'But she has been selfish and foolish in ways that will be hard to mend.'

'It would make a difference if you defended her.'

'I said you didn't understand, and you don't. What do you think I'd be defending? Her behaviour runs counter to everything I believe in.'

'She defended you.'

He turned toward me now. 'What are you talking about?'

'When I was little you were in trouble and needed help.'

He pursed his lips. 'That Bible,' he said.

'Yes, you brought it home from Chapel and father found it with someone else's name in it. 'Presented to…' it said and then that person's name. Father asked you why you had it, and you managed to tell him before you began to cry.'

He stood up suddenly from his chair. 'You've a good memory,' he said. 'A boy had laughed at me because I was silently mouthing the verses from Exodus about the Commandments that father had woven into his sermon. He sat across the aisle and mocked me by opening and closing his mouth like a fish. When his parents were talking to father after the sermon, I bumped into him outside and his Bible tumbled into the bushes. He couldn't find it, but I did without telling him and put it in my pocket.' He walked over to the window. *'Thou shalt not steal,'* he said, and I could hear father's voice echoing his all those years before.

'And Lettie argued with father that the boy didn't deserve his Bible if he was going to mock God's words. The thief on the cross was saved, she told him, through Christ's mercy. She said she would go with you to return it quietly. I'm not remembering this all by myself. Lettie told me about it when I was older.'

'My big sister,' Ernest said. 'If she hadn't spoken up father would have made a public example of me. We found the boy with his parents in the high street and I explained, as she had suggested, that I'd found it in the bushes outside the Chapel. The parents were happy, and the boy relieved that he'd avoid a scolding. He said nothing, of course, about our altercation.'

'She's still your big sister,' I said.

He gave a little smile. 'It's not that simple, Horace. She hasn't taken the Bible, she's disobeyed it. A woman is meant to be betrothed to a man, not to another woman!'

I didn't know my scripture like Ernest does his so there weren't any verses at hand to give him pause. But there was something else I could say.

'Isn't it up to God to judge Lettie?'

He tapped the window pane softly with his knuckles. 'Leave her to Heaven, then?' He was asking himself the question, but I had the answer.

'God's already forgiven her,' I told him.

I went out to a farm with Mr. Peverel for the last time. A cow was having trouble giving birth.

'Sometimes we can help and at others we just have to wait and see,' he said.

We arrived at the stall with the cow on her feet as the calf's front hooves then its head appeared, the farmer's look of concern giving way to one of relief.

'It's been hours with no sight of life at all. Your coming must have prompted her,' he announced.

It was too late to get her to lie down. Mr. Peverel rubbed some jelly on the entrance to her birth canal and stretched it as best he could. Then one of his hands cramped up and he told me to reach in, grasp the calf's neck, and pull. I could feel it through my fingertips moving slowly out of its confinement and heard the mother grunt even as she kept quite still. I couldn't believe the shoulders and hind legs would get through such a tiny opening despite my efforts. Everything was slippery and wet, and there was blood dripping from my wrists as I tried to brace my feet against the floor boards and tugged as hard as I could. The calf's eyes were as round as saucers and fixed on a distant point in the world it was trying to enter. I think my own eyes must have been bulging with the strain, and I heard Mr. Peverel tell me to ease off for a moment and see if nature took its course. I let go and sure enough the two front legs unfolded into the air and the rest of the body slid out with a smacking sound and tumbled to the straw, followed by the after-birth. The mother moaned loudly, and Mr. Peverel clapped my back. 'Well done, Horace,' he cried. He wiped some fluid from the creature's mouth as the mother turned to lick its glistening hide.

'That's the first time I've seen anything born,' I said as we walked back to town. 'Other than a butterfly from a cocoon Norman brought home.'

'Most people go their whole lives without knowing the miracle,' he replied. 'Once you've witnessed it, everybody and everything is precious.'

Arthur

Deeper now than ever before
First lightning strike, then wave's last crash
And all this life that asks for more
Beyond the pane, beyond the sash

The way the bird rests on the wing
Or grace is granted seals on swell
The way a woman learns to sing
Refusal of death's lonely knell

My sister's eyes are like the sun
They burn alike in sea and sky
Where blue surrender to be won
Forked bolt, flocks, and voice give cry

I have enough poems now for a small volume and will send them out to John Murray when I get home. The publisher should know I am Yorkshire born and bred rather than from this obscure group of islands, though as I've found there's much more here than meets the eye. Who would have guessed Mr. Brechin would carry Shelley with him to Papa Westray or Lettie discover the love of her life in a boat called *Tom Paine*? I should not have written what I have without the inspiration of sea and sky or my sister's and youngest brother's adventures. The lesson I have learned above all is that you must step off the path of your usual ways, not just through books, and be willing to explore the new. Back home I would never have had the courage to get around father and cross even the county line, let alone board a ferry to parts unknown. I can see this expansion of horizons in the entire family.

Father's involvement with the fishermen and the courts has taken him far beyond his ordinary pulpit from which he declaimed weekly verses that affected but a handful of people. I don't see how in the future he will be able to ignore any injustices, large or small, that come to his attention. In the outside world, that is. As far as his own family is concerned, he and mother have agreed that Lettie should be left to her own devices if she does not repent, a clear injustice if there ever was one.

On the surface, mother has changed the least, remaining the loyal helpmate and shepherd to her flock, and our house, as always, is a refuge from passing storms. Except, of course, from the cloud that is her daughter. She does not seem to realize there will be no atonement and return to the fold (unlike father who, I think, begins to suspect the worst), and when that blow finally lands as she boards the train it will break her heart. I will have to serve as go-between and encourage reconciliation no matter how long it takes.

Ernest will be no help in this whatsoever. I swear his sense of righteousness outweighs father's most days, and he will not forgive her trespass on unconsecrated ground. Bertie, on the other hand, to my great surprise visited the cottage and seems to have made his peace with Lettie. I'm sure it has something to do with the end of his unquestioning allegiance to Alice McBride. Once his eyes were opened he was able to see other matters more clearly. I don't know what changed, just that when I asked him how she was doing with her husband in gaol, he replied without hesitation that she had her own life to live.

Horace, bless him, has been to see Lettie as much as me. She loves him unreservedly, which is as it should be, good-natured soul that he is who prefers to see the best rather than the worst in others. I have little doubt he will come back to the island once he turns sixteen. He's told me of his plans to build a dwelling near their cottage and work with Mr. Peverel. One day, no doubt, he'll take over the old man's practice, license or no license. People trust Horace and will certainly give him their trade. As for Clem, he's always been rather predictable when it comes to family relations. The creative side of him has often yielded an aloof attitude that might be somewhat offensive in a grown man but is merely annoying in a youngster. I've told Lettie my words might never see the light of day, but his music, I'm confident, will be bathed in brilliant sunshine. I just hope if he gains any fame it will rest easily on his shoulders and not cause them to stiffly shrug off any well-meaning admirers. Norman escaped this place with his life, but his vision of the selkie and his innocent love of nature in all its forms are a kind of protective shield that wards off dark thoughts. His Mr. Garson has had a beneficent effect on him, whatever mother thinks.

My sister has stepped from behind the arras that supposedly divides right from wrong or, if a more dramatic image will better serve, she has crossed a bridge above a bottomless canyon and watched her parents cut the ropes behind her. This separation pains her, I know, but her love for Margaret Muir has called her to another level of existence where the arras or bridge or any other border is finally inconsequential. When I see them together, their bodies move as one while their hearts and minds interweave without obstruction, not always in agreement but never in competition or discord. God willing (now there's a phrase I should suspect!) I'll one day find a woman as bright and beautiful as Lettie or Margaret and write a poem for her. *Though the sound overpowers,/ Sing again, with your dear voice revealing/ A tone/ Of some world far from ours,/ Where music and moonlight and feeling/ Are one.* Yes, something like that.

Ernest has shocked me, which I never thought possible. He has visited Lettie, not as a messenger of father and mother but of his own volition.

'What on earth did he say to you?' I asked her later that same day.

We had walked down the hill to the water. *Tom Paine* was rocking gently, and a small sea-bird was trying to maintain its balance on the tip of the mast.

'He said he wanted me to know that while what I had done was difficult for him to understand, he would try and, above all, he would defend me against father and mother's condemnations.'

'Did he say why this change of heart?'

'He asked me if I remembered the thief on the cross beside Christ and how he was taken into Paradise despite his transgression.'

'I'm not surprised he'd quote scripture at you, but what has that story got to do with anything?'

'When we were young, Ernest took a Bible that didn't belong to him. Let's say that father…well, he wasn't Christ-like in his response.'

'Few are,' I said, forgetting for a moment my own distance from the Book of John or any other part of holy writ.

'No, and I don't think we should expect them to be. Anyway, I persuaded father that forgiveness was in order and went with Ernest to return the Bible to its rightful owner.'

'So, it's that simple? One good turn deserves another?'

'No, Horace gave him something else to think about as well.'

Now I couldn't be so cynical. If Ernest had listened to Horace, only good could come of it. 'What?' I asked.

On the path to the wharf she must have picked up the smooth, flat stone which she was playing with now between her fingers and thumb. Swiftly she drew back her arm and flicked her wrist. The stone went skipping over the water making a dozen soft indentations on the surface before it disappeared with a tiny splash.

'Leave supposed sinners to Heaven,' she replied, turning to me with a smile. 'It's a good notion, don't you think?'

Thomas

Taggart spoke from the pulpit on Sunday about the need for islanders to stand together against the punishment of Rory Parker and for the fair settlement of the dispute with the fish buyers. He took as his initial text Matthew 7:12 – *So whatever you wish that others would do for you, do also for them, for this is the Law and the Prophets.*

'Ask yourselves,' he said to the congregation whose members had filled the pews and were standing in the side aisles, many in their rough weekday attire because they could afford no finery, 'what the fishermen have done for you, and seek to return their favour according to your abilities. They have braved the seas in fair and stormy weather, risking their lives daily to put food on your tables. They have asked nothing in return except the right to feed and clothe their own families and keep their boats in the water for a fair price. Their struggle to do so has been life-long, but now has been worsened by those who will not pay for their work what it is worth. Unless they are to return to the sea after all these weeks with their tails between their legs, beaten and never to raise their heads with self-respect again, all of you must act. I am calling on those with shops to close their doors to any of Her Majesty's hirelings in any capacity, be he soldier, custom's man, tax collector, or just plain supporter of Edinburgh or London's ways, for, if the buyers will not act, it is up to the government to resolve this dispute and return our lives to normal. Those of you whose only doors are those of your homes, bar them equally to anyone who does not support the rights of Rory Parker and the fishermen's association. It is time for the good people of these islands to stand up and be counted!'

There was a shapeless silence behind myself, Elizabeth, and our sons as the crowd took in his words. No one could properly be blamed, I thought for refusing to serve a customer on his own premises, but the shunning he called for was a different matter, an insurrection of turned backs instead of the turned cheeks authority had come to expect. Then he exhorted them further and although it was a holy edict he gave them, I feared the lesser law's response.

'Remember Ezra 10:4, he cried, *Arise, for this matter belongeth to thee... be of good courage and do it.*'

By association with him I would share any guilt for such incitement, but I was more than willing. I took Elizabeth's hand in mine and we bowed our heads together. Then someone yelled from the back of the Chapel that we should stand fast, and I heard the commotion as a hundred people or more rose to their feet, boots shuffling and dresses swaying, and waited on their minister, ourselves among them.

'I can think of no better time for a hymn,' he told them. I suddenly realized then there was no one at the organist's seat, and heard Taggart announce that since Mr. Locke had unfortunately sprained his wrist this past week he would ask Mr. Larsen's son Clement to accompany the congregation in their singing of 'Onward Christian Soldiers.'

Clem did not hesitate but marched to the console as if carrying Christ's banner on his fingertips and, at Taggart's nod, began to play. Never was I a prouder father, and never did enlistment in God's army seemed more apt – *We are not divided, all one body we/One in hope and doctrine, one in charity.*

Once outside after the completion of service, our enthusiasm was tempered somewhat by our realization of what we had signed up for in the quotidian world. There was no one in our sphere I could think of whom we would have to spurn, but my support of Rory Parker and of Taggart would be on trial soon enough. Elizabeth had not let go of my hand even as we conversed with several elders and their wives on the Chapel steps. The boys had walked on ahead, though I couldn't see Clem. I wanted to tell him how well he'd done.

In the next three days it became clear that Taggart's words had had their desired effect, and not just in Methodist circles. Presbyterians joined our cause as well, at least those of the lower orders, for there were wealthier families in that faith whose connections to Queen and country could never be abandoned. There were enough sympathizers, however, to disrupt routine proceedings of government business, including the courts. Although the magistrate was prepared to sit, his clerks and bailiffs were not, so our case was postponed until volunteers could be brought in from the mainland or our '*happy throng*' of Christians could no longer continue on its chosen path. All this meant our plans for a return to Yorkshire were delayed, but we were in the hands of the Lord.

The local newspaper took up our cause, calling for a just arrangement with the fishermen and that the charges be dropped against Rory Parker who, after all, had only briefly grabbed an official's ankle. Furthermore, the editorial stated, without naming names, anyone who had 'not prevented Mr. Parker from leaving the island' should not be held responsible for his taking a boat to ports unknown. The authorities were helpless in the face of any non-violent deeds. No one took to the streets, and no one other than Taggart openly promoted dissent of any kind. Individual acts of protest that occurred on private property or through simple refusals to engage in conversation could hardly be prosecuted, but they added up to an overall warfare against those who would not deal justly with the working-man and his family. Although there were some tavern scuffles and one half-hearted attempt to damage a craft in Stromness harbour, the citizenry by and large remained united. After just six days, with the government making noises about stepping in, the buyers agreed to bring the price for a full catch back to where it had been in the spring and promised a small percentage increase every three months as long as the stocks did not diminish. The fishermen, to their credit, accepted this offer provided Rory Parker was free to return and resume work like the rest of them. The courts were drawn into the final resolution and saw the wisdom in dropping the charges against him. As a result, Taggart and I could hardly be put on trial. At least that is what we thought.

The day after the boats were back on the water and everything seemed to have returned to normal Taggart was summoned before the magistrate and charged with having used his pulpit to disturb the public peace. No mention was made of the fishermen or of Rory Parker. It was that Her Majesty's officers had been prevented from carrying out certain of their duties due to the minister's spurring of his congregation. I accompanied him to the courts along with Mr. Campbell and Bertie who had advised him it was just the authorities' way of indicating they were still in charge and that a small fine would be the extent of punishment handed out.

'I will not pay it,' Taggart stated flatly.

Before Campbell could speak, I replied, 'I do not believe you will have to.' I turned to the barrister and asked him whether a witness would be able to speak on behalf of the accused.

'Most certainly. And I take it that would be yourself?'

'Yes,' I said, knowing exactly what had to be done so that the victory of the fishermen and those who had supported them would not be tainted.

When Campbell introduced me as a witness for the defence the magistrate asked me what I had to say.

'Only, your honour, that since Mr. Taggart will refuse to pay the fine, you will have to gaol him. Then this Sunday coming I will stand up in his pulpit and call for a repeat of the shunning of government officials. If you are able to bring in assistants from the mainland, you will have to gaol me as well. The next week my son Ernest will preach that the opposition to your punishments continue and perhaps become more stringent, and you will have three of us imprisoned. Meanwhile, there will be an ongoing disruption to civil exchange on this island such as you have not seen before.'

'You are threatening an officer of the law, sir!' the magistrate expostulated.

But Peter and the apostles answered, 'we must obey God rather than men.' I thought, but for the moment did not say.

Clearly he was angry, but it was also clear we and the principles we were defending were not worth this trouble. I watched as he pondered his options. Even if he was prepared to drop the proceeding against us, he still had to save face and be able to say something had been paid.

'Mr. Campbell, do you think your client and perhaps his supporter here might see fit to make a small contribution to the fund for the maintenance of Kirkwall harbour?'

Taggart nodded. Campbell looked at me and I beckoned him close to whisper in his ear. He smiled when I had done.

'Given the circumstances, your honour, Mr. Larsen would prefer his money went to upkeep at Stromness.'

The magistrate did not smile, and I thought perhaps I had gone too far. 'So be it,' he said after a long pause, and rapped the bench with his gavel.

All this time Lettie was arraigned in my mind.

Ernest

Thank God father and Mr. Taggart were not found guilty, else I might have betrayed their expectations of me in the pulpit. It would have been up to me on the third Sunday to urge continuance of the behaviour that had resulted in a fair price for the fishermen and halted the persecution of Rory Parker. But father's firm stance gave the courts pause. The result is he is home safe and sound, his pockets five quid lighter, and we are making preparations to return to Yorkshire. All except Lettie, of course, who has left the women's work to mother.

I say 'betrayed' for two reasons. First, I might not have been strong enough in my role to be convincing. Father and Mr. Taggart are born leaders whose conviction and manner of speaking spark the dry wood that waits to be fired on any significant occasion. I have not their strength of character and fear I would have been perceived as going through the motions as I tried to urge my congregation, and the others listening beyond the Chapel doors, to stay the course. But even if I had found my voice of persuasion, there would still have been my doubts.

I cannot speak with father about these, given his natural assumptions about our shared, unwavering faith and its irreproachable place in the daily lives of our parishioners. The rightness of Rory Parker's cause has always seemed self-evident to him so there has been no real need to discuss it with me or to justify it to the rest of the family. We are all together in the combating of injustice with the Holy Word. Now that Mr. Parker has returned to Stromness and the fishing fleet is spread out among the islands, we can look to our equally common future with the satisfaction we have served the Lord and the Orkney citizens to the best of our abilities. Perhaps so, but then why am I not entirely mollified by the outcome, as positive as it appears to have been for everyone? Is it because scripture may have been bent to suit the occasion? The only person I can approach with this troubling notion is Reverend Scott.

I have not been inside the cathedral since we spoke about the contradictions of faith some time ago. Then I had been dazzled by the stained-glass reflections of Viking saints and the sheer strength and size of the Presbyterian bastion. Now, though there is no lessening of my awareness of history's beauty and dimensions, I am preoccupied with more immediate concerns.

'Well, Ernest,' he greets me. 'You must be highly pleased. With your father's support, Mr. Taggart's daring oratory moved islanders regardless of their faith and together they have undoubtedly made the Orkneys a better place.'

'At what cost?' I reply, determined to go straight to the point.

'I'm not sure I know what you mean.'

'Well, Mr. Taggart used Matthew 7:12 as his text and made it clear that the fishermen's bravery deserved reciprocation from those who never left the shore. We were to become Christian soldiers in a holy war against all manner of officialdom that opposed fair prices for the fish and turned Rory Parker into the chief scapegoat.'

'Yes, and the war has been won, But for some reason you object to this?'

My throat feels constricted, and I have to force the words out like a parched desert traveller asking for water. 'It's just that the Bible asks us to consider so much more, doesn't it? Mr. Taggart didn't refer those verses in Matthew that immediately precede Christ's direction to *do unto others*. It's as if he left them out deliberately.'

'Go on.' Mr. Scott sits beside me in the front pew, his hands clasped in his lap and his cassock hem not quite covering the tips of his shoes. I see that one is more polished then the other and wonder if he had been interrupted in his personal tasks that morning by someone as demanding as myself.

'Well, the first words of Matthew 7 are *Judge not that ye be not judged.* Then Christ goes on to ask *Why beholdest thou the mote that is in thy brother's eye, but considerest not the beam that is in thy own eye.* He does not want us to put ourselves above the ones we condemn for their different opinions. If we do so his admonition is even harsher – *Thou hypocrite, first cast out the beam out of thine own eye; and thou shalt then see clearly to cast out the mote out of thy brother's eye.* In other words, we should tend to our own flaws before we criticize our neighbours' faults.' I stop there for the moment, anxious for his reply.

He does not immediately respond, rubbing his interlacing fingers against one another, and I can hear my watch in my waistcoat pocket ticking away the seconds. Then he turns to face me. 'You are forgetting one thing, Ernest. The Lord guides us in His wisdom to interpret scripture so that good may be done. We are all, compared to Christ, hypocrites whose eyes are filled with motes, but we must still try to see according to His light.'

I am not satisfied. 'But there is Leviticus, as well. 19:18 – *You shall not take vengeance or bear a grudge against the sons of your own people, but you shall love your neighbour as yourself.* How do we square this message with our shunning of those who disagreed with us about the fishermen?'

'I would take the last as first and the first as last in that verse. If you truly love your neighbour as yourself, then your actions will not be vengeful; indeed they cannot be. The Bible can be all things to all men, Ernest, if they forget it is the Lord they serve and not themselves, but there will be no answers given to such reprobates. Rather it is those who truly seek the Lord in all his glory who will benefit from that same chapter in Matthew – *Ask, and it shall be given you; seek, and ye shall find; knock, and it shall be opened unto you.*'

'You're surely not saying that all those who turned their backs on the officials can interpret Matthew and Leviticus as you do?'

'No, that is why there are churches and chapels and guidance offered from the pulpit. People often act according to the will of God without knowing that they do so. They may not see the truth of their actions here on earth until the final day of Judgment.'

There is no doubt that the outcome of the fishermen's fight was a good one. Who could argue with food on the table and the keeping of good men from prison? But when each of us uses scripture to justify our actions in the world isn't that dangerously close to the means justifying the ends? I know if I am to continue on the ministerial path this is a question I will have to struggle with for a long time, perhaps until my soul leaves my body and all doubts vanish. In the meantime, pulpit or no pulpit, I might ask and seek and knock as much as I like and never find the open door.

'I can see you're still troubled,' Mr. Scott says. 'I think you should talk things over with your father.'

We would have to have our own compartment on the train south. Even then, I would not know how to begin.

Horace is the true minister among us.

Clem

'I don't see how you can't include them,' Mr. Berry says.

We are sitting in the front pew of the cathedral where I thought I would never return. I have just played the 'Lettie' section on the organ, and his enthusiasm is evident. I don't fill him in on the background, but there's probably no one on the island who doesn't know of my sister's behaviour.

'You're writing this music because of your family. Together your relations are speaking to you through your music, and your parents are part of that voice. If you left them out, the work would be incomplete.'

I know he's right, but I'm afraid of falling under their sway completely, of bending the notes and chords to their will. When I tell him this, he nods.

'If that's what happens in their section, so be it. Perhaps you need to compose according to their influence over you throughout the piece. That, after all, is the reality of your relationship with them, and properly so. But I'm confident there will be enough independence in your score that will keep your head above water, so to speak. You are who you are largely because of them, but in this case they would not exist without your music. And you are a true musician, Clement. Your ear is tuned to something beyond parental sway.'

I am thankful for his advice and support and can already hear father's weighty presence on the keys and mother's less obtrusive but equally firm attendance. I am about to take my leave when he speaks again.

'I have only one question for you now we've settled that matter,' he says.

I am afraid it will involve my sitting at the organ during a Presbyterian service. 'What is it?' I ask with some trepidation. He's been so kind to me I don't like to refuse him again, though I knew I'll have to.

'You've told me about all the different sections, but one.'

I can't think of what he means. Everything is in order.

'You, Clement, you. How are you going to display yourself?'

I stare at him fixedly. There are my sister and two eldest brothers on one side of Horace and Arthur, Norman, and myself on the other. I know now the way my parents have to sound and am already planning how to intersperse them throughout the entire piece. But it's true, I've given no thought to my own composition. If that has been partly because I've been so busy arranging the others, isn't it also because I've been avoiding any pinpointing of myself like one of Norman's butterflies on the page? Mr. Berry hasn't really been expecting an answer only an evasion, and I provide one that prompts him to clap his hands together and laugh loudly.

'Like a ghost,' I say. 'I'll be there, but no one will be able to see me.'

'They'll have to hear you, though, won't they? You won't deny them that phantom pleasure?' I think he's going to laugh again, but his next words to me are more serious than any he's spoken before.

'You're very reserved in regard to the world around you, Clement.'

I'm about to object, but he holds up his hand. 'Don't mistake me. Such distance is necessary in a creator. The contradiction is that you can't get close unless you're far away. But you'll have to find a way to be truthful to yourself as well and not skip over passages in your thoughts and feelings to leave a gap in your achievement.'

On my way home, I think over what he'd said. Aren't I present throughout the entire piece by virtue of having written it? Can't that fact stand in for my own separate section? I know Mr. Berry is right. There'd be a hole big enough to drive a horse and cart through, and listeners would envisage me with a whip in my hand pummelling the poor beast of my avoidance without mercy. That might tell them a great deal about me, but it isn't what I want them to hear.

Who is Clement Larsen if I look at him as I have my brothers and sister? I ponder how I pressed the keys to one or two main features of their characters and subsequently have been able to play them with confidence. They were exposed by their strongest notes, ones that can't be denied. How can I apply this method to myself? I walk right by the door to our house so involved am I in this puzzle, when suddenly I remember hiding from Ernest behind the console screen that morning in the cathedral when I longed to touch the organ keys. I see myself kneeling before the priest who turned into my father and opening my mouth to sacrilege and salvation. After a moment or two of fear and then elation, I glimpse the way to revelation. I won't be a ghost but a figure with the courage of a Viking warrior who will re-enter the dream and for one short movement claim the spirit of a forbidden faith as his own.

Lettie

With Arthur I sent a note to father and mother asking if I could meet with them before they left. I told him not to make any special plea on my behalf. They'd have to decide, I said.

'Everybody's on your side, Lettie, even Ernest. They'll have to give in if only to combat that fact.'

'I don't want them to give in. I want them to understand.'

'Now you're asking too much. You've gone against their Christian conscience, and that's something they'll never grasp or put aside even if they make an effort to keep their daughter. No, what I mean by 'give in' is that they'll agree to see you, if only for the satisfaction of being able to say they offered the course of salvation tried right up to the end.'

He was right. There was nothing in the return note other than agreement that I come to the house the next afternoon, the day before they were to take the ferry to Thurso and the train south.

'Remember, Lettie, gently,' Margaret said as we clasped hands by the door.

'I'll try,' I replied, then hugged her for all the world.

When I arrived, the entire family was in the parlour. Norman clutched me around the waist, his head buried in my skirts, and wouldn't let go until father told him off.

'I felt everyone should be here to begin with,' he said to me, 'because, as I guessed correctly, you have not brought your baggage and mean to stay behind. Therefore, before your mother and I have a final word with you, your brothers can bid you a proper farewell.'

If my decision to live with Margaret had given father the shock of his life, what happened next must have jolted him nearly as much.

'If you don't mind, father, we'd like to stay.'

He might have expected such resistance from Arthur and been prepared to reprimand his insubordination, but it had been Ernest who spoke up, his Methodist heir who should have been wholly on side. Before he could reply, Bertie added his support.

'You may as well know it, father. I have been to visit Lettie and Miss Muir.' He glanced at Ernest, who nodded. 'As has Ernest.'

There was no need to mention Horace whose loyalty to me was never in question.

Mother gave a little gasp and pressed her handkerchief to her lips. Father, arms crossed over his chest, surveyed his flock. 'Clem, Norman, you will leave now,' he said firmly. They looked at me rather than him, and I knew he noticed their allegiance was almost as strong as his command.

I wanted them there but knew Norman especially was too young for what was to come. 'I'll see you both before I leave,' I told them.

'Promise?' said Norman.

'Yes, cross my heart.'

'I want to play something for you,' Clem said, 'else you'll never get to hear it. At Mrs. Drever's house, alright?'

Father looked as if he were under siege and all his soldiers deserting him. Mother was weeping quietly but refused the cup of tea Arthur offered to make. I knew I was largely responsible for this disintegration of the old order but felt it had always been an enforced union held together by chains of righteousness that frayed the finer cords of love. It had taken this trip to the islands to reveal our imprisonment. Father might not have to go to gaol, but he had confined us under lock and key until the sea and sky and unreserved people here had led us along our various paths of escape. It wasn't just Margaret who was a guide to freedom but, in their ways, Alice MacBride, the man on the distant island who had met Shelley, Mr. Spence and Mr. Peverel, and Mr. Garson. I don't know who had shown Ernest and Clem the way on, but it was evident they had accompanied us on our journey as well. Even father himself, as was clear from his involvement with Mr. Parker and the fishermen, had expanded at least some of his Christian horizon so his voice from the pulpit could never be the same again. I suspected mother, on the other hand, had moved the least. She had always taken her direction from the one she had been married to these twenty-four years and would continue to do so, even though her decision to spy on myself and Margaret, as troubling as it was, had occurred without father's knowledge. Now here we all were at very likely our final family gathering that, despite our individual advances, was bound to end in resentment and sadness.

When Clem and Norman had gone, father took his stand. 'Well, Lettie, I see you have not come to your senses.'

'On the contrary, father, I have found my senses at last and only wish that you and mother would appreciate this.'

'You want us to give you our blessing, is that it?'

'No, that is too much to expect. But I would ask that you not to think ill of me and do not keep from Norman the letters I will write him.'

'How can you treat us so, Lettie?' mother cried. 'It is you who think so ill of us that you would go against everything we have ever taught you.'

Despite Margaret's parting advice, I had thought about what I needed to say when confronted in this fashion, but it wasn't easy, and I almost faltered. 'It's true you taught me to expect nothing but a proper marriage and settled life that would produce grandchildren and little else.' I hadn't meant it to come out as such an accusation, but I was angry now and refused to bow my head and accept chastisement. Father provided it, nonetheless.

'*The head of every man is Christ; and the head of woman is the man,*' he said, reaching for his usual conviction, but for the first time such words did not suffice and Ernest seemed to know this.

'Why did the Lord send Lettie and Miss Muir together to save Norman if they didn't have His blessing?' He asked his question calmly and of everyone in the room.

'Because He doesn't condemn them,' Arthur declared. 'I don't believe every aspect of the Lord is contained within ancient verse. Otherwise Norman would have died on that beach.'

I could see Bertie agreed with him, but it was Horace who offered the next surprise.

'I will come back here, father, no matter what you say. And I will live by Lettie and Margaret and keep them from any harm.'

'Horace!' father rebuked him. 'Remember your place.'

'I think what Horace is saying, father, is that his place, like Lettie's, is here,' Arthur said.

'You will have only the clothes on your back if you leave home against my will, any of you.'

'*And having food and raiment, let us be therewith content,*' Ernest replied.

Father jerked back to have scripture and his eldest son reprove him so bluntly. But he was not to be swayed from his mission.

'I ask you for the last time, Lettie. Will you renounce this woman and return to your family where you belong?'

'Please, Lettie,' mother said. Then, as if reminding herself who was in charge, she added vehemently, 'I will not speak to you again should you not do your duty.'

'Your silence I will regret most of all, mother. But my duty, as you call it, is to peace and happiness on this earth that I believe are reflections of Heaven's promise.' I turned to my brothers. 'Thank you for standing by me. You are every one of you welcome in our home, and I will write to remind you as often as I can.'

They all hugged me while over their shoulders I watched father move to stand resolutely behind mother's chair, his eyes everywhere but on our mutual affection. If it was to be the last time I saw them together, I would remember their dignity in the face of so much they could not abide.

'Next summer.' Horace whispered.

'I will see you again,' Bertie murmured.

'I hope there's a place for me at your Christmas table,' Arthur declared for all to hear.

Ernest held my hands in his. If I was expecting another biblical verse, however well-intentioned, I was wrong.

'I'm sorry I wasn't there for you when it mattered, Lettie.'

'You are now,' I replied, and leaned up to kiss his cheek. 'Please tell Norman I'll be at Mrs. Drever's with Clem.'

I looked at my parents withdrawn behind their veil of rectitude and wondered at the price paid for such decorum, almost screaming aloud at my ability to love two things at once and their incapacity to do the same.

'Goodbye,' I said, without any rancour in my heart, 'God bless you.' Then I closed the front door on what could never be retrieved. The sound of a distant piano drifted on the Orkney winds.

Norman

It is sad to say goodbye to Mr. Garson. Today we went out in the field where I found the Tortoiseshell butterfly with its big yellow and blue wing-spots to frighten the birds. It died in the bottle and is pinned on Mr. Garson's board. I said back then I wanted to make sure there was another one, but after I heard about the selkie I didn't look very hard. We didn't have our nets with us, and I was glad. Whatever was resting on the stinging nettles or flitting over the stalks of grass could stay free and carry the pollen so new flowers can grow. If I could talk to a butterfly, I'd ask it go to the beach and tell the selkie I won't forget her. There's no net could catch either one.

'You must promise to write me, Norman,' he said, 'and let me know all your news. Even if you're not going to keep butterflies anymore, make sure you have your notebook so you can record their colours and habits. And let me know, as well, what else you discover on your Yorkshire moors.'

'I will send you letters, but mother and father won't let me go out on the moors by myself. I'll have to wait until the insects and animals come into our garden or the park down the road. I saw a fox in the park once. Horace says there's deer too, but I've never seen one.'

'I think if you look close to home, you'll find all sorts of creatures, more than are here really because there's better shelter and the winds aren't as fierce – deer, foxes, hedgehogs, even badgers.'

'If I was like Arthur, I'd write books about wild creatures. I don't mean just what they look like and what they do, but stories.'

'That's a wonderful idea! And don't worry about being like your brother. You know enough about butterflies to tell him a tale or two.'

I was excited now and said it would be the first thing I'd do after I got home, and I'd send everything to him before anyone else got to read it. 'I'll write a story about the selkie too,' I proclaimed.

'Be careful with that one,' he said.

'Why?'

He looked up at the sky then down at me. 'Because if you say too much about magical beings, they become ordinary and get taken for granted. Either that or they want nothing more to do with you and disappear altogether.'

'So I should keep her to myself?'

'I think so.'

'But if you'd done that I never would have found her on the beach.'

'You're right, Norman, but I should have said too much magic is dangerous as well. You almost died and your sister and Miss Muir could have perished as well. That's not what stories are meant to bring about, is it? Selkies aren't like butterflies or the other creatures I mentioned, living where we can easily find them and open to observation or capture. You don't want children reading your story and trying to climb down cliffs to the sea, do you?'

I wanted to tell him if I had enough rope and we weren't leaving so soon, I'd go back to the cliffs and find her again. I wanted to see if her face was still Lettie's. But he was right. I didn't want to take anyone with me, not actually and not in words either. She was mine alone, and I couldn't share her if that was so. It was going to be hard to be a writer, I decided.

'I have something for you, Norman.'

From his jacket pocket he took a round pebble dotted with silver glints. 'It's from our beach,' he said. 'I've had it for almost sixty years. There's no children to hand it on to, except you.'

It was such a very special present, and I had started to tell him so, when I caught a rusty-red movement out of the corner of my eye. Mr. Garson saw it too. 'My God!' he cried.

The largest butterfly I had ever seen rose from the grass, then hung so still in the morning glow it looked, as Mr. Garson said later, like a painting without a frame.

'It's a Tortoiseshell,' I whispered, though he didn't need my help. 'How did it get so big?'

'I think it's very old, Norman.'

I remembered he'd told me that butterflies don't usually live more than a month, but sometimes they could last almost a year. This one had been around for a long time, and I was happy that it must have a large family.

It hovered there for a few moments then sailed upwards on a current of wind. The sun was in our eyes and we soon lost sight of it in the twirling motes of light.

'All alone. Maybe the very last one. Now that's worth a story.'

But I knew now the selkie took different forms and there weren't any words to capture her changes.

'Thank you for the stone,' I said.

I'm sad, too, that mother and father won't let me visit Lettie, and that she can't come here unless she says she's sorry. It's not fair that Horace and Arthur can see her and not me. We'll be gone soon, and I'll have to be big before I can come back here again. Horace says Lettie is thinking of me. She told him so. I liked Miss Muir when I was in her cottage. Mother and father don't like her, though. They say she's taken Lettie away from us. Why would Miss Muir do that when she helped Lettie save me? I asked mother, and she said just because Miss Muir could sail a boat didn't mean she was a good person. But I know she's a good person because Lettie wouldn't love her if she wasn't. I write a note to my sister and tell her a story.

Dear Lettie

I miss you and wish you were here. It will be worse when we go home because you'll be so far away. Mother and father say things about you and Miss Muir, but Horace and Arthur tell me not to listen to them. Even Ernest, who always talks with them about the Bible, sat down on the end of my bed and said you were my sister and nothing could ever come between us. Last night Bertie got in an argument with father, saying he'd take your view of the world over any that condemned you. I don't want you to be condemned. That's what Bertie says they do to bad people. I wrote this story for you.

Once there was a girl butterfly who had lived a very long time. She liked living in the field where the grass grew and the sun shone. When it was too hot she settled on a cool flower stem, and when it was too cold she flew south with her family. Her wings were very pretty and the different colours scared the birds so they didn't eat her. One day her family decided to stay in the south but she did not want to stay there so she flew back north where her home was. After everyone else had died she was the last one. But a man and boy saw her and put her in their memory.

The Frame

That's it, then, everything based on a photograph I'm holding once again in my hands. The only thing I know about them for certain is that, like Norman's butterfly, they're all dead. The last one, Ernest, went home to Glory when I was eighteen years old. Why is it that I waited so long to raise them from their slumber and reshape a long-vanished reality? Has there been a common strand of DNA at work encoded with genetic instructions to tell a particular family story out of all the tales that could be spun from human interaction? Or has it just been a personal reaction to the shabby treatment of my mother by my grandfather? If he has been the chief impetus, it seems that I've become interested in the background to *his* side of the story, though some of her view of his character has certainly rubbed off in my portrait of him. Maybe it's because I visited Grimsby not long after Ernest died and stayed in the house Clement ruled for so many years, shocked by the physical resemblance between my mother and my step-grandmother who was no biological relation. I was taken to various other houses to meet friends of the family, but the only blood relative I encountered that summer in England was great-cousin Enid when I went to Leeds. I asked no one any questions about the lives of my great-aunt and uncles or about my great-grandparents. My banished mother had a nostalgia for things English, and an unquestioning admiration for her older brother, but for all her memories of her girlhood (school, poems she'd read, the stretching-away sands at Cleethorpes) she said very little about that group in the garden photo.

My excuse is I didn't know what to ask, having no idea before the internet and its ancestry sites where and how all the brothers had lived. There were no boxes of letters in Grimsby or Leeds to which I had access. Great-cousin Enid would never have placed any private information in the hands of such a disreputable young man as myself. If I had told her that one day I'd write a novel about the family in which a character based on her mother was a crucial figure, she would have laughed (I don't want to say derisively, but there it is) and then she would have told me I had no business doing so. What good could ever come of such an intrusive act? In our technologically-adept world in which pictures are snapped for every minor and even inconsequential occasion, we take for granted a lasting record of ourselves. And it may be true that the sheer numbers of visual representations will mean the long-term survival for the reproduction of our features in some no-longer-recognizable place. But eventually our names will fall away from our facsimiles, and we will be left like the family Larsen in a frozen moment only imagination can unthaw. Despite some changes, I have depended heavily on real names and dates in my story, and without these I don't know whether I would have written anything at all. Of course, anyone else could come along, pick up the photograph, and invent a tale. But I doubt their connection with the framed subjects could be more intimate and revelatory than mine.

Just as my recreated family members are stepping off the Orkneys (where I doubt no one of their real counterparts ever ventured), I must step off my fiction and look at each of them again, albeit it through a double opening – the lens of the original camera and the aperture I have manipulated to shape my characters almost from scratch. It's not easy because I haven't really been fair, imposing my own slant on just about every aspect of their experience from religion to poetry, gender relations to fishermen's collectives, and imposition of authority to resistance of it. They're looking at an 1890s lens first of all, but that's long gone. As I'm the only witness left, they're also looking at me after I've said what I've needed to about them, and their gaze isn't the same as it was before I began.

The issue of Thomas's unswerving faith lies at the heart of the story. It's astounding to me that my great-grandfather (who died one hundred years ago as I write this) could have been a Methodist minister with all his attendant beliefs and convictions having no formal place in my life. My mother went to church twice on Sundays under Clement's aegis and sent me and my sister to Sunday School until we decided, as young teens, we didn't want to go anymore. I have my Bible from 1956, and I can still recite a lilting verse that lists all the books in the Old Testament. That, I suppose, is partly the basis for my employing biblical quotations rather liberally in my text, though I'm confident they would have passed readily through Thomas and Ernest's lips. On the more negative side of religion, there is Clement who became a choirmaster in the Grimsby Methodist Chapel, lauded, as I've said before, by his colleagues and the children under his direction. Despite and because of his own principles and persuasions, he imperiously abandoned my mother to the fate she had chosen over his undoubted plans for her – an English husband and regulated life nearby, much like those Lettie rejected – and went off to his Maker with apparently no misgivings or thoughts of forgiveness (including hers of him), unless her dream the night he died was his visitation of penance.

The elder siblings in my version of the family break from this rigid conception of the way things must be, and I'm fairly certain this is because of my own engagement with powerful cultural changes during the 1960s. On the Orkneys, Lettie secedes in charged and irreversible fashion. I wrote her partly in tribute and partly in precursory opposition to Enid, who never rode the swells of sea or love in quite the same way.

Thomas died when Enid was fifteen, so he wasn't around to condemn her eventual 'sinful' behaviour. Since Elizabeth's death date is 1930 she probably had plenty of time to see where Enid was headed. But whatever fractures in the family structure Elizabeth may have encountered, moral desertion was not one of them (death in childbirth was hardly Letitia's fault). In the photograph both my great-grandmother and great-aunt return the lens' stare with remarkable self-assurance and look alike more than any other two figures in the garden that day.

While it is a known fact that Ernest followed his father into the church, there is no extant record of what happened to Bertram, Horace, and Arthur. Physical appearances are dubious sources for the reading of a man's character and career, but, given all the conventions within which we operate, Bertram with his straight shoulders and clipped moustache does look more like a lawyer than a poet. Yet I have him breathless with idealized love for Alice, unable to provide adequate testimony. Arthur, with his fine features and open collar, appears to be more sympathetic to Shelley than to Blackstone, and his unwavering defence of all things unbound is overly romantic at times. Thickset Horace is right in the middle of the photo with his feet (though they're not visible) squarely on the ground. He may have been the brightest of them all in real life, but with his steadfast connection to the material world around him my Horace isn't given to abstract thought. Clement I've spoken of in no uncertain terms, but my Clem is a prodigy with the redeeming grace of musical ability that is beyond mere talent. The implication is that he will amount to more than a hypocritical choirmaster. From the photograph he stares at me quizzically, and I have no idea whether I am to be slotted with my supposedly wayward mother. As for Norman, his spectacles hide his eyes, but give him an erudite look even at his young age. I wanted there to be someone in my family almost entirely outside the boundaries set by the Chapel. His vision of the selkie and wonder at the butterflies indicate a freedom of belief not yet circumscribed by age and parental expectation.

They all haunt me, but have I been able to haunt them wherever they are?

14. Afterlife

Ernest 1964

I am the last one. It's been two years since Clem passed on, and this month marks the seventh anniversary of Norman's death. The others went long before that. There are grandchildren and great-grandchildren, of course, but not as many as you would expect. Bertram's son had only one child who seems indisposed to marriage, while Clem's son has remained a bachelor, and his daughter lives in exile with her two children in Canada. I don't have many family visitors now that Anne is gone.

My health remained strong so I preached every Sunday until my eighty-fifth year, my memory for scripture intact and my keenness to exhort others to follow God's holy word as sharp as when I first began my ministry. Of course, I was tested along the way, not least by those caught in the assault of earthly empire against the Kingdom of Heaven. Their damage was beyond measure. I remember a young captain sent back from France because of a nervous condition whose eyes were empty pools and whose mind, or what he revealed of it, was a scarred wasteland of mud and slaughter. As for his soul, I was not able to reach it and give him hope for a better world above where wars did not exist. For all this he remained terribly lucid. Once when I tried to assure him everything he'd seen and endured was part of God's plan, he laughed bitterly.

'Tell me,' he asked when his resentful mirth had subsided, 'was it God's plan that I see my sergeant's head blown off three feet from where I was standing?'

I started to answer, but he was not yet finished.

'It rolled toward my feet and settled there like a bloody football I was meant to kick down the trench so others could play. The whistles were blowing, chaplain. Would you have played or pretended it wasn't there?'

There were not many who spoke out like him. Most broke down and sobbed uncontrollably, unable to provide coherent tales. It was up to me to fill in the gaps with supportive comments, and I tried as best I could, but often came away with the overwhelming feeling that no words could suffice to counter the horror these men had suffered. I couldn't imagine what it would be like to be with them at the front before and after attacks or to crawl out into the carnage to bless the wounded before they died. The Lord had seen fit that I serve Him on this side of the Channel, but the war came home to me every day in no uncertain terms. Perhaps had I been witness to just one conflict of such magnitude my own trial might have been more bearable, but the next great battle, only twenty-one years later, took an even greater toll because of my age and the fact that bombs were falling all over England.

I was in Coventry in November 1940 when the Germans sent over five hundred bombers in waves of assault, destroying the entire city, including the great cathedral dedicated centuries ago to St. Michael. My job was to comfort those in distress, but that night I huddled with them beneath the exploding skies and prayed desperately for our survival. The following morning my hands would not stop shaking and my mind was unsettled. I could not recall the whereabouts of my own Chapel and did not want to be near or speak to anyone. For hours I wandered through the rubble, my collar giving away my identity so people called to me for spiritual aid I could not provide. When some of my compatriots found me, I was sent to a hospital in the countryside where I spent several weeks recovering beside those very soldiers and civilians I was supposed to help.

This led to a crisis of faith, though I could not have called it such at the time, so far was I from any rational assessment of my condition. I remember repeating lines of what I thought was biblical verse but could have been sheer nonsense so little did they do to relieve my sense of desolation. Gradually, I came to my senses, which did not mean the awful scenes of flame and carnage disappeared, only that their actuality hardened into inescapable forms to twist my emotions and hold me in thrall for many months. For the rest of the war I was assigned to a small community miles from the city where the bombs could be heard only from a great distance. My congregation was nearly all my age or older, and when I led them in prayer for our brave men overseas I'm sure many of them saw no farther than Ypres or Passchendaele.

When it was over I returned to Yorkshire and took up my old Chapel duties, but so many of the men and women I encountered were veterans of the two wars, in one way or another, that I could not rely on my usual authority or even on the usual truths to placate their troubled spirits or my own. This forced me to look deeper than ever before at the lessons the Lord means us to learn in life and at the words written to shape our journey and its inevitable end. To do this I had to try to take my parishioners out of themselves and their terrible recollections. '*Trust in the Lord with all your heart,*' I told them, perhaps contradicting my own need for insight, '*and lean not on your own understanding; in all your ways acknowledge him and he shall direct thy paths.*' I did believe that, but it was never easy.

I loved and respected my parents and always felt close my brothers no matter our very different ways. Next to father and myself, Clem was the most religious, but his faith was always bound up in his music. Sometimes when he visited we would discuss the hymns he had written, and he would leave me with the scores of his most recent efforts. Mostly I found a conflict between the simplicity of the words and the lavish sounds, but never wanted to hurt his feelings by saying so. I rarely saw Bertie except at occasional holiday gatherings while mother was alive. The legal life in York took its toll as he wasn't yet sixty when his heart gave out. Arthur lived in self-imposed exile in the Lake District where he taught school, never forgiving father for his treatment of Lettie, though he was pleased when mother travelled to her funeral and began her correspondence with Miss Muir. He and I had the least in common. I could not tolerate his reliance on literature as replacement for true faith, and he viewed my devotion as foolish tribute to what cannot be proven. Horace, of course, went back to the Orkneys and never came south again. From what I was able to gather, his experience in the first war was very different from my own. He died not much older than Bertie when Hitler was threatening invasion. As for Norman, he became quite a successful naturalist and the most highly educated of us all. His work at Nottingham University was renowned throughout the country, and a species of rare butterfly is named after him though he always maintained his old mentor, Mr. Garson, deserved it more.

There is the one photograph taken just before we went to the islands in which Lettie leans against the back of father's chair with the trace of a smile on her lips. I have many pictures of the rest of the family sent to me over the years that marked changes in their features and always animated my sense of passing time, but even though I visited her twice after that fateful summer, and had my final glimpse into her coffin, my lasting image of her remains frozen in the garden of our Yorkshire house. I shall always be grateful to Horace for showing me the way to Margaret Muir's door and to my relationship with the two of them that would otherwise have been cut off by my own shortcomings. Father never took a similar journey of reconciliation because he made it plain the Lord's judgment, as always, took precedence over his own. The trouble was in this instance he shaped that judgment as he saw fit, looking only to those verses that would justify his inability to forgive her. I tried more than once to speak with him about this confusion of Word and word, and about the contradictions Mr. Scott and I discussed with St. Magnus looking on, but on each occasion failed miserably to influence him.

Mother's behaviour reflected his own until Lettie died. He did not openly order her to stay in Yorkshire when Horace's cable arrived, but she defied any unspoken demand. Though she must have desperately regretted the wasted years, her Orkney farewell and subsequent bond with Margaret surely lightened her heart. When she saw the inscription on the headstone in that tiny cemetery above the sea, I believe she finally understood how splendid Lettie's freedom was before she found eternal peace.

Horace 1942

It was a bitter day in the midst of the coldest winter I had ever known on the islands. A thin layer of ice had formed on Scapa Flow and sloshed around the hulls of the fleet. We were loading horses aboard a transport ship that was making ready for France. Cavalry mounts they were, sleek and well-muscled but skittish until you got them settled below. We brought them out in groups of ten or twelve on a flat-bottomed barge, tied a rag over their eyes, wrapped the leather bag around their bellies, and hooked up to the winch. They rose without ceremony, their legs dangling and steam pumping from their nostrils like smoke from a stack, and they were probably in the air for no more than a minute or two before disappearing into the hold. On this trip the last one gave some trouble, rearing up and flashing out with his hooves so it was all I could do to cling to his halter and keep him from tumbling over the side. I short-hauled him bringing my fist on the rope right up under his chin, talking quietly to him all the time, and gradually he calmed down. But as luck would have it the harness buckle failed to close properly and the boys on the deck above swept him up before we could call them off. You could see he wasn't going to make it as he was listing sideways just a few feet out of my grasp, and I prayed when he tumbled that he didn't hit the side of the barge or fall from a greater height and meet his fate against the ship's rail or deck.

Suddenly, as the winch swung him out over the water, the buckle gave way and he slid off the tilted bag like a sled down a frozen slope and crashed into the sea. The men above and below were shouting and carrying on but unable to make sense of one another as I waited for his head to surface and to see if there was any chance of looping a rope around his neck. When he came up he was too far away and thrashing in desperation at his plight, struggling against the currents and the cold. I suppose I reacted to the certainty of him drowning there in front of me because I leapt in without thinking, the shock hitting my chest like a sledge-hammer, my extremities already numb before I cleared the surface, trying to track him down through the salt film over my eyes. The men's calls filled the air like the cries of seagulls, and someone tossed a life-buoy that floated away on the tide, a broken piece of rope trailing fuzzily in its wake.

I shook my head to clear the haze and saw the stallion sunk to the withers a few yards off, its foreleg hooves thrust out uselessly in front of its muzzle as if they might gain purchase on a solid piece of air. The frigid water was quickly sapping my strength, and I cursed my saviour impulse that had brought me to this end and to leave Althea a widow at thirty-six. I thought of Margaret warning me years ago of the sea's indifference to our fate as we thought to test it on a run to Shapinsay with the storm-clouds all around. I couldn't lift my arms, and my boots were like lead weights four feet beneath my slowing heart. The horse was still there, reaching for the sky, but the barge and ship had disappeared into the empty expanse, and we were two tiny figures lost in the shared solitude of our dying. It was then I heard her voice. It came from no direction and every direction at once and it was clear as a bell.

'Swim, little brother,' she said. 'You can help one another.'

Somehow my arms began to pull me along while my boots kicked out against the depths. The chop was in my mouth and the brine coated my cheeks and eyelids, but I kept on for what seemed like hours and eventually drew up on the flailing creature. I circled him warily, keeping my distance until I could lunge out and grab a handful of his mane with one hand. He panicked further, dragging me under and against his pulsing barrel before I could fight my way back to breath and secure my hold. Finally, I managed to swing a leg over his back and find an imaginary saddle. The barge came back into view and I could hear the men yelling. Reaching out for the bridle I yanked his head around in the direction of their noise. In our common fear and refusal to relinquish our new-found grip on life, we moved as one and reached the shore.

The men told me later I had been in the water near to ten minutes and it was amazing I hadn't turned to ice. They had wrapped us both in blankets and given me some hot tea. As I lay there with the warmth slowly returning to my limbs, I saw some were preparing to hitch him to the winch again and could see his legs trembling though he was quite subdued from shock and did not resist their efforts.

'No,' I called. 'Leave him be. He's been through enough today.'

Just then an officer with a megaphone shouted down from above that we should stop wasting time and get our last bit of cargo aboard. 'That's an order, sergeant!'

I couldn't see his face but could bet from the sound of his voice he wasn't more than a stripling. There were too many of them at the front, I'd been told, but I wasn't about to argue my way into military prison.

242

The others looked at me and I nodded. The horse swung towards the heavens, and it hit me that had I waited in the water for some sign from above I would be floating face-down now beside a dead stallion. But something had saved me for another fate. It was only then I remembered her voice.

That night I told Margaret my story. She listened in silence as the fire crackled with a few pieces of dry wood I had thrown on top of the peat.

'I do believe she was there with you,' she said when I had done. 'And that she's here with us every day. That's my idea of God.'

'Maybe He gives us one chance after you die to come back and make a difference.'

'No, Horace, I don't think the dead ever leave us. Your father and Lettie were so unlike, but they are surely together now and his voice was part of hers that you heard. They both loved you and would want you safe on this earth.'

I told her it was nice to think so, then pointed out what passed between us the last time I saw each of them.

I went back to Yorkshire with the family certain I would soon return to build that cottage next to Margaret's. But father had other plans. He said he would pay for me to train as a vet's helper if I would promise to stay home until I was eighteen, a proper age for a young man to set out on his own, though he hoped I would see that my prospects would be better advanced close by him and mother. When I told him that while I appreciated his support I could not make that promise, he told me I could remain in the house but find any available work on my own. He would expect a weekly contribution to household expenses since I was determined to be independent. It was obvious that since I was also expected to attend school I would be able to save no money to pay for the train north or anywhere else for that matter.

Father did not count on Mr. Peverel. I wrote him explaining my situation, and he replied he would be happy to lend me the fare that I could work off in his employ. But he was adamant I accept father's edict for the next year. He had consulted with Mr. Campbell, he said, and the age of majority in Scotland was generally deemed to be sixteen. Reaching that, if I took up residence in the Orkneys and held a steady position Father would have great difficulty in persuading any judge I should be returned to his care. The result was I became a stable-boy for a successful farmer on outskirts of town who quickly discovered my way with animals and put me in charge of his livestock. I made more than I expected and even after giving mother a set amount for my food and board had a little to put aside. They thought I would come to my senses, as I was always respectful. Waiting confidently for my conversion, they could not see me biding my time.

On the Saturday I turned sixteen, Arthur came home from Keswick where he was teaching school and Bertie from York where he was studying for his barrister's exams. Ernest was away in Lincolnshire, but Clem and Norman were present for the tea with cake mother had prepared. Everyone raised a glass of punch and wished me well. Then father decided to seize the bull by the horns, thinking no doubt that with others around I would not dare to argue.

'Well, Horace, I have made some enquiries on your behalf at our local college, and it seems you will be able to obtain a certificate there as a veterinary assistant despite your average grades. It will mean full-time attendance so you will have to give up your farm work, but your mother and I feel you have made great strides in your maturity over the past year and will be pleased to assist you.'

I had been prepared for something of the kind, and the certificate was a strong temptation. But I had my answer ready. My letters to and from Lettie gave me the strength and belief in my direction. I thanked him but said I would be returning to the Orkneys at the end of the month. Mr. Peverel had work waiting for me there.

'You will defy me, then, just like your sister!'

'It is her I wish to be near,' I told him.

'Be warned, Horace. Like her you will not see this house again.'

'Father,' Arthur remonstrated, 'don't you see this is a way back to Lettie?'

'I don't need such direction,' he said dismissively. Then he looked at me harshly. 'If you're leaving,' he said, 'it might as well be immediately. *One day is as a thousand years, and a thousand years as one day*, saith the apostle.'

'He can stay with me,' Bertie said.

'Father,' I began, not wishing things to end this way. To my surprise he held out his hand for me to shake, which I was glad to do. 'Goodbye Horace,' he said. 'May the Lord be with you always.' Mother hugged me, but she was not completely on his side as she asked that I write. Then they left the room and I never saw him again. She, of course, came to Lettie's funeral, and after that our letters were frequent.

I did not expect Lettie would die of her illness, which was why I sent a letter rather than a cable to father and mother. Three days after I put it in the post, she was gone, and I walked in a fog to the telegraph office hardly able to fill out the form. *Lettie passed away from infection. Stop. Will hold funeral until sure of your plans. Stop.* My tears smudged the form, and I had to ask for another.

My cottage was several hundred feet from theirs and there was soon a well-worn path between the two. Mr. Spence found several young lads like myself to help build it, and I was settled in shortly. Mr. Peverel, true to his word, hired me the day after my arrival and paid me a wage that kept me in what Ernest and the Bible had called 'food and raiment.' On Sunday afternoons after Chapel, weather permitting, my two sisters took me sailing, and I quickly learned to know and love the ocean, which stood me in good stead years later on Scapa Flow. Arthur, Ernest, and Bertie came to visit more than once, and one summer when Clem was sixteen he turned up with Norman, mother apparently having stood by them and given them the fare. It was a full three years since she had seen her youngest brothers and Lettie cried with joy. All of our visitors spoke of father's refusal to bend. He seemed to accept he had lost control of his family on this issue, but felt something akin to his honour, or the Lord's honour, was at stake, and he was not going to change. Naturally, I never forgot him, but as time passed he became more like a distant relative than a parent.

Lettie and Margaret were very happy together. Their only disagreements were over the suitability of the weather for a sail or if one of them stayed in the garden too long under the afternoon sun. Lettie took in private students, young girls who needed some extra attention even though it was assumed they would only go so far in school before becoming wives and mothers. She told me that one day women would gain the right to vote and so influence their own futures, and, of course, she was right. When it happened in 1918, I walked with Margaret to the polls where we cast our ballots for a local man who was demanding independence for the Orkneys. He lost, but Margaret said it felt good to contribute to such possibility.

Until the day the infection struck her down, she remained healthy and full of strength. The sun bronzed her face and arms which she bared to its rays without any inhibitions. When Margaret told me she was resting in bed one day, I was surprised but not alarmed. I had come down with the grippe occasionally and had to inform Mr. Peverel I was not available. But then things took a turn for the worse, the doctor was summoned, and Lettie drifted in and out of a deep sleep, sometimes making no sense with her words at all. I sat by her, spelling Margaret when she needed to lie down, and heard her talk to herself as if from a dream.

'No,' she said, over and over again and her brow was furrowed. Then she smiled and opened her eyes. 'Yes,' she said to me, and I felt she was back because she called me by name and asked for Margaret whom I went to rouse from her slumber. When we got to the door she was by the window that looked down to the sea.

'Lettie,' Margaret cried, 'you'll catch your death!'

'I'd like one more sail,' she said in a voice clear as a bell, moving her arms back and forth above her head as if in imitation of billowing canvas. 'Stay here and wait for me.'

I ran and caught her as she slumped toward the floor.

Everyone but father came north for the funeral. When he died at the beginning of the war, I did not attend his. Now we are in the midst of another conflict and there is no use for horses anymore.

Elizabeth 1930

I have lived a long life, and many years without my husband by my side. Thomas died at the beginning of the war and missed the horror that claimed so many young Englishmen and their comrades from France and the colonies. What I will never understand is how our beloved Queen's grandson could be so evil as to attack members of his own family and those they ruled. I was proud of our children. Ernest volunteered as a chaplain, but did not cross the Channel. Instead he was assigned to meet returning troops at the docks, especially the wounded, and provide spiritual comfort to them. Horace enlisted in the Royal Navy but never went far from the Orkneys, thank God. He was put in charge of horse transportation between the mainland and ships in Scapa Flow and rose to the rank of sergeant. Mr. Spence wrote to tell me of how highly the officers thought of him and his work, and at the end of the war he received a Distinguished Conduct Medal for his service. The other boys stayed home. Arthur wouldn't fight whatever the circumstances, but his age and teaching position exempted him from conscription, otherwise he would have registered as a conscientious objector, a shameful position to many and certain to anger his father since it wouldn't have been sought for religious reasons. To his credit, though, he did volunteer in the York hospital wards housing the injured and dying. Bertie stayed with the Home Office, advising the Minister on matters of law and order. When Clem attempted to enlist the doctors discovered he had a weak heart, so he stayed in his Lincolnshire parish where he organized concerts for the families of men at the front. Norman, because of his eyes, was allowed to remain in his laboratory at the university, but halfway through the war the government decided learned people like himself could get together and contribute to the writing of pamphlets and speeches that supported our troops. He told me of meeting Kipling and Conan Doyle on several occasions.

I stayed with Ernest and Anne throughout the conflict that went on so much longer than anyone expected, and I have lived in their house ever since. My three grandchildren visit often, Bertie's boy, Gerald, who has become a barrister like his father, and Clem's two, John and Elizabeth, who are still very young. I am delighted by their company, and my namesake, in particular, is a free-spirited and intelligent girl, even if somewhat headstrong. Clem will have to watch her when she is older though I hope with some indulgence. It is a shame Horace and Norman have no children, though Norman's wife Catherine confided to me, as this newer generation is wont to do, that in their case it is not from lack of trying. Arthur, meanwhile, has remained a bachelor all these years. I do think it has something to do with his poetry not being well-received, a lack of confidence perhaps, but I would never suggest this. He has continued to write, he tells me, but nothing has been published except for one or two bits in local magazines.

One of my great satisfactions for almost thirty years has been my continuing correspondence with Margaret Muir. I have not been back to the islands since Lettie's funeral, but we have become quite good friends through our letters that come and go every month or so. I spoke only briefly to Thomas about my trip. There was no point in confronting him since he had long ago taken an irrevocable position when she refused to bend to our authority and her duty, and he was not about to change his mind. I was angry with her then and for a great while after, but when she died the tight coil around my heart was torn asunder and I could no longer turn away from the one with whom she had chosen to share her life.

I hardly remember the difficult train trip north, and it was a good thing the boys were with me, the older ones from Edinburgh on. We arrived in Kirkwall where, our old house under lease, a suitable bed and breakfast was found for me facing the harbour. Arthur went to Horace's home. Ernest and Clem, to my surprise, had written to Presbyterian acquaintances from the cathedral, and stayed in with them. Bertie lodged with Mr. Campbell. Norman, to my consternation, announced he would be at Mr. Garson's house. I had never quite forgiven him for leading his naive pupil to that cliff-face, but my own sorrow was so strong I could not dwell long on that part of the past.

The next morning Ernest offered to accompany me to the cottage where Lettie lay waiting, but I said I would prefer to go alone. I was fearful I would break down when I saw her, but Miss Muir and I had much to say to one another as well, and so raw would be our shared feelings that I doubted even Ernest, for all his compassion, would be much good. I walked slowly down the beach, my boots sinking in the sands of time, recalling how we had all trodden this path together before our conflict. Following the rising path through the fields where Norman had hunted his butterflies, I looked north to the spot where his selkie had saved him and Lettie and Miss Muir had provided his escape, closing my eyes in the bright sunlight and seeing their shadowy shapes in that frail boat as it rode the swells to safety. Another ten minutes on the path and the cottage appeared, unchanged but for a fresh coat of green paint on the front door and sashes, with the boat still bobbing beside the wharf below.

She answered my knock, the depth of pain and sorrow in her eyes vanquishing any tension I had felt in my approach or uncertainty as to our association. We had both loved Lettie, loved her still, there could be no doubt of that, and we were here to give one another what consolation we could rather than fight over the past or any present remains. Without speaking, she grasped my hand and led me into the front room where Lettie lay unadorned in her plain coffin. She was thinner than when I had left her and there were small lines by her eyes and the sides of her mouth that spoke to ten years of country life and much time on the water. I wept uncontrollably as I bent to kiss her cheek and called out her name repeatedly. Hardly knowing my whereabouts, I was guided me to a chair in another room where a strangely comforting Scots burr pulled at my attention.

'She went quickly and without suffering, just a shortness of breath at first then a slight fever for a day and night whose power we could not anticipate. The doctor was here, of course, but there was little he could do against the infection.'

I did not reply for a few moments so lost was I in my grief that I had kept bottled up on the train for the sake of the boys. They had their own feelings to deal with, all of them having seen her fairly recently when I had not. Gradually I came to my senses and through the blurring of my tears saw Miss Muir seated by me in the kitchen, a woman whose beauty I had not noticed all those years ago because of my umbrage at having been wronged and, yes, by my jealousy.

'I'm sorry,' I said.

'For what?'

'For letting each of you down. Not in the beginning, because I couldn't understand what was going on. But before it was too late, I should have quelled my resentments and reached out to you both.'

'You did in your way by helping Clem and Norman to visit us.'

'I couldn't keep them from her.'

She smiled and glanced at the coffin. 'It was like sailing the boat into waters that had never been explored before. We had to keep an eye on where we were going, not on where we had come from.'

'As when you rescued Norman.'

'Yes, something like that. Only there I had a feel for the tiller and a sense of the currents. When Lettie and I struck out alone we were like beginners, the first sailors on a strange sea.'

'But you were happy.' It wasn't a question I was asking but, I realized, an admission it had taken her death to draw forth.

'Yes, we were happy, and have stayed so until just a few days ago.'

She made some tea and told me of Lettie's tutoring of young girls who came to the cottage for lessons in literature and mathematics to supplement their schooling.

'They were very loyal to her, as were their parents, because she obviously cared for their well-being and tried to give them some skills beyond those they would acquire in the classroom. Two of them are now studying to be nurses in Inverness and another has become a teacher here herself. It is not easy for girls to rise above their expected station on the island, you know. Lettie was a leader for them, and an example.'

I stood and walked into the room to where she lay, trying to think of a sacred verse to say over her, one that would do her justice and not damn her for her supposed sins. The idea that she was in some burning pit because she had flaunted biblical law seemed itself heretical to me, and I dismissed it with every fibre of strength in my being. Nothing came to me immediately, just bits and pieces like flotsam and jetsam on the waters before the creation of the world as we know it or perhaps after its end. I tried to conjure up some response to Thomas's constant scriptural condemnations of her before we left the islands but could not. When I explained my frustrations to Miss Muir she rose and disappeared upstairs. After a minute or two I heard her footsteps on the stairs again and looked up to see her holding out a framed piece of coloured needlework.

'This has been on the wall of our room since Lettie came to live here. It is from the Book of *Romans*.'

'Our room,' I said to myself and was grateful I could touch a part of it. She set the piece on my knee and the letters there divided light from darkness.

Do not be conformed to this world
But be transformed by the renewal of your mind,
That by testing you may discern
What is the will of God
What is good, and acceptable, and perfect.

I met with Horace the next morning and was introduced to his fiancé, Althea. He hadn't changed much in all his time away but had grown into manhood as I had always expected he would, possessing a quiet strength and sense of purpose that served him with people as well as animals. He and Mr. Peverel shared a practice together, and I knew the domesticated island animals were the better for it. When we spoke there were no words of blame for me or his father, just a quiet resignation that Lettie had gone before her time. I can see Althea is a caring woman who shelters his tender spirit.

That afternoon as I entered the Kirkwall Chapel, Mr. Taggart approached and expressed his sympathies. When he shook his head in disappointment at Thomas's absence, I could not tell whether his gesture contained disapproval as well. He was followed by a tall, weathered man who introduced himself as Rory Parker and said that with her help to the islanders Lettie had been her father's daughter. He enquired after Thomas's health then stepped away without further comment. There were more people present than I could previously have imagined had known her, including many former students and those still in school who had benefited from her instruction.

Ernest conducted the service with great sensitivity, telling the story of Christ's meeting with the woman at the well to whom he gave the water of life. The coffin lay beneath the altar, and when all the holy words had been spoken and the hymns sung, with Clem at the organ for *O God our help in ages past*, Arthur read a poem in which he compared Lettie's eyes to the sun burning in the sea and sky. I have the copy still. Bertie stood briefly to mention her last words to him when we were leaving her behind eight years ago. 'A lesson to remember when we judge others,' he said to the mourners, and I knew he was including his father in this remark. Then Norman rose to speak so beautifully of how his sister was like his beloved selkie that I almost believed in that mythical creature myself. There was no need for Horace to say anything. As much as his own need for freedom, his love for her had brought him back to the island. The boys carried her to a cart that bore her past the main cemetery and out to the cottage property where she lies overlooking the sea. 'She makes it hallowed ground,' Ernest assured me, 'and it's where she wanted to be.'

He spoke briefly at the gravesite and we recited the Lord's prayer, Margaret, Mr. Taggart, Mr. Parker, the six boys, and their friends and protectors – Mr. Garson, Mr. Spence, Mr. Peverel, Mr. Campbell, and the Minister and organist from the cathedral. The stone had been prepared at Margaret's behest with Lettie's name and the dates of her birth and death. Arthur told me the inscription beneath was from a poem by Christina Rossetti, chosen by Margaret, and it revealed for me and for all to appreciate the blessedness of their love for one another. As she was lowered into the ground, I wept for the last time, then transformed my grief into support and affection for my new daughter whom I would never let go.

Thomas 1914

I am seventy-three and poorly. The Lord is waiting for me as the world slides into darkness. Last month the prince of Austria-Hungary and his wife were killed by a madman, and now we are at war with Germany. The boys are surely too old and settled to consider volunteering, though Ernest has indicated he may well put his name forward as a chaplain. Bertie has an important position with the Home Office where his legal skills are needed. Arthur, whose teaching duties are not so vital, says he will avoid service under any circumstances as he abjures appeals to God and country. 'A bit too much like *Deutschland uber alles*,' he says, adding that the anthem was written by a German poet on a North Sea island belonging at the time to England. I do worry about Horace. He has written his mother from Kirkwall that the army will need men to work with the horses hauling the guns and other heavy equipment, not to mention the finer breeds of the cavalry. I will try to dissuade him from any personal sacrifice, but my opinion has not meant much to him for many years. Clem is a choirmaster in Louth, and I cannot think how any of his musical abilities could be of service at the front, though I suppose bands will be necessary to celebrate our victories. As for Norman, he's as blind as a bat without his spectacles and would be utterly useless even if he could tear himself away from his studies.

Everyone has turned out well, though Elizabeth frets about the lack of grandchildren. There have to be more marriages first, I remind her. Ernest, Horace, and Bertie have been to the altar, but only the latter, with the warm-hearted Jane, is a parent (of Gerald, a tow-headed lad of eleven with a sunny disposition like his mother's). Fatherhood does not seem likely for Ernest at his age, though Anne, a little younger than him, is a wonderful helpmate at his Chapel and always very kind to us when she visits. I have not met Horace's wife, Althea, nor do I expect there will be any such acquaintance before I leave this earth. He has never forgiven me for Lettie. Somehow Elizabeth has escaped his censure, likely because she traveled north when his letter and cable arrived.

Eight years after our summer on the Orkneys and our daughter's distressing choice that kept her there, she contacted an infection of the lungs and died in the cottage to which she had retreated. It all happened so fast, Horace's telegraphed announcement of her death came the same day his longer missive about her illness was delivered in the mail. I prayed for her soul that night while Elizabeth packed. I said I would not accompany her though Clement and Norman told her they would, and the others made their plans separately to meet their mother in Edinburgh. They had all visited Lettie over the years. Elizabeth offered no explanation except to say she would not allow her daughter to be consigned to that cold island ground without farewell. Neither did she weep, at least in front of me, but her grief was evident in every weighted step she took and in her last words as she prepared to board the train.

'We should never have let her go.'

'It was her decision, Elizabeth.'

'Yes, and once she had made it we should never have let her go.'

I understood what she meant but told her I did not see what could have been done given our conviction. Lettie's was a sin only the Lord could forgive, I reminded her. Why else had we not broken the silence between us and the islands during the past decade?

Her tears fell now as she held my hands in hers. 'I believe this is the Lord's punishment on us, Thomas, and we must bear it for the rest of our lives,' she said, naturally distraught as any mother would be at the loss of her child, no matter her behaviour. I assured her we were not to blame and reminded her gently that '*The Lord giveth and the Lord taketh way,*' but she would not be comforted. The truth I did not utter was that Lettie was dead to me almost a decade before.

A cable came from Clem late the next day to say they had arrived safely, then for two weeks I heard nothing more. I busied myself with my work and tried not to dwell on her absence or the reason for it. Finally, I sent a cable to Horace asking that she inform me of her return. To my relief, he replied she would be leaving the next day, with a stop in Edinburgh, and provided the time of her arrival at our station. When she stepped to the platform with our youngest boys at her side, I could see her tiredness from the journey in her features, but also a distance from her surroundings and, indeed, from me as I kissed her cheek and took her arm.

'Was all as expected?' I asked as we walked to the line of cabs, Clem and Norman trailing behind with a porter and the luggage. The rain was pattering on the cobblestones and running in rivulets along the cracks and around the horse's hooves. It suddenly came to me how little it had rained that summer on the islands, and for a moment I wished I could see that bright and blustery convergence of land and sea once more. But there needed to be no return to summon up the enduring image of Lettie walking out from our house into an improper life. It had come to me unbidden often enough, and all the sights and sounds of the Orkneys or more familiar countryside could not wipe the consequence away.

She looked up at me with a sadness of expression I feared would never vanish. 'Thomas,' she said with a quiet determination I could not ignore, 'we will not lose anyone else.' Apart from a few words about the funeral after we were warm and dry at the house, we never spoke of Lettie again.

Now I am afraid the war will take others. We are told foolishly it will be over by Christmas and there will be no need for most volunteers to cross the channel. It may be that chaplains will be pressed into service to console the injured and bless the dead. I retired from the pulpit some years ago else I would have to devise a suitable sermon to speak to these troubled times and urge the congregation to keep their faith in our Queen and her generals. There was a time, of course, when I was prepared to shout them down in the name of justice for the fishermen and their families, but that was but a skirmish compared to the continental battle to come. I learned from Mr. Taggart that after his return to a hero's welcome Rory Parker had formed a fishermen's union to ensure a future of fair prices and practices. Undoubtedly, if he has the strength, he is leading the struggle still.

My thoughts of the Orkneys are quickened by reports in the *Times* that the great bay to the south of the main island is to be used as a base for the fleet to guard the entrances to the North Sea. Ernest tells me its name, Scapa Flow, is from Viking days, and that it can hold hundreds of warships. Horace will be influenced by the appearance of destroyers and battleships, and he is bound to make enquiries about the transportation of horses. Hordes of sailors on shore leave will change that peaceful place, but I suspect they will limit themselves to the streets and pubs of Stromness and Kirkwall, and the beach and fields where we walked will remain unsullied. I trust Norman's cliff will remain untried from above and feel certain no enemy could come ashore at its foot unless, of course, he possessed Miss Muir's skills and Lettie's. They did save Norman, that I cannot deny, though it would have been enough had they simply sailed together then gone their different ways. Elizabeth told me her grave is on the hillside above the wharf where the boat is tied, marked by a simple stone with her name and dates and two lines from a poem by Miss Rossetti. It perturbs me deeply to admit this, but I find them almost beautiful as I do those troubling verses in The Song of Solomon.

I cannot love you if I love not Him,
I cannot love Him if I love not you.

After her return, Elizabeth began a correspondence with Miss Muir that continues to this day. I have never asked her what passes between them and have no intention of doing so. When I queried Ernest about the funeral service, he replied that he had conducted it and that Mr. Taggart, Rory Parker, and many other islanders had been in attendance. I praised him for accepting his ministerial responsibilities in the face of his grief, and I thought but did not say such a crowd showed great respect for myself and the family. As if wanting to correct my reading of events, he replied, 'You can't imagine, father, how she was loved.' Miss Rossetti and my own earthly judgments aside, now my own time is near, I pray the Lord *has* forgiven Lettie so He might teach me to do the same when we meet in Heaven.

Bertie 1934

The night before my sister's funeral I did not dream of her but of Alice MacBride. On my previous return to the island with Ernest, she had been away with her girls on the mainland. I had a good talk with Jamie then who told me their marriage had outlasted the gossip and her spontaneous show of feelings for Roger Nicholas. The dream was quite vivid, and when I woke in the morning in Mr. Campbell's spare bedroom my cheeks burned with the thought I had slept with her during the night. Happily engaged to Jane for the past year, I hadn't thought I'd be haunted so.

First things first, however. If I may be permitted a barrister's point of view, Lettie made a binding choice, one that could certainly be challenged but never overturned except by her own judgement. Father did appeal her decision on grounds of grievous wrong, but when the jury, consisting of the rest of his family, ruled against him, the cost was very high. He left the courtroom of his own construction intact and in his own mind could not let the case drop. In the end he was the guilty one and the prisoner, not her.

Enough with legal masks! The simple and painful truth is that he could not accept her love for Margaret Muir, and I believe he paid greatly for this. He didn't know his own heart, and so could not know Lettie's, relying instead on lukewarm scripture and cold authority to quell her passion.

Her death was a terrible shock to all of us, mother especially. When we met her in Edinburgh she seemed a ghostly figure called into this world without comprehending why. Her black raiment and the veil that hid her face suggested otherwise, but when she first tried to speak her words mingled instantly with the columns of steam from the engine like wispy phantoms of sound without substance. Ernest took her arm and directed her to the station dining-room where we would share a table before taking the overnight train through Inverness and on to Thurso. Horace had invited her to stay at his cottage near to Miss Muir, but she declined, saying she needed to rest and gather her strength, so we found her a tidy bed-and-breakfast not far from the Kirkwall Chapel. We had arrived separately in Edinburgh, and there had not been much opportunity to speak among ourselves on the train given mother's frail disposition, so once we had her settled, we all went for a bite to eat and some verbal sustenance. I would have preferred something stronger than teas and crumpets, as would Arthur, I knew, but we had Ernest and Clem's tastes to contend with as well as Norman's youth. Horace had joined us so we six were together for the first time in many years.

'Father remains the same, then?' Horace asked.

'Yes,' Arthur replied. 'Unrepentant and unbending.'

'That's not quite fair, Arthur,' Ernest said. 'I'm sure he is suffering now, not least because he is alone.'

'That is his choice, is it not?'

I weighed in to keep things on an even keel. 'It's not father we should be concerned with but mother, who is here and needs our support.'

'I offered to accompany her to Margaret's, but she said she wanted to walk alone,' Ernest said.

'How is Margaret?' Arthur asked Horace.

'Well enough, I suppose. When I saw her this morning she enquired after mother and the rest of you.'

'It isn't fair,' said Norman. 'Lettie was so happy here.'

I heard Clem clear his throat. Nodding at Norman, he said, 'When we saw her last she took us for a ride in the boat. Margaret didn't even have to come along, Lettie was so accomplished with the sails and tiller.'

'Yes, we sailed right by the cove where I saw the selkie.'

I looked at him amazed. Here he was almost nineteen years old and still believing in fairy tales. Ernest brought us back to earth as our food and drink arrived by saying he would meet with Mr. Taggart that afternoon and arrange the service for the next day.

'I'd like to play something,' Clem said. 'Perhaps I can discuss the choice of hymns with you and Mr. Taggart.'

'And I have some verse I'd like to read,' Arthur added.

Ernest looked at him sharply. 'Not Shelley or the like?'

Arthur smiled. 'Same old Ernest,' he said. 'No, in fact it's something I wrote for her when she made her choice.'

'Does anyone else want to speak?'

Horace and Norman shook their heads.

'Bertie?'

I was used to speaking in public, but addressing the law on behalf of a client with your brief prepared was not the same as finding the words for what your sister meant to you. I remembered what she had told me before we all returned to Yorkshire. 'O Bertie, you should just love us and forget about the rest.'

'Yes, about a gift she gave me,' I told him.

The next morning we walked to Margaret's cottage to accompany the cart that would convey Lettie's coffin to the Chapel. Horace was right. Margaret's strength was carrying her through the storm of feelings, and when she hugged each one of us I felt she was passing it on so we could ride the waves together. It was difficult to see Lettie so pale and still and to close her in the coffin for the rough journey along the track to town. We walked slowly toward a life without her, and I felt like a clod of earth crushed beneath the turning wheels of our sorrow.

Ernest chose as his text the story of Jesus meeting the woman at the well and how he broke custom by speaking to her though she was a Samaritan and traditionally an outcast. He asked her for a drink of water from her supposedly unclean cup and said he would give her 'living water' so she would never thirst again. 'Christ welcomed her into his fold,' Ernest emphasized. I wished father had been there to hear it. Mother wept quietly while Ernest told the tale and stressed the lesson of forgiveness, then Clem played *O God our help* gloriously and there were one or two other hymns I cannot remember. Arthur and I went separately to the pulpit to say our goodbyes, his something quite lovely about the sun in her eyes. When we had done, to our surprise, Norman raised his hand and Ernest nodded that he should come forward. But he simply stood and turned around, his spectacles glinting in the dim light as he faced the crowd.

'When I was a little boy,' he said, 'I thought my sister was a selkie who pulled me away from the waves.'

There was delighted laughter from the many children for whom magical creatures still had a place in the world, but Norman, as I quickly realized, was speaking to young and old alike.

'Now I know that selkies are who you need them to be, and sisters are who they have to be. Sometimes they come together, and you are lucky if you can be there when it happens.'

'Good for you, lad,' someone said quietly, and I was sure it must be Mr. Garson.

We walked again beside the cart as it made its way to her chosen burial site, my arm linked with mother's who told me she would stay with Horace that night. Our best island friends were at the gravesite, including Mr. Parker who had, with father's help, escaped the local law so a higher one could presumably prevail. The words on the stone said clearly that Lettie had known her own heart, and as she disappeared into the ground, I knew Norman was right. I had been lucky to be there when it was so.

Alice had not appeared at the funeral, but I did not need to see her, dream or no dream. She was no selkie even if she had once assumed that form for me. She was not my sister either, but I recognized she had been what she had to be. Perhaps I finally knew my own heart as well because all my yearnings were for Jane and home. I told myself if we ever had a son I would keep him away from the sea. Because of Lettie, if we were blessed with a daughter I wasn't sure what I would do when the water called.

Arthur 1947

Just yesterday, this couplet:

The sky lowers, but birds still sing
Dark feathered rain, they will take wing.

Not much by itself, I admit, but I lack the energy these days to pursue the flock. Not long after we returned home from the Orkneys, I sent my sheaf of island poems off to John Murray. The rejection slip wasn't long in coming, and without any explanation. After that *Blackwoods* and several other magazines turned down my individual efforts, including what I thought my premier poem to Lettie that I would read at her funeral. Bemoaning my poor reception, I fell in with a group in York that spent more time complaining about the lack of appreciation for their work than in actually producing it, and after several months of such gloom and bad influence withdrew to my study where I have remained ever since as far as my verse is concerned. Still, I have always been delighted by the emergence of images and metaphors from my mind whatever their lonely fate. What matter they have rarely been discerned by the powers that be and it sometimes seems I am the only writer left on earth? When I read Robert Bridges' commentary on his publishing of Hopkins poems, I felt a kinship with that long-dead Jesuit visionary unheralded for over thirty years.

Knowing I would never earn my living by the pen, I decided that teaching would suit me best. I would stay in touch with all forms of words that way and be inspired by children's innocent glees and sorrows at their performances on the page. Reading them *Ode to the West Wind* and *To a Skylark*, along with Hardy's melancholy stanzas to test their enthusiasm, and revealing the joys of rhythm and rhyme, kept me sane in a world that has twice descended into hell. Both times I volunteered for hospital work, in 1914 since I could never serve such madness on the front, and twenty-six years later because, though old, I could not simply stand by. I saw the Kaiser's and Hitler's horrors inflicted on the bodies and minds of men so much younger than myself, many of them boys not much older than my students, and I did what I could to help them live or die with dignity. These things I wrote of because I had to and did not bother to send them out.

Wrapped in white gauze but for his eyes
He blinks at me in pain and fear
But also there a need to prise
The conflict's soul into the clear

The tearing, ripping cry goes on
Each night and day to sound the same
He cannot call midnight or dawn
A war by any other name

At his bed's foot there is a sheet
To tell the tale who, what, and when
White-coated figures all so neat
They cannot mend the soul again

Not Sassoon or Owen, I am aware, but I was at least one man's witness whatever my talent.

In the years before her death, I visited Lettie three times, staying the nights with Horace in his cottage and glorious days with her and Margaret rambling about the island or in the boat between the wharf and Shapinsay. Over the years, under Margaret's tutelage, Lettie became quite adept at handling the *Tom Paine*, and we spent many hours together sailing along the coast and out in the middle of the channel where the winds whirled like dervishes, setting our course into new worlds of space and time marked only by lines of foam and the sun's slow sinking in the western sky.

One evening during my first visit the four of us sat by the fire and Margaret listened to our talk of how fortuitous father's property inheritance had been, the Orkneys not on any of our childhood maps, and how each of us – Ernest, Bertie, Clem, and Norman, as well – had found something here to sustain him when the sojourn was over.

'I once saw a map of Britain,' Margaret said, 'that showed everything from a northern point of view.'

'What do you mean?' I asked.

'Well, the Shetlands and the Orkneys were huge as was most of Scotland, but then things gradually started to shrink until London and southern England were just barely visible dots.'

'So Yorkshire was somewhere in between?' Horace said.

She laughed. 'I suppose so, yes, but I must admit I didn't pay much attention.'

'Brobdingnag and Lilliput,' I remarked.

'We all became Gullivers of one kind or another, didn't we?' Lettie said.

'It's a very apt comparison to a point, if you think about it,' I told her. 'We had to deal with our own version of the Houyhnhnms in the form of father and mother, the perfect rulers who kept us lowly Yahoos under their sway.'

'O Arthur, I will not condemn them that way. We are all true to our natures, and they were simply being so to theirs.'

'They abandoned you, Lettie.'

'But none of the rest of you did, and that is what I prefer to dwell on.'

'Thank God, you can. Remember, Gulliver retreats to his stables and converses with his stallions and mares, slowly going insane, which is what would have happened to us all if we had not seen your light.' I imagined Horace musing on the strange combination of madness and horses.

The next morning we sat on the wharf watching the gannets fold their great wings as they dived into the waves, staying submerged for the longest time before appearing with a cod or herring in their beaks, the doomed scales glinting in the sunlight.

'They can go down for thirty feet or more,' she said. 'So there's not much place for the fish to hide. Apparently they lay only one egg at a time, and it takes years for the young to mature.'

'You've become an expert in all sorts of ways.'

'You know as well as I do it's just a matter of paying attention to what goes on around you. Horace and Norman do it the best of all.'

'And me?'

'You, Arthur, are my visionary brother, and every sister needs one. But your words help keep you harnessed to the world.'

'More like Breugel's ploughman than Icarus, then?'

She smiled. 'What will you do with the rest of your life while the crops of poems are growing?'

'I don't know. Teach, perhaps. I can take a year's course work at college in York and get my licence. There's nothing else I'm fit for, really. Besides, I'll get several weeks holiday every year and can visit you then.'

We were talking too much about me, and I wanted to hear of her own situation.

'How are you, Lettie? It's been two years. Is everything the way you thought it would be?'

She sat with her knees drawn up to her chin and her arms wrapped around her legs as if she were cold, though it was a warm July day and there was not a cloud in the sky.

'It has been more than I dreamed though I sometimes wonder at the price I paid, that we all paid in our different ways.'

'You may have lost father and mother, but you didn't lose your brothers, not a single one of them.'

'But everyone was changed by what I did. You cannot tell me the family is the same.'

'No, that's true. But I think you gave us all a sense we could be what we wanted to be and not depend on direction from the pulpit.'

'I had no intention of turning anyone away from mother's and father's guidance. It was just that they had nothing further to teach me. Clem and Norman mustn't branch out on their own too soon, and when they do they must know where they are going.'

'Oh, I don't think there's any worry about Clem. There's too much of the Methodist in him for any foolishness. As for Norman, he'll be a man of ideas as well as a chaser of butterflies and selkies, so father won't be able to keep up after awhile.'

'You know, when I made up my mind to stay, it was only Margaret I was thinking of. The Orkneys are part of me now, but back then I could have been anywhere with her – the colonies, the Sahara, it wouldn't have mattered.'

'And you're happy?'

She nodded. 'If happiness means a sharing of your innermost thoughts and feelings with someone you love and the daily contentment that results. We have our disagreements, of course, and it is frustrating that we cannot walk arm in arm in the high street.'

'Not like sisters?'

I saw a flash of anger and immediately regretted my words. 'We are *not* sisters, Arthur, and our public affection would clearly indicate otherwise. People here exhibit good will, but, except for our friends, it comes from tolerance rather than approval. We walk a finer line than you think.'

'I'm sorry,' I said. 'I should have known better,'

'There's something else, as well.'

A gannet plunged perilously close to the wharf and came up with an empty beak.

'I may have spurned conventional marriage to a man, but I have always wanted a child. And now it is impossible. If we were sisters we could adopt a girl or boy from the orphanage in Thurso, but since we have never denied our true relationship, we have blocked that route.'

'I didn't know, Lettie.'

'How could you? How could anyone except Margaret? That is one of those rare innermost thoughts almost too painful to share. So tell our brothers, as I have told Horace, that I want to see as much of my nieces and nephews as possible, especially while they are growing up.'

Alas, she did not live to see Bertie's or Clem's children, and Horace, who would have been the perfect provider, dwelling so close-by, didn't marry Althea until after the funeral. Not that it mattered in the end as, like Ernest and Anne, Norman and Catherine, they were childless. I've often wondered if there was a curse placed on us for so determinedly following our own paths during and after our Orkneys sojourn. Perhaps Lettie's action did the most to alter things as far as father's and mother's prospective role as grandparents was concerned, but that doesn't explain the biological facts. As for me, I never married, though I have remained wedded to my efforts at verse and hold them as near to my heart as any imagined lover despite their ineffectual ways. Regardless of my failures, the most sublime address to the Spirit of Beauty might as well be my own. *I vowed that I would dedicate my powers/To thee and thine – have I not kept the vow?*

Clement 1962

My side of the story won't be what my descendants hear. My son, who has been to Canada, tells me his nephew considers me as the one who unfairly disowned their mother. In other words, I have become my father who renounced his own daughter because he did not approve her choice of a mate.

I have never forgotten Lettie and what she suffered because father could not reconcile her love for Margaret Muir with his biblical precepts. There have been those, more than one of my brothers among them, who have accused me of being too much the minister's son, and certainly my role in the Chapel all these years would seem to support such a view. But it is Ernest who followed father into the pulpit, a place that allows no contradictions, while I chose another road, one filled with the precision and passion of music. Two opposing elements, you might say, but surely the trick or the talent is to harmonize them in the same composition, whether it is in praise of the Lord or of family. I have written many hymns and more than a few classical pieces, not least of which was my first with its eight individual movements that revealed the prominent characteristics of my siblings and parents, as well as my own somewhat troubled features. Who was Clement Larsen, I had asked, and found myself again in that dream of forbidden communion and the accompanying desire to play the St. Magnus organ for a rival congregation. How could I ever forget the trespass and presumption that ultimately provided me with the strength to believe in myself? How could I deny such conviction to anyone else, let alone my own daughter?

Towards the end of the war my daughter, a nurse's assistant in a children's home outside London, met a Canadian airman, a ground crew member who serviced the planes flying out of a base in East Anglia. When she brought him home that summer after the German surrender, and announced they were to be married, I did not consider she might have been already with child. Would that have made any difference in my initial response to this lack of consultation with her step-mother and myself? To part of me, perhaps, if only because there had been so few children granted to my brothers, Lettie, and me, and this would be the first of the next generation. But I did not know and therefore had to judge the proposed union on its visible merits.

Her preference had been born to a northern coal-miner's family. He had emigrated to Canada as a young man and become a citizen of the colony. I would not apologize for thinking she could do better and told her this without hesitation. Since her mother had died when she was just a girl, I was her only true guide in matters spiritual and practical, so it was my duty to speak my mind. It is one thing to succumb to a passing fancy under the pressures of the war and quite another to base your entire life on such an escape whatever the emotional needs at the time. In her defence she brought up her long-deceased aunt, having been told the story in detail, I had no doubt, by Arthur. Apart from Horace, he was the one who had remained most fond of the Orkneys and Lettie's memory there. I was so startled at her using the past to defend her own actions that I never thought to question the source who, I found out much later, had actually been Ernest.

'Aunt Lettie left home when she was no older than me, and you supported her decision.'

'I was far too young to comprehend the meanings of her choice, and I could not understand father's objection. When you're a boy, you resist what you cannot grasp.' I didn't mention how I had visited Lettie with Norman.

'Well, I cannot understand *my* father's objection to what everyone else would consider completely normal behaviour. I want to get married. What's wrong with that?'

'Nothing is wrong with marriage. It's just that the war created special circumstances – countless young men facing death turning to young women for comfort, and the young women afraid there would be no record of their affection except on a license.'

'But Ted wasn't in danger. He never left England.'

I tried to stay calm as my object was to convince her to slow things down and see how she felt in a few months. 'All right, then, let's consider the licensed future you propose. He'll be shipped home sooner or later. Will he come back here or will you go to him?'

'We want to live in Canada.'

This seemed so much farther than the Orkneys were for father and mother that I could not imagine ever seeing her again. She was twenty-one, and I could not block their union even had I wanted to. I simply did not want to lose her, and for perhaps the first time understood father's extreme anxiety. My sister would be relatively nearby geographically, but the step she had taken with Margaret Muir had been into another world altogether. My daughter would not only be an enormous distance away but in a place where, from what I had heard, two hundred years of subduing forests and crossing endless lakes and rivers had crippled any efforts to preserve English affiliations and propriety. The year after her birth, the Canadian Methodists decided to join up with Presbyterians and form what they call the United Church. Was that what she would attend or would she be pulled toward another denomination with no ties whatsoever to her upbringing? I tried to keep our exchange on an even level.

'How will he support you there? What is his training?'

'Before the war he was a teacher just like Uncle Arthur. He can go back to that.'

'I doubt anyone is just like Arthur,' I said, trying without success to lighten the mood a little.

'He is being sent home almost right away. I won't go over until the spring, which will give plenty of time for him to get settled.'

'And where will you live until then?' Though I knew the answer.

'If you will not have me here, I will find a room in London. There will be plenty of children to care for there.'

They would be married, true, but if he was absent for that long then perhaps she would recognize where she really belonged. The wedding was a quiet affair at their request. It did take place in our Chapel, which was my wish, and his parents did make the trip from their town, shy people who didn't want to be a bother. Arthur and Norman attended, but Ernest's duties kept him away. Bertie had been gone for many years, and Horace had an early Orkney grave. Nonetheless, I could not help but be pleased she had not simply eloped to Canada without any attention to family expectations. It was several months before I was made aware of her condition by her step-mother.

My main concern was for her health and safety as she was determined to leave just a month before her expected date. The seas would be rough at that time of year, and I attempted to dissuade her on those grounds alone. But I now was also perturbed by my discovery that she had likely been with child before the wedding and the accompanying probability that impending motherhood had forced her into matrimony. It was my mistake to voice this issue directly rather than attempt to draw it out and let her see the light.

'I love him, father. The baby is the result not the reason for it.'

'Think on it. He has been gone a longer time than you managed to spend with him in England. How can you know either of you is the same person who committed to the future under war's shadow? At least have the baby here. Perhaps then you will have a better grip on where your duties lie.'

'To you, you mean.'

'No, I mean to your child.'

'He will need a father.'

'He?'

'He or she. It will make no difference.'

'What if you get over there and things are not as you expect? What happens, God forbid, if the marriage fails? What happens to fatherhood, then?'

'Failure may be what you wish, but it will not happen.'

I cannot say I wished it, but I had a foreboding she would end alone in a country where she knew no one and with no family to reach out to. It was this troubling thought that forced the unintended words from my mouth.

'Do not expect to return here easily if you are wrong.' I meant, God knows, that time and distance could well intervene in unassailable ways, but she took it as a statement of severance and turned away. It was my weakness that I could not immediately retract or explain, and, as the days passed, I confess that I felt such an extreme indication of my unhappiness might serve the purpose of convincing her to stay. But from that day forward a gap opened between us that could not be closed. I further compounded my mistake one afternoon by offering to pay for her return voyage should she find herself in desperate circumstances.

'You would buy me back?' was her reply, and I knew there was nothing more I could say or do without being pre-judged.

When she left the house that April day for the train to Liverpool and the ship to Halifax, I asked her to write. There were a few brief letters to her step-mother, and she kept up a lively correspondence with her brother who has visited her once. I took no pleasure in the accuracy of my prediction when her marriage dissolved after only three years.

It has been sixteen years since she left, and I wonder, now my time is nearly up, if father considered what might have been as his own death approached. The difference is, of course, Lettie died too young and robbed him of any opportunity to reach out. Given my own longevity, I have had ample opportunity to do so, and it is likely she will live her own long life with my failure in mind. Her brother has given me her address, and I will send my conductor's baton to her, the one presented to me by the orphaned children's choir. It is for my grandson, I will tell her, perhaps to hold high one day and part the air of memory.

Norman 1957

The one who most affected my Orkneys experience and influenced my subsequent life was Mr. Garson. It was he who, while I was in Sixth Form, encouraged me to pursue my scientific interests at a higher level. I was fortunate enough to win a scholarship to study entomology at Edinburgh University, and four years later I went on to graduate studies in lepidopterology. My laboratory was a busy place for many years, but I always preferred outdoor work, which I carried out all over the British Isles and even, for several summers after the first war, on the continent. It was strangely beautiful how the butterflies hovered over the poppies between the rows of crosses. Now, of course, I am an aged emeritus professor with a tiny office where I go to read the publications of others rather than prepare my own. Mr. Garson died not long before father. I'd been back to see him at least once a year since Lettie's death, eventually accompanied by Catherine who deemed him a perfect nineteenth-century gentleman. He was always interested in my discoveries and those of my colleagues around the world. We would walk out into the fields to see what we could see and were usually rewarded by the flittings of Meadow Browns and Common Blues and the occasional *Aglais urticae* with its black and yellow wing markings.

'As you know, Norman, I don't collect anymore,' he told me the last time I saw him. 'I leave that to you professionals. But I do like to study photographs of those that never fly this far north. Some of the early colour plates are quite handsome.'

'You must realize how grateful I've always been for your friendship and guidance,' I'd written clumsily to him before that final visit, but when I tried to express my appreciation more elegantly in person he'd replied that the gratitude was all his. In my caterpillar stage, he said, I'd been a delightful near-sighted boy, precocious and full of enthusiasm, who then turned into a splendid butterfly scholar with a true vision of nature's place in God's scheme. 'And to my mind, as to yours,' he declared, 'that scheme has never included blind dominion over every living thing.' Then he smiled. 'Including selkies.'

At his funeral soon after I provided examples of his keen mind and good heart to those present to celebrate his long life, as well as of his sharp eye that could spot a Small White in a vast field of sneezewort. When I was a boy, I told them, he took me under his wing until I was ready to fly on my own. When that day finally arrived, and I was off to other landscapes, he never left my side.

There was one thing I never shared with him because I did it for Lettie and no one else. When all the words had been spoken and we had lowered her into the earth, mother retired to Horace's cottage for the afternoon, attended by Ernest. Arthur sat with Margaret while Bertie went off with Mr. Campbell. Clem asked if I wanted to come along to the cathedral with him, but I declined, and I suppose he assumed I'd go off to Mr. Garson's where I was staying. I did go back there but only to change into some old clothes and tell my host I needed a bit of time alone.

'She was a rare flower,' he said as I left. 'It's a shame your father could not see her qualities.'

'He is but one of nine.' I replied. 'The rest of us always saw them well enough, now even mother.'

I walked to the chandler's shop and purchased a sufficient length of thick manila rope along with a pair of leather workman's gloves and a couple of other necessary items. Then I headed down the beach and up the path towards the cliffs with the rope and my canvas bag over my shoulder. On the train north I had thought over what I wanted to do and why. All my brothers had plans to pay tribute to her with words or music. I didn't know about Horace. When Ernest asked if I'd like to speak, I shook my head, afraid my emotions might get the best of me.

'That's alright, Norman,' Arthur whispered. 'You'll find a private way to honour her.'

I did stand up in the end, but what I found myself saying only spurred my plan.

When I got to the declivity in the rock face it was as if I had stepped back in time. There below me was the narrow entrance to the cove the boat had slipped through, the rocks waiting for others mad enough try. I couldn't see the beach but heard the booming from the caves as I secured the rope around the jutting piece of stone and tightened the thin cord that held my glasses in place. I wasn't concerned for my safety because I was older and stronger than before and knew what was waiting. I might have asked myself if I possessed this knowledge why I had to make the descent, but, if so, it was only a fleeting consideration. To be this close to her again was the only homage I could make, and I was determined to leave a sign.

My downward progress was slow and even, the gloves protecting my fingers and palms and my arm muscles permitting precious seconds to find purchase with my boots. Still, it was only a matter of minutes before I was on the strand, my feet sinking into seaweed and kelp as I dropped the rope end and stepped towards the shore. There was little wind, but the swells slowly rose and fell with great curved power and indifference to my gaze. At their height in this calm weather they were taller than a man, and I knew their weight beneath was to be measured in tonnes. I lay again in the bottom of the boat as its captain and my sister rowed against all odds. Before that I had seen Lettie's face and the selkie's as one, and now seeking the source of that convergence I turned towards the caves.

There was no easy path to gain entrance. The sea encroached on the pebbled edge of the land, blocking any dry access and threatening submergence to the hesitant or timid. I took the plunge to my knees and holding on to the protruding rock face waded into the unknown. I don't know what I was expecting, but certainly not the dimensions I found in a capacious, high-ceilinged chamber whose size seemed to absorb the thrust of the swells. On its far side, however, was a series of smaller, receding antechambers where light poured through a wide breach above the weighted water slamming into their back walls with enormous force and reverberation. The very air was shaking, and I knew I could be disoriented by such pounding if I stayed too long. I made my way through the dark shallows to the rear of the main cavern and up onto a narrow shelf at the foot of a flat slab of stone. It was here I would leave our mark.

Taking the chisel and hammer from my bag, I began to tap out the proof of our shared triumph well above the waterline all those years ago. Nothing fancy, just a few letters and numbers to last as long as anyone's myth.

Lettie
Margaret
Norman
1894

When I got to the top of the cliff I unhitched the rope and watched the sea rolling in and out eternally. Only one pair of eyes would ever glimpse what I had left behind, and she had her own face now.

Lettie 1902

Last week, on the eighth anniversary of our companionship, Margaret and I lay on our backs on the wharf and watched a meteor shower unfold above us. We held hands as those tiny pinpricks of light tumbled across the heavens and suddenly disappeared, their brief beauty reminding us of our own time together, fragile and finite in such a vast expanse.

'It's like a door in your head opening onto something sacred.'

'Yes, but no more than the sea on a wind-blown day,' she replied. 'Or a gull soaring in that same wind above a fish swimming in its element below.'

'It's all connected, isn't it?'

'If Arthur were here he'd remind us. *Nothing in the world is single;/ All things by a law divine/ In one spirit meet and mingle.*

'Well, he's not, so it's I who must remind you of what comes next: *Why not I with thine?*

'Yes,' she said, the rough planks beneath our bodies a bed for our embrace.

Tonight I'm low with a fever and don't care much for meteoric displays or measurements any larger than the distance between my hand and the glass of water on my nightstand. Neither have I a taste for passion, though Margaret's kiss before turning down the lamp cooled my forehead wonderfully. I lie here quietly thinking about the past decade in which we've been so happy and tallying up the cost. How do you weigh the gain of love against the loss of those who bore and raised you?

I suppose I didn't want to see it as a choice in the way they did. All their yesterdays added up to tell them what was right and wrong while my tomorrow subtracted from such certainty. There is a photograph of all us taken in our garden not long before we left for the Orkneys, seven planets orbiting around two great stars in a private universe before it collapsed and vanished. Mother and father shine so brightly we cannot see beyond the wheel of our own turning, our surfaces serene while at our cores small fires work to burn the glare away. If you had questioned me as to the nature of my own flames at the time, I would never have replied that my refusal of parental marriage plans was a refusal of *all* men. But, even so, not only hadn't I met one with whom I wanted to spend the rest of my life, I couldn't *imagine* one. The alternative to matrimonial prison was self-reliance, not another woman. Margaret was as big a surprise to me as she was to everyone else. Her warmth and intellect drew me, as no man had been able to do, and above all her generosity of spirit that happened to be in a woman's body. When you fall in love, the outer form of your desire is mere reflection of the inner radiance.

Each of us found a freedom here to question old habits, from Ernest who recognized contradictions in himself and began to carve out his independence to Norman who was too young to do anything but follow his innocent nose and blessedly survive. Afterwards, they all stood by me, which must have made it terribly hard for mother and father who assumed the black sheep would be left alone in the distant, rocky field until she returned to the fold where she properly belonged. And they have all come back through the years to stay with us, singly and in pairs, to build a new kind of family whose faith is in discussion rather than decree. Horace's nearby presence has helped greatly because he is a brother and friend to us both, and while the others of necessity come and go his down-to-earth constancy replenishes our well of being daily.

When they visit, my other brothers reveal how they have grown. Ernest preaches from a more flexible pulpit than that of his predecessor. Bertie balances legal certainties with his hard-earned knowledge that the courtroom is not the only space where truth resides. Arthur will be a starry-eyed idealist until he dies, but he is also an avid listener, never quite detached from his immediate surroundings and their influence on him. Clem is the one I worry about most as his compositions, at least the ones I have heard, do not shake the soul but play to its expectations. Because of the religious nature of much of his music, he remains to no insignificant degree under father's sway, and I hope that a wife and children will one day expand his composition of the world. As for Norman, Mr. Garson assures he is on his way to great success, and I can see his confidence behind those spectacles as he excitedly describes his insect studies.

'There are millions of them and just a few of us.'

'Like stars in the sky,' I answer.

'Yes, and we will outlive neither.'

My face must fall a little because he quickly says, 'Don't worry, Lettie, you'll be the grand old woman of these islands long before that happens!'

I catch a glimpse of myself older than mother, butterflies nesting in my grey hairs and a numberless brilliance overhead.

I'm feeling chilly now and pull the blanket up over my shoulders. Margaret has promised to bring some hot broth soon and read to me of Mrs. Seacole's adventures in many lands.

Made in the USA
Middletown, DE
04 May 2019